Doris H. Gray is Associate Professor at Al Akhawayn University Ifrane, Morocco. She holds a Ph.D. from Florida State University and is the author of *Muslim Women on the Move: Women in Morocco and France Speak Out* (2008).

BEYOND FEMINISM AND ISLAMISM

Gender and Equality in North Africa

DORIS H. GRAY

I.B. TAURIS

LONDON · NEW YORK

New paperback edition published in 2015 by I.B.Tauris & Co. Ltd
6 Salem Road, London W2 4BU
175 Fifth Avenue, New York NY 10010
www.ibtauris.com

Distributed in the United States and Canada
Exclusively by Palgrave Macmillan
175 Fifth Avenue, New York NY 10010

First published in hardback in 2013 by I.B.Tauris & Co. Ltd

ISBN: 978 1 78453 006 8
eISBN: 978 0 85773 503 4

A full CIP record for this book is available from the British Library
A full CIP record is available from the Library of Congress

Library of Congress Catalog Card Number: available

Typeset by Newgen Publishers, Chennai
Printed and bound by CPI Group (UK) Ltd, Croydon, CR0 4YY

CONTENTS

ACKNOWLEDGEMENTS

Cross-cultural dialogue is always fraught with complications. It means looking in from the outside. We cannot easily shed biases we have been inculcated with since early childhood. Nevertheless, understanding that which is different is an exciting process that allows us to get a sense of 'the other' as much as re-evaluating our own understandings. The Moroccans who have shared their viewpoints and opinions generously with me risked being misunderstood or misrepresented. In exploring Moroccan gender discourses, I have tried to have an open mind and faithfully report and analyze what I have heard and read. As social and cultural transformations are a fluid process, we can observe them as they unfold but things may have changed from the time we focus on a given moment. This has certainly been the case in North Africa in general beginning with the revolution in Tunisia in January 2011 culminating in the overthrow of the regime of Zine El Abidine Ben Ali on 14 January 2011. Less than a month later, Egyptian dictator Hosni Mubarak fell. Mass demonstrations calling for democracy, transparency and an end to corruption started in Morocco on 20 February, followed by the announcement of King Mohammed VI promising sweeping changes. The terrorist attack on the popular Café Argana in Marrakesh on 29 April that same year slowed the movement down. At the time this book went to press, the outcomes of events in Morocco – as in much of North Africa and the Middle East – were not yet clear. What is apparent, however, is that Morocco will not be the same again regardless of the exact nature of changes set in motion during the Arab Spring.

Several people have helped in exploring the themes of this book. My friend and colleague Souad Eddouada has spent countless hours discussing ideas, challenging them and adjusting my focus. We talked in cafés, in offices, even while sweating in the hot steam of a *hammam* and she never got tired of my questions. She introduced me to several people, all of whom were intent on helping me understand their vision of gender equality and justice in their country. Various women's rights activists have shared their ideas with me, trusting that I report faithfully what they have said. Maria Marsh of I.B.Tauris was an enthusiastic supporter of this project early on. I am also indebted to the Fulbright International Exchange Program that awarded me a senior fellowship for my initial research. The American Institute for Maghrib Studies also provided a grant that allowed for further exploration. Of my colleagues at Florida State University, Drs. William Cloonan and Alec Hargreaves have offered support and advice. My editor Jayme Harpring has helped shape this book beyond what is normally expected from an editor. As always, I am thankful to my daughters Tunuka and Khadijah who keep me from becoming complacent. Their youthful optimistic view about changes that are possible in the life of individuals and on a larger scale is an inspiration. I am grateful for the patient encouragement of Michael Painter.

Parts of Chapter 3 of this book appear in a chapter of an edited volume *Contemporary Morocco: State, Politics and Society under Mohammed VI*, published by Routledge, 2011. All translations from French into English are mine.

O Mankind! Fear your Lord who has created you from a single soul, and from it He created its mate; and from them both, He brought forth multitudes of men and women. Be mindful of Allah through Whom you demand your mutual (rights), and revere the wombs that bore you. Surely, Allah is ever watching over you.

(An-Nisaa' 4:1)[1]

NOTE ON TRANSLITERATION

In the absence of a convention on how best to transliterate into English Arabic terms used in francophone North Africa, I have used French-based transliteration of Arabic names and terms as these reflect the actual usage within the region. In case of inconsistent use even in local transliteration, the most commonly used spelling has been adopted.

PREFACE TO THE
PAPERBACK EDITION

Books on themes relating to current affairs that analyse facts and events occurring during a particular period face a dilemma: by the time a second edition, such as this one, is published, some things have changed. While the substantive analysis of this book remains valid, several unrelated events in Morocco pertaining to individuals profiled in this text have occurred since the publication of the hardback edition. The most important examples are noted as follows.

Sheikh Abdessalam Yassine, founder and leader of the Al Adl wa Ihsane (Justice and Charity) movement died on 13 December 2012. As anticipated in this book, conflict between the Sheikh's daughter, Nadia Yassine, head of the women's section, and the new secretary general, Mohammed Abbadi, has resulted in a dissolution of the women's section she built and led. For the time being, Nadia Yassine has stepped off the public stage. The director of the women's section, Merieme Yefout, has left the movement and has dedicated herself to her career as a scholar, exploring new concepts of gender equality.

Khadija Moufid, founder and leader of Al Hidn, has established a new association in Casablanca that is focusing more on research than social action.

Bassima Hakkaoui, a member of the ruling Justice and Development Party (PJD) was appointed as Minister of Solidarity, Women, Family and Social Development in January 2012, and hence is presently the single most prominent and influential female PJD member. She has had a rough ride in public office because of some unfortunate statements she has made on women's rights issues, which have sometimes been misquoted or given out of context. She has thus been reviled by more secular-minded women's rights advocates.

Asma Lamrabet was awarded the Organization of Arab Women's Sociology Prize in 2013. She has become an increasingly prominent figure both locally and internationally, speaking on women's rights issues within a Muslim context.

These shifts demonstrate the dynamic nature of women's rights advocacy. As the political, religious and social landscape changes, women move in and out of certain positions, associations and movements in hopes of increasing their effectiveness.

The post-revolution unrest and economic instability in Tunisia, Libya and Egypt have left Moroccans thinking of ways to move their society forward while at the same time maintaining stability and security.

INTRODUCTION

Research for this book was conducted in 2009 and 2010, before the occurrence of any of the remarkable events that took place in North Africa in the spring of 2011. A wave of persistent mass protests in Tunisia and Egypt overthrew their respective dictators or rocked governments in Libya, Bahrain, Syria and other countries of the Middle East and set their countries on a path of tenuous democratization. Internal dissent was evident prior to these eruptions, of course, but no one could have foreseen that average, courageous civilians – led neither by the military, political leaders, nor Islamist radicals – would take matters into their own hands in such a show of force throughout North Africa and the Middle East. In chronicling some of the debates on women's rights, roles, and status that are taking place in Muslim-majority countries such as Morocco, this book hopes to provide insights as to the dynamics among activists – from secular to Islamist – in trying to develop a new vision for the society in which they live.

When the status and the role of women becomes one of the most hotly debated topics in a country, change is in the air. When women's rights become the linchpin around which major national discourses revolve, it is a sign of movement and reorientation. Such is the case in the North African kingdom of Morocco, where one of the most frequently discussed and controversial issues is *women.* Why is this North African Muslim monarchy so concerned with the status of women? The answer to this question is multifaceted, comprising economic and political questions and issues related to human rights, national and cultural identity, post-colonialism, and religious principles.

At present, debates about gender issues are a dominant feature of public discourse in Morocco. Particularly among young Muslims, both male and female, there is a desire to know how Islam applies to the here and now, and how changing conceptions of gender relations affect their daily lives. An emphasis on religion enjoys increasing popularity among the young in Morocco. Secular feminists with an overt Western orientation often find themselves out of touch with this reality, and the number of young Moroccan activists who belong to secular organizations is today less than in religion-based associations. In fact, the performance of religious observance is evident in the increasing numbers of young women wearing the Muslim *hijab* (headscarf) in the bustling modern urban centres of Casablanca and Rabat. At the same time, King Mohammed VI is pursuing a modernizing agenda for his country, and supports research into new religious interpretations that lend credence to a more gender-egalitarian agenda.

Civil rights and women's rights

The first decade of the twenty-first century has been a time in North Africa that is reminiscent of the 1960s in the United States. During that period, the civil rights movement in the United States of America arose from a quest for rights for African-American citizens. Yet the discourse about rights for this minority went well beyond issues of equal opportunities and legal rights for a certain segment of the US population. The civil rights movement unleashed a national debate that exceeded the demands, aspirations, and visions of inclusion of African Americans; more broadly, the civil rights movement raised questions of identity and about the future inclusiveness of a previously discriminated and marginalized population group in the United States. The civil rights movement was not a broad mass movement; it was comprised of courageous individuals from a minority population and their supporters who rose to the forefront and publicly questioned the status quo. For their actions, they were ridiculed, attacked by police dogs, sent to prison, and sometimes killed. In response to the upheaval, even moderate Americans feared a disintegration of society, as they knew it.

In retrospect, it is easy to overlook the enormous perseverance and courage required to achieve rights and protection for minorities. Further, many who in those days stood at the sidelines now claim to have been part and centre of the struggle. Such distorted views of history are held by segments of the majority population, even today. As civil rights became more and more the accepted norm it became problematic to admit to having opposed rather than having promoted the movement. It is commonly held that people like to side with winners. Nevertheless, while the civil rights struggle was ongoing, many stood on the sidelines, waiting for the outcome. Once Martin Luther King Jr. became a national hero (especially after his violent death in 1968) and once civil rights became widely accepted, many among those who sat on the fence claimed to have always been enthusiastic supporters. Thus, though movements for positive change may start small and often face great obstacles, those who remain uninvolved or even in opposition to them will in the end also enjoy the results. This is as true in the West as it is in the Muslim world, where forces of change can easily be underestimated.

The expansion of rights and freedoms for African Americans, then, led to an improvement of rights and freedoms for the majority population in the United States. Further, in the wake of the civil rights movement, the women's rights movement became invigorated and emboldened, and the sexual revolution broke with previously held sacred customs – changing America forever. The fact that white middle-class women were beneficiaries of the civil rights movement whether they participated in this particular struggle or not illustrates the point made above. In this, the great effort and broad consequences of the civil rights movement in the United States provides a point of comparison and perspective on the struggle for women's rights in Morocco. Obviously such a comparison is limited because of the very different nature of American and Moroccan society, as well as the structure of their respective governments and constitutions. Yet, there are similarities that make for an interesting analysis.

In the early years of the twenty-first century, the Moroccan monarch Mohammed VI responded to demands by women's rights associations and spearheaded the quest for gender equality in his country. In a comparable way, the then US President John F. Kennedy called for a civil rights bill in 1963 that was signed in 1964 by his successor Lyndon B. Johnson. In both instances the heads of state used their positions of authority to push through legislation that emerged from grassroots organizations but which did not have the support of existing established power structures. To the extent that the struggle for minority rights ushered in a profound change of North American society, it is not unlike the women's rights challenges faced today in the Maghreb. The Maghreb comprises the North African countries of Mauretania, Morocco, Algeria, Tunisia, and Libya, though conventionally Maghreb (Arabic for West) refers to the former French colonial territories of Morocco, Algeria, and Tunisia.

Modernity and tradition

Women's rights are a contentious issue in the North African kingdom of Morocco. Many men and women alike do not quite know what to make of demands for equal rights. Some fear social disintegration and prefer the status quo, even if it comes with undeniable injustices. Others advocate for change – for instance, reform of certain laws – but there is no overall consensus on the role and status of women. Discourse on women's rights is not limited to what women do or do not want (of course women do not constitute a homogeneous population); it extends to the direction of an entire country, caught between various notions of modernity and tradition. This is because equal rights for women eventually will lead to rights for ethnic, religious, and sexual minorities, and the majority of men from socially disadvantaged backgrounds. The Moroccan government is seeking to increase its alignment with the highly industrialized, secular West – Europe in particular – while at the same time staying true to its own cultural and religious identity. The question of women's rights is the tightrope of this balancing act. Friction, dissent, and above all uncertainty pervade the various discourses on women's rights among ordinary citizens as well as the ranks of those in government and religious circles.

The path to modernity is not a one-way street designed by the West and to be followed by the rest of the world. Each nation must map its own way to that destination. While activists and policy makers in Muslim-majority countries may take Western models into consideration, they can create a successful policy that does not cause irreparable internal tension only by finding a balance between modernity and tradition. Admittedly, the concepts of modernity and tradition are problematic as there are no universal definitions for either; the terms merely describe certain tendencies and trends. In this book, I refer to modernity as a phenomenon that is most commonly associated with the industrialized world, or the West, although Japan belongs in this category as well. Modernity generally refers to dynamic societies, oriented towards the future and open to transformation, and is often associated with the nation-state and democracy. The hallmark of societies referred to as traditional is that customs, practices, and social norms are passed on from one generation to the next and are highly valued. There also is an emphasis on collective cohesion, which is seen as threatened by an overt stress on individual rights. Countries of the global South, including predominantly Muslim societies, are often viewed as holding to traditionalism. In this book, the terms global North and global South describe on one hand industrialized, so-called modern countries and on the other those often but erroneously still referred to as the third world – after all, the Soviet Union, once the 'second world', no longer exists. The term West, as used in the book, refers to North America and Western Europe.

Another scramble for Africa

In our increasingly interconnected world, unprecedented advances in technology facilitate the movement of peoples and ideas. What happens in one corner of the world inevitably reverberates in other parts as well. Globalization is a fact of life and the economic dominance of the West over the rest of the world has long been a reality. However, so-called BRIC countries (Brazil, Russia, India, and China) are increasingly challenging Western dominance. Throughout Africa, Morocco included, the Chinese presence in particular is increasingly visible. Yet China's dealings and trade come without political demands. There are no expectations for democratization, no required alliances in the war against terrorism, no demands with regard to human rights. The involvement of China in Africa follows a different trajectory from that of the West, which is saddled with colonial guilt and notions of having to spread the new gospel of democracy and human rights. As elsewhere, African markets are increasingly stacked with cheap Chinese goods, replacing local crafts and pushing out indigenous production in which women play a major part. Nevertheless, Chinese encroachment in Africa has gone largely unchallenged by African leaders and the cultural, social, and economic impact of the Chinese presence on the continent has yet to be determined.

Historically, the scramble for Africa describes the years from 1881 to the beginning of the First World War in 1914, when European powers invaded, occupied, and annexed African territory. The second scramble for Africa refers to the post-colonial era around the 1960s when the United States and the Soviet Union sought influence over newly independent African countries and used them as pawns during the Cold War period. At that time, new indigenous African governments in turn scrambled to fulfil the great hopes of the African peoples for socio-economic and political progress.[2] In the aftermath of the fall of the Berlin Wall in 1989 and the subsequent collapse of the Soviet Union, new fault lines eventually emerged, leaving Muslim-majority countries pitted against the West. In today's world, however, such demarcation lines have become less meaningful because of the transnational flow of capital, people, and ideas. Further breaking down such dividing lines is related to the economic power that flows from the global North to the global South while the migration of people generally moves the other way.

Today, Morocco is in the uniquely difficult position of simultaneously being a *sending* and *receiving* migration country. About three million Moroccans – that is, 10 per cent of the population – currently live beyond Morocco's borders, mostly in Europe, Canada, and the United States, and many more hope to leave Morocco in search of better economic opportunities abroad. At the same time, in recent years Morocco has become, however involuntarily, an importer of human resources. With its proximity to Europe, Morocco has been a traditional place of transit for Africans from south of the Sahara who wish to migrate north. Those migrants are often refugees, fleeing war or political conflict in home countries such as Congo or the Ivory Coast, or economic refugees who are attempting to escape poverty. Since the European Union has put in place progressively tighter border controls in an effort to stem the continuous stream of migrants and refugees, Morocco has become a final destination for those arriving from countries south of the Sahara. The majority of these migrants are non-Muslims who are, in effect, turning Morocco into a religiously pluralistic society. Having to come to terms with this unexpected, steadily growing influx of foreigners – the majority of whom are black and Christian – adds yet another dimension to issues of individual and minority rights. In the case of Africans from south of the Sahara, this situation poses a particular challenge because until the early part of the twentieth century, dark-skinned Africans, women especially, were kept as slaves in Morocco.[3]

One can argue that though women are not a numerical minority worldwide, they long had, or in some countries still have, the legal status commonly ascribed to minorities. They are not in all matters the legal equals of their male peers and do not have comparable personal and professional opportunities in the same way that the African-American minority in the United States did not enjoy the same rights as Caucasian citizens. Hence, the issue of women's rights is linked to minority rights in general, which, in Morocco, includes the rights of sub-Saharan migrants, rights that were until recently largely ignored.

The West, in particular the United States with its history of civil rights battles, knows how divisive, confusing, and emotional debates about minority rights can be. Although women in the United States were subjected for centuries to an inferior legal and social status similar to that of minorities, today most young women in the West take equal rights for granted. And yet it should be noted that despite all the advances in women's emancipation, gender is not a passé issue even in the very modern, highly industrialized United States. The furore surrounding first Hillary Rodham Clinton's candidacy during the US presidential campaigns in 2007–2008, followed by the choice of Governor Sarah Palin as a vice-presidential candidate, serves as a reminder that complete equality has not yet been attained even in places that pride themselves as beacons of gender equality.

Morocco at the crossroads

Many of the worlds' pressing problems of the twenty-first century are embodied within Morocco's borders, including tensions between the West and the Muslim world, minority rights, legal and illegal immigration, the role of religion in a modern society, and the issue about which this book is chiefly concerned: women's rights. Morocco is uniquely situated at the crossroads between Africa, the continent on which it is located, the Middle East North African region (MENA) to which it belongs culturally and historically, and Europe, from which it is separated by the nine-mile wide Strait of Gibraltar. At the northern tip of Africa, Morocco has the unique feature of being the only African country that shares a common border with Europe through the Spanish enclaves of Melilla and Ceuta (also spelled Septa), two cities on Moroccan soil that are pre-colonial holdovers still belonging to Spain. This oddity has its counterpart in the city of Gibraltar, located within Spain, but part of Great Britain.

Though Morocco lies on the African continent its economic, cultural, and political reference points lay beyond Africa. Morocco is oriented towards the North – namely Europe – and the East – that is, the Arab world. For centuries, the historic trans-Saharan trading routes enabled the movement of people, goods, and ideas across the desert. Today, black Moroccans – for the most part descendants of slaves or trans-Saharan traders – are the most visible testimony of this interaction. Though recently scholars have shown a renewed interest in exploring the West African connections with and influences on Moroccan culture, especially in music and visual arts, Moroccan scholars have shown remarkably little interest in their African neighbours. While educated Moroccans are well informed about events in Europe, the Middle East, and North America, many draw a blank when it comes to countries on their own continent. So northward looking is Morocco that the term mixed marriage, for instance, refers to the union of a Moroccan and someone from a European country or North America, but not from another African country, as such marriages occur so rarely. In the same way that Western mass media routinely portray the so-called third world and third-world women in reductionist terms, Moroccans frequently have an equally limited view of 'black Africa'.

The perceived or real conflict between the West and the Muslim world plays out in unique ways in Morocco. The country's official name, *al-Mamlakah al-Maġribiyya*, is Arabic for Kingdom of the West, meaning it is west of what was the centre of the seat of Muslim power at the time of the Arab/Islamic invasion. Morocco is the westernmost outpost of the Muslim Arab world. The country's name is indicative of its identity, in that it conceives of itself in relation to the Arab/Muslim world. Though Morocco is a member of the 22-nation League of Arab States as well as the largely defunct Arab Maghreb Union, it is the only African country that is not part of the African Union.[4] Yet ironically, from a Western point of view, Morocco historically has been considered part of the impenetrable, mysterious Orient.

Morocco has been most influenced by the Arab Middle East through the Muslim invasions that began shortly after the inception of Islam in the seventh century. At that time, one of the founding fathers of the Moroccan dynasties, Moulay Idriss, a supposed great-grandson of the Prophet Mohammed, settled among the indigenous Berber (Amazigh) populations of North Africa. Today, Arabic is the only official language in Morocco though Berber languages are also recognized as national languages. In the early twentieth century, Morocco was part of the scramble for Africa when France (and to a lesser degree Spain) declared it a protectorate. As a result, Morocco today is a country of polyglots. Any educated Moroccan speaks at least three or more languages fluently: *derjea*, the local version of Arabic, as well as modern standard Arabic, French and/or English, Spanish, and one of the indigenous Afro-Asian Berber languages. Nearly half of the Moroccan population of 33 million inhabitants is of Berber origin, a Greek and Roman appellation connoting 'barbarian'.[5] Though the term Berber is still commonly used, Berbers refer to themselves as Amazigh, meaning free people. Because a substantial portion of the Moroccan population is of mixed Amazigh-Arab origin, Moroccans are sometimes referred to as 'Arabized Berbers'. Both Tamazight and French have influenced the local *derjea* language, or dialectical Arabic. Hence, Morocco encapsulates African, European, and Middle Eastern cultural and linguistic traits. It is for these reasons that the country is particularly well situated to develop a discourse that bridges cultural and religious divides and dispels old dualistic ways of seeing the world.

In modern history, Morocco was a French protectorate from 1912 until its independence from France in 1956. While France dominated the largest part of the country, the northern regions of Morocco were ruled by Spain. Unlike most of its neighbours in the Maghreb – Mauretania, Algeria, Tunisia, and Libya – Morocco was never part of the Ottoman Empire. Historically inhabited by Jews, Christians, and Muslims, Morocco today is mainly comprised of Sunni Muslims. Christian churches (mostly Catholic) and synagogues can still be found throughout the country but are visited mostly by expatriates. Ethnically, Morocco contains various Berber ethnic groups and Arabs. The unifying trait of North African Imazighen (plural of Amazigh) is a common linguistic bond, not a race or skin colour, since Imazighen come in all shades – from black Tuareg, the blue men of the desert, to light-skinned, green-eyed Imazighen of the Atlas mountain range. Imazighen inhabit mostly rural areas in the Atlas mountains, the Sahara, and the Souss region in the South, whereas Arabs settled and established urban centres along the coastline and in Fes. The interior old imperial city of Fes is host to the Al-Qarawiyyin University and mosque. Established in the ninth century by a woman, Fatima al Fihri, it is one of the oldest continuous degree-granting institutions in the world.

This blending of cultures and traditions is evident in everyday activities. While traditional Muslim custom dictates strict separation of men and women, Moroccans – men and women – routinely kiss each other on the cheeks several times as is the custom in France rather than shaking hands or avoiding physical contact. Simple daily habits reflect a mélange of cultural influences that set the Maghreb apart from the Mashrek (the Muslim East). Morocco is the western outpost of the Muslim Middle East and at the same time it is the northernmost country in Africa and the one closest to Europe. One could say that Morocco, along with Turkey, another Muslim-majority country aspiring for closer links with the European Union, is one of the bookends of the Mediterranean region.

West meets East

Its blend of historic and cultural influences has made Morocco a country whose people by definition have multiple identities. The tensions of the modern world play out on its soil, making it an important – and fascinating – place to observe. Women's rights are an integral part of contemporary modern societies; therefore the question of women's rights is a vital indicator of social change. Both religion and feminism are 'controversial, emotion-laden systems of belief that directly affect people's lives'.[6] Feminism, though often vilified, does provide a lens through which one can approach issues of societal change. Feminist theory is credited with introducing the now widely accepted notion of gender differences as a cultural construct while recognizing sex as a biological fact.[7]

The question of women's rights is one of the most controversial topics in Morocco. This is not surprising, since the challenges associated with women's rights touch on the foundations of any society. Talk about women's rights in any social context goes to the heart of social structures, culture, the conception of the nuclear and extended family, and matters of authority and power. The issue of women's rights – whether in Muslim-majority countries or elsewhere – also involves human relationships in the private and the public spheres as well as fundamental questions about representation, religious interpretation, and sacred law. In addition, there is the question of the role of individual agency versus the importance of maintaining a collective culture. The West's antagonism with the Muslim world revolves, to a great extent, around women's rights. Western governments see democracy, economic progress, freedom of speech, and legal reform as intrinsically linked with the status of women. Though the current extent of women's emancipation in the West was unheard of a mere 50 years ago, it is now often portrayed as if this had always been the case. Further, Western governments, mass media, and popular perceptions frequently portray the Muslim world as having irreconcilable differences concerning the status and role of women. Muslim-majority countries are viewed as propagating submission and second-class-citizen status while the West is seen as offering liberties, freedom, and equal rights.

There is a project underway in Morocco that some are calling a 'third way'. Using religion as the basis for advocating gender equality, it is chiefly concerned with new interpretations of Islam's sacred scriptures. In this way, the religious resurgence that is sweeping through Morocco is being harnessed to promote a new vision of a more egalitarian, modern society. In the following, we will present some of the main actors of this third way.

Overview of the book

First, it is important to discuss the definitions of the terms Islamic, Islamist, and Muslim. Islamic and Islamist are frequently used interchangeably and incorrectly. In general, Muslim refers to an individual who either by faith or by birth has Islam as religion or cultural background. Islamic refers to concepts and articles of faith deriving from the religion of Islam. Islamist refers to a phenomenon that arose in the wake of the Iranian Revolution in 1979 that marked a revival of religious identity based on Islam. Islamist pertains to people for whom religion is the main reference point. In the context of this book, Islamist is used with regard to decidedly non-violent actors, though Morocco has experienced its share of murderous terrorist attacks perpetrated by self-proclaimed, radical Islamists. In my opinion, it is inaccurate to use the term 'Islamic country'. Though Muslims may constitute the majority of a given population, this margin does not make it an Islamic country. Islam refers to a divine revelation that provides guiding principles to its believers, who apply these to their respective circumstances, which may differ from time to time and from one geographic region to another. Hence, a more precise appellation than Islamic country is Muslim-majority country.

Chapter 1 begins with a discussion about how women in general have come to bear the burden of social change, change that frequently has little to do with what they do or do not want. This is followed by an analysis of how the 'woman question' in the Muslim world has preoccupied the West for more than a century. The chapter further chronicles early twentieth-century Moroccan discourse on women's rights and shows that many issues of concern – the veil, polygamy, female illiteracy

– have been enduring topics for nearly 100 years. Finally, a lengthy interview with Fatima Mernissi, the *grande dame* of Muslim feminism, sheds light on the evolution of gender debates in Morocco. Chapter 2 describes the role of secular women's rights activists in bringing about a major reform of the Personal Status Code in 2004, which raised the legal status of women significantly. Chapter 2 also contains an examination of the reasons for certain Islamist opposition to legal reforms and how their approach differs from that of secular activists. Both a detailed description of the largest Islamist movement and interviews with its leading female members offer insights into Islamists' platform on women's rights, particularly their emphasis on gender justice versus gender equality. Chapter 3 explores a new, emerging 'third way' concerning gender equality, one that straddles Islamism and Western-inspired feminism. As in many parts of the world, Islamism in its moderate expression has become increasingly popular in Morocco. This is not simply a return to the 'old-time religion' as it were, but a new approach stressing personal choice in matters of religion. On a scholarly level, it comprises of a re-reading of sacred texts using the method of *maqasid*; that is, an exploration of the spirit or meaning of Islamic precepts. Chapter 3 also explores similarities between Catholic Liberation Theology and this third way. It offers a description of women's organizations that apply this approach in their daily work as well as discussions with leading proponents of this paradigm in Morocco. Chapter 4 concerns the way forward based on an authentic women's rights debate within the Muslim world. Formulating a platform that takes into consideration issues such as high unemployment, illiteracy, and poverty requires collaboration between different factions. This chapter also offers some very preliminary assessment of the historic events that are variously called Arab revolution or Arab Spring. I refrain from using the term Arab awakening as this sounds as if people throughout North Africa had been asleep prior to their uprising.

In all, reductionist views of Muslim women do not contribute in any meaningful way to the debate about women's rights taking place in Morocco. The erstwhile dichotomy between the West and the Muslim world should be drawn into question and not only since the recent massive push for democracy in North Africa and the Arab world. A reform that takes both the religious and cultural dimensions of Morocco into consideration may be slow in the making but ultimately may have a greater chance of creating a more gender-egalitarian society.

Countries far and wide are engaged in their own social experiments concerning women and minorities. This book zeroes in on Morocco, one country currently undergoing deep-seated changes. It highlights various facets of the contemporary discourses on gender that shape the debate concerning women's rights and its larger implications for this country. This book is not a general discussion of Muslim women, nor is it a broad discussion of Islam and women's rights. Instead, it focuses on the actual discourses on women's rights that are taking place in Morocco, and in so doing illustrates their complexity. In its specificity, the book counters reductionist views and generalizations about the Muslim world that actually hinder rather than enhance a greater understanding of the complexities of societal changes.

CHAPTER 1

AND GOD CREATED EVE . . .

The quest for women's rights and equality is commonly associated with the West. In the United States, Germany, Great Britain, Nordic nations, and other countries around the world, human rights advocacy groups and feminist movements have pushed for the past 50 years to create gender-egalitarian societies. As a result, in the United States, for example, women now make up 50 per cent of the workforce. Women not only constitute the majority of university graduates, they also can expect to find jobs commensurate with their education. The British weekly *The Economist* called women's empowerment 'the biggest social change of our times' and finds this societal transformation all the more remarkable because it 'has been achieved with only a modicum of friction'.[1] Thus, relative gender equality has been accomplished in the West without causing any significant social unrest or resulting in an anarchic, disorderly society.[2] Today, whatever their religious, political, or ideological leanings, not many men or women would advocate turning back the clock and relegating women solely to their traditional roles of mother and/or housewife. The benefits of gender equality to society are obvious – with few exceptions – to all citizens.

There is one arena in Western countries that has successfully resisted gender equality, however. While anti-discrimination laws restrict blatant gender bias in the secular sphere, the same cannot be said of the religious domain. Despite laws that prohibit discrimination in the workplace, a woman has no legal grounds on which to sue the Catholic Church, for example, for denying her the right to become a priest. Secular civil rights laws do not apply within the confines of a religious denomination. Thus, churches, synagogues, temples, and mosques may – and do – discriminate based on gender, sexual orientation, and occasionally race, without the threat of legal sanctions. Exceptions also are extended to privately funded institutions affiliated with religious denominations. As recently as the year 2000, Bob Jones University, a Christian college and seminary located in Greenville, South Carolina, that seeks to 'develop Christ-like character' in its students, banned interracial dating. Bob Jones University does not receive federal funds and therefore is not required to adhere to civil rights laws.[3]

In Western countries, the system of separation of church and state makes it possible for officially recognized religious organizations to be shielded from laws that apply to the public sphere, and has led to the view that religion is a private matter. Religious affiliation or identity is seen as a matter of choice; if one does not like the discriminatory practices of the Catholic Church, for instance, one can leave it and join another religious denomination. The separation of church and state gives the state limited legal influence over religious matters and vice versa, leaving individuals with the freedom to practise their faith in most any way they choose. This does not mean that the interests of church and state do not overlap and intersect. Perennial disputes arise as to how the US Constitution applies to matters closely linked to religious convictions, such as abortion, school prayer, or more recently gay marriage – none of which are explicitly addressed in that founding document. Because legislation on such issues cannot be based on religious teachings, proponents seek justification for their respective positions in the Constitution. Naturally, there are distinct differences among Western countries. Although in the United States explicit pronouncements of faith are generally frowned upon in the workplace, among strangers, and in the classroom, religion is still a topic addressed with much greater ease there than in Western Europe.

In the United States, the Jeffersonian principle of separation of church and state has enabled feminists to promote a women's rights agenda without having to defer to religious dogma and practices. According to the First Amendment of the US Constitution:

Congress shall make no law respecting an establishment of religion, or prohibiting the free exercise thereof; or abridging the freedom of speech, or of the press; or the right of the people peaceably to assemble, and to petition the Government for a redress of grievances.

Conversely, religious institutions and authorities may hold little sway in legal discourse on women's rights, since gender equality generally is conceptualized within the framework of human and civil rights. In Morocco, however, religion and the state are more closely intertwined.

Islam as state religion

In much of the Muslim world, the demarcation between religion and state is either non-existent or much less obvious than in Western countries. Changes to laws and societal norms must be consistent with religious doctrine in most Muslim-majority nations. In Morocco, Islam is the state religion, and the Moroccan monarch has the dual function of head of state and *Amir al-Mu'minin*, or 'Commander of the Faithful', making him both the political ruler and the highest religious authority in the land.[4] In addition, he carries the title of *sherif*, meaning descendant of the Prophet Mohammed. His rulings are taken as sacred and he is believed to enjoy special *baraka* (divine blessing and grace) by virtue of his lineage and office. Thus, religion, the state, and the law are officially connected in Morocco. In the absence of a central authority figure for all Muslims worldwide, the Moroccan king has the right to proclaim new religious interpretations of sacred texts for his country.

The importance of Islam for national cohesion in Morocco is paramount because religion is a central marker of national distinction. Though religion, culture, and customs are closely intertwined in any country, in Morocco there is an official link between religion, the state, and the law. This link makes Morocco different from countries with separation of religion and state where religious beliefs may influence matters of state but cannot be their explicit basis. The absence of a barrier between state and religion in Morocco is also reflected in daily life, where religion is anything but a private matter.

In most of the Western world it is unseemly for a stranger to inquire about a person's religious convictions, while in Morocco this is quite common. Foreigners from Europe or the United States often find it unsettling that a Moroccan would ask – within moments of becoming acquainted – about their faith. In Morocco, religion is not a highly private topic; to the contrary, it is one of the most common themes in daily conversation. Religion plays an important role in national discourse, in private and in public life, and is probably the single biggest factor in defining Morocco's national identity. This is not to say that religion does not play a major role in other parts of the world, but the degree to which there is consensus in Morocco on the importance of Islam, as a marker of both personal and national identity, cannot be overstated.

Though there is no separation of religion and state in Morocco, however, one can identify a demarcation between the public and the private spheres of people's lives. Whereas one's private life is conducted according to clear codes and norms and within well-defined relationships, male–female interaction in the public sphere is marked by an absence of particular norms and rules. In general, then, the public sphere is considered a male domain, the private sphere a female one. Sons show respect to their mothers, aunts, female cousins, and sisters within the home, yet once out in the street those same men may whistle, harass, and affront women. Similarly, women may defer or even submit to their husbands, brothers, or fathers in the private domain, but once out in public, where unrelated men and women mingle freely, these same women can become ferocious negotiators with male vendors in the market, or vigorously push and shove their way to the front of the line (more of a clump, really) at a post office, bank, or bus stop. Conceptualizing the Muslim world through the binary lens of the public versus private sphere actually reflects more the Western tendency to categorize than the reality of life in a Muslim-majority country, where gender-related behaviour is fluid and depends on context. Still, flawed as they are, categories do provide a useful tool for the purpose of analysis.

The boundary between public and private becomes even more blurred when the state interferes in previously unheard-of ways on private matters, such as when it enacts new laws regulating private behaviour, like those that render domestic violence a crime. Domestic violence legislation undermines the established patriarchy and traditional hierarchies in a country, as it eliminates a man's right to behave violently towards his wife, thus narrowing the range of acceptable behaviour of the men in a family. In Morocco today, criminalizing domestic violence is a hot topic and one of critical importance in expanding women's rights.

Patriarchy

A central feature in the quest for gender equality and justice is the dismantling of patriarchal structures. Most female Moroccan activists across the spectrum, from Islamists to secular or liberal women's rights advocates, embrace this pursuit because patriarchy is seen as the major stumbling bloc to the advancement of women's rights. When using the term patriarchy in this book, I refer to the work of Allan Johnson, who described four principal aspects of patriarchy:

1. Male domination: Most prestigious and powerful roles are held by men.
2. Obsession with control: Women are devalued and subjected to physical and psychological control. Violence or fear of violence is present in women's everyday life because of ideological need for men's control, supervision and protection.
3. Male identified: Most aspects of society that are highly valued and rewarded are associated with men and identified with male characteristics. Any other attributes that are less valued and rewarded are associated with women.
4. Male-centricity: Public attention (e.g. media, public spaces) is often granted to men and women are placed in the background and on the margins.[5]

At issue here is the superior social status associated with maleness and the abuses such superior status allows. As the name suggests, patriarchy (from the Latin word *patriarch*, meaning father) is experienced in the smallest unit of society, the family, and extends outwards to the larger society. Patriarchal structures also hinder genuine solidarity among women, and are reinforced through an educational system in which boys and girls are taught gendered rules for acceptable behaviour. Nedjma Plantade, an anthropologist of Maghrebi descent, described the aims of traditional North African education with regard to gender roles:

> It is clear that educational rules have the following goals: for a boy to become a man endowed with three fundamental qualities: honesty, family values and disinterest in women and sexuality, for girls to become obedient women, submissive, polite, respectful and self-effacing.[6]

Plantade also argued that in North African societies, because a woman's standing in the community is under constant scrutiny and observation and her value derives from approval by men, women tend to view other women as rivals rather than as potential allies.[7] Such competition between women is evident in contemporary rivalries between the leaders of various Moroccan women's associations, be they Islamist, secular, or in-between. Across the board, disagreement often exists based not on some larger philosophical outlook on gender but on conflicts of personality both within and between secular and religious activist groups. Regardless of such differences, however, the gender discourse is always situated within the context of Morocco's Muslim identity. Though secular women's rights associations were instrumental in passing the landmark 2004 Personal Status Code reform – a topic to which we shall return later in this chapter – today they often find themselves at odds with an increasingly popular performance of religious observance among women.

Secular associations refer to organizations that use universal human rights as their guiding principle in advocating for women's rights. This is not to say that the Moroccan women who lead such associations do not value or practise their religion. When speaking of Islamists in this book, I mean individuals, both male and female, and organizations that use the religion of Islam as their primary reference point. Islamists in Morocco are not a uniform group; instead, different Islamist organizations hold widely differing views depending on their particular interpretation of the sacred scriptures. In Morocco, Islamist pertains primarily to non-violent religious activists. Though there are small criminal groups that have appropriated Islam to justify their actions, these are rejected by the vast majority of Moroccans, non-violent Islamists included. Where appropriate, I use the terms Muslim culture and Muslim-majority countries instead of Islamic culture or Islamic countries because it is humans who create cultural patterns and states, and their views and practices change according to eras and to societies. Modern challenges are posed to and by Muslims and not to Islam as a faith.[8]

The West's obsession with Muslim women

One of the main challenges faced by Moroccan society is the status and role of women. Today, the most intense discourse about 'the woman question' actually occurs within Muslim-majority countries like Morocco. Such discussion often revolves around the role of individual agency versus the importance of maintaining collective cohesion. Significant differences on this issue exist among such Muslim-majority countries as Saudi Arabia, Afghanistan, Turkey, Mauritania, Mali, and Indonesia. Even within the North African region, attitudes about women's rights differ from Tunisia to Algeria to Morocco and are manifest in vibrant debates within each country. The Muslim world is not a monolithic bloc, nor is there a general consensus within a given country. In fact, the discourse on gender is probably one of the most divisive and controversial in Morocco. Not a week goes by that issues related to women are not discussed in the media, at one academic conference or another, in a mosque, in parliament, or on the street. The current internal discourse within Morocco has much to offer the Western world, where the debate about Muslim women is often conducted with a kind of tunnel vision.

Westerners often see the West and the Muslim world as having irreconcilable differences concerning the status and role of women. They view the Orient as propagating submission and conferring the status of second-class citizenship, and the Occident as offering liberties, freedom, and equal rights. (Yet even in the West, women's emancipation is a relatively recent achievement.) Dating back to the colonial period, Western Europe in particular has had something akin to an obsession with Muslim women. While the American public was propelled to acknowledge the existence of Muslims in the aftermath of the 11 September 2001 World Trade Center attacks in New York City and in the course of the two subsequent wars in Afghanistan and Iraq, Europe has had historical interactions with the Muslim world for centuries. In fact, the sometimes contentious relationships between colonial powers and previously subjugated countries have resulted in sporadic terrorist attacks on European soil for decades. This has been the case especially in France. The Algerian civil strife of the 1990s between government forces, militias, and armed Islamist extremists spilled over into the hexagon, as metropolitan France is often called, resulting in a string of terrorist assaults. Since the 1960s Europe has been home to a significant and steadily increasing Muslim population. In 2009, nearly 10 per cent of the French population was of Muslim immigrant background, followed by Germany, Great Britain, and Italy.[9]

Within the last several years, there has been a shift in the European discourse about these minorities. While in the past, immigrants were identified by region or country of origin – North African, West African, Asian, Turk, and so on – today they are jointly referred to as Muslims, connoting a false sense of homogeneity and unified otherness. As a result, Islam has inserted itself into Western European public debate, with religion and women a central theme. Indicative of the real or perceived conflict between Western and Muslim mores are the fervent debates about women's dress, in particular the headscarf and the full-face veil. In 2004, France banned in public schools the 'wearing of ostentatious religious symbols', which, for all intents and purposes, refers to the Muslim headscarf. Six years on, parliaments from liberal Netherlands to Belgium and Germany are back at debating Muslim women's attire, only this time questioning the wearing in public of the full-face veil, be it the Afghan style *burqa*, or the piece of clothing that covers everything but the eyes, the *niqab*.

In April 2011 France became the first European country to ban the full-face veil and make wearing it a punishable offense. Women seen covering their face in public are to be fined the equivalent of $217 and required to receive instruction in citizenship. Further, anyone found forcing a woman to cover her face risks a fine as large as the equivalent of $43,400. Even Muslim-majority countries such as Egypt and Tunisia have implemented laws banning this form of dress in certain places. Muslim women have become central to domestic discussions on national identity, integration, and *Leitkultur*, the German term for the Judeo-Christian primary or lead culture. The acrimonious climate between majority populations and minority Muslim populations in the West reverberates throughout the Muslim world and fuels the momentum of their own gender discourse.

One may wonder why it is that 'women' have to bear the burden of discussions on economic development, unemployment, the process of democratization, integration, assimilation, and questions of national and religious identity. Certainly the issue of religion and women, or more specifically women in Islam, is a topic that never ceases to inflame, incite, and provoke public discourse and vehement expressions among those of all shades of the spectrum. Why are women at the centre of debates concerning all manner of issues that are not necessarily linked to gender? There is no definite answer to this question but it is possible to venture some guesses. Though their legal status and actual treatment is that of a disenfranchised minority in many places around the world, women make up roughly half of the world's population. Every human being is linked in some way to a woman: a mother, sister, wife, daughter. Beyond political, social, and economic experts with specialized concerns, then, every human being has a vested interest in the role and the status of women.

Women's rights touch on private as much as public matters. In private relationships important questions arise, such as how is one to raise a daughter, what is the relationship with a sister, and, most crucially, how would an altered legal status and public role for women affect the most private of relationships – namely, between a couple? For many men, their most important emotional investment is in women, first and foremost their mothers, and then their wives and daughters.

Because these relationships deeply involve issues of power and domination, sexuality and morals, legitimacy, secrecy, social norms, and economic questions, there is no clear dividing line between private and public when it comes to discussions about the status of women in a society. In addition, religious interpretations are often central to understandings about the position of women. Their role as mothers, wives, and daughters is addressed in the holy books of all monotheistic religions. Historically, men's dominance over women has been understood as being divinely ordained. Even in cases where men question their status of superiority, faith can push them to assume a dominant status just as women may accept their inferior status as a religious duty, be they Jewish, Christian, or Muslim. Religiously sanctioned male privilege has remained intact for centuries; therefore, discussions about women's rights are linked to the reinterpretation of sacred texts. As scholar of Islam Tariq Ramadan wrote:

> It may well be over the women's issue that tensions, contradictions, and concerns are most frequent and complex. This involves human relationships, deep-seated representation, and relationship logic that, beyond scriptural sources themselves, have to do with age-old cultural and social heritages that remain deeply ingrained and highly sensitive. Speaking about women in any human group means interfering with the groundwork of social structures, of cultural symbolisms, of gender roles, of the position in the family unit, and of authority and power relationships.[10]

Ramadan's assessment implies that rights and freedoms accorded to men are an indisputable fact of life. Further, the implication of Ramadan's assertion is that, whether justified or not, the conventions of male domination ensure some measure of stability in the home and in society at large. It is only when the status and role of women are at stake that questions about the social order arise. How many domestic and international debates have dealt with men's suitability to occupy public office, men's privileged access to professional advancement, men's innate qualifications to handle public or private finances, or to hold political office? How often have theologians or social scientists warned that peace and social cohesion may be at stake once men contribute to household chores or take an active role in raising their children? It is worth pondering these questions, ridiculous as they may seem, if only to demonstrate the depth of our assumptions about male superiority and of our acceptance of their suitability for a privileged status.

Closely linked to theological considerations about women is the perennial nature versus nurture debate. In today's West, there is widespread agreement that biology does not determine an individual's legal standing nor his or her capacity to pursue a chosen private or professional path. In Morocco, however, the discussion about women's rights frequently refers to biology. Unlike opinions based purely on faith, opinions based on biology and proven sexual differences provide scientific underpinning for religious positions on women.

Feminism before feminism

However fervent the contemporary discussion about women's rights in Morocco, this debate is not new. In modern Moroccan history it dates back to the period 1912–56, when the country was a French Protectorate. In 1935, Algerian legal scholar Tahar Essafi, who spent much of his time in neighbouring Morocco, observed: 'North African women doze in semi-permanent hibernation of uniform traditions. Legal liberation is held hostage by habits, morals and customs passed on from time immemorial'. Essafi described the need for some form of feminism (a term he used as early as 1935) and warned that conservative Muslims perceived emancipation as threats. In the foreword to Essafi's book, *The Moroccan Woman: Morals – Social Conditions – Evolution*, Ginerva Hubac wrote: 'To be a feminist is first and foremost wanting dignity for women. Dignity through freedom, dignity through equality. North Africans should not be terrified by these concepts. However, evolution progresses slowly.' This text, written nearly 80 years ago, puts into perspective current discussions of women's rights in Morocco and the larger North African region. Essafi's arguments are as current today as they were at the time of his writing, a pertinent reminder of *plus ça change, plus c'est la même chose.*[11] He wrote then as one would nowadays:

> The condition of Arab women – the woman in Islam – has always been confused, mixed in with all sorts of other problems. Questions about Islam are so-to-say *à la mode* just as the question of the veil, polygamy and emancipation.[12]

This observation shows that today's discussions about women's rights are not original; rather, they are a continuation of a theme that has been played out in North Africa for a long time. However, the contemporary debate is more far-reaching and broad-based than ever before and not confined to small, exclusive scholarly circles. Essafi described other themes that are as current today as they were nearly a century ago, namely religion and law and the rural/urban divide. He argued that religiously based law stood in the way of emancipation and progress in general, and that allowing rural areas to apply 'tribal laws' was an impediment to national development. Among the issues Essafi raised, the only one that has been resolved since the time of his writings concerns slavery, which was a common practice in Morocco in the early part of the twentieth century.

A contemporary of Essafi, French legal scholar Octave Pèsle also studied the situation of Moroccan women in the early twentieth century. Pèsle emphasized the need for urgent legal reform, particularly of the Personal Status Code, or family law. He specifically recommended abolishing the legally sanctioned practice of *talaq* (repudiation), whereby a man can unilaterally declare a divorce from his wife. Pèsle also suggested eliminating the system of guardianship that stipulates that a woman is under the lifelong tutelage of a *wali* (male guardian) whose permission she needs in order to marry and to make basic decisions for her life.[13] Pèsle wrote this in 1944, just around the time when women in his home country of France were about to gain full citizenship, including the right to vote. As Morocco was then a French protectorate, Pèsle believed that rights granted to women in Europe should be extended to women in French-occupied territories as well. But things would evolve differently in North Africa. The French occupiers were not keen on granting the indigenous population such rights, and upon independence in 1956 post-colonial Moroccan authorities were preoccupied with tasks other than gender equality. It was not until about 60 years after Pèsle's admonitions that the practices of repudiation and the guardian system were abolished as part of the Personal Status Code reform of 2004.

For Pèsle, female slaves were also of concern. These were mostly black African women from countries south of the Sahara. Slavery was formally abolished in Morocco in 1926, but continued in some form for decades afterwards. Today, slavery itself is no longer an issue, yet another equally disturbing practice has replaced it, namely that of *petites bonnes* who do the work formerly provided by slaves. *Petites bonnes* refers to girls, some as young as eight years, who work as domestic servants in middle- and upper-middle-class families. Primarily daughters of large, poor, urban or rural families, often they are kept in appalling conditions, underpaid, overworked, and frequently sexually abused by their employers.

A look at the annals of history reveals that some discussions have a long history, and that the same arguments have been used time and again to justify certain positions. During the early part of the twentieth century, when France insisted on ending slavery in its colonies and protectorates, some local leaders opposed this reform, arguing that 'the abolition of slavery is in total contradiction to the Muslim religion and will therefore be widely unpopular'.[14] An eminent pioneer of Muslim feminism, Fatima Mernissi, researched reports dating to that period and found official statements opposing the end of slavery: 'Slavery is part of our tradition; human rights and democracy are in contradiction to our sacred values'.[15] Mernissi advocated for legal reforms that would advance human rights and combat violent acts against women 'that are part of the traditional landscape'.[16]

The debates about slavery in Morocco in the early twentieth century have application to the current discourse on women's rights there. Though few people today would argue that slavery was an institution worth preserving, some Islamists use the very same arguments once used to oppose ending slavery to rail against gender equality. While no one now would dispute that the abolition of slavery in Morocco, for males and females alike, was a necessary step towards modernity, it is useful to recall that many there previously opposed the elimination of this practice in the name of religion, culture, and national identity. Still, while slavery no longer exists, permutations that allow for the exploitation of underage girls and women continue to pose a serious problem.

In the early part of the twentieth century, progressive Moroccans also pushed for improving the legal status of women and discussed the merits of feminism. This was, we should remember, long before the term feminism had become part of the vocabulary in the United States. In his book *Feminisme, Islam, Soufisme* (1997), Moroccan sociologist Abdessamad Dialmy documented the evolution of the effort to achieve rights for women in Morocco since the 1920s. According to Dialmy, at the time when Morocco was under French rule, proponents of feminism were mostly men whose attempts at reform were decried as being in contradiction to the religion of Islam, just as in contemporary discussions. Like many modern theologians, these early supporters of women's rights in Morocco insisted that the second-class status of women was based on a 'flawed interpretation of Islam'.[17]

According to visionaries of that period, the subordination of women was due to 'deviant, even heretic masculine interpretation of sacred texts'.[18] Thus, they proposed, though largely in vain, a new scriptural reading of the Qur'an and Hadith. In 1927, Mohammed Allal al Fassi (1910–74), Islamic scholar and one of the founding fathers of the Moroccan movement for independence from France,[19] submitted a petition to the municipal council of his hometown Fes in which he denounced excessive demands for dowry. In addition, he chided local authorities for continuing to permit the practice of putting blood-stained linen on public display after the wedding night so as to prove the virginity of the bride. Sadiqi and Ennaji noted that although al Fassi also opposed essential Muslim practices like polygamy, for the most part this opposition was not because he was concerned with the development of women as individuals. Instead, he believed that marrying multiple wives tarnished the image of modern Islam.[20] More recently, Muslim modernists, or purists (depending on one's point of view), were preoccupied with initiating a fresh discourse on their religion in order to promote development in their country. Though the emancipation of women was not central among their concerns, it happened to be part of an overall modernization agenda. Similarly, in proposing a more egalitarian agenda, al Fassi sought to liberate Moroccans from all forms of slavery and exploitation.[21]

Others did see an explicit need for reform that would specifically elevate the status of women. In 1938, Islamic scholar and jurist M. El Hajouri presented a statement to the Franco-Moroccan club of Casablanca in which he argued that Islam was in the process of producing its own feminism. According to contemporary sociologist Dialmy:

Modern feminism, which had ardent defenders in the West, was gaining ground *peu à peu* in the Muslim world where it began to have no less audacious supporters. The Muslim world needs to take the example of the West and bring forth its own champions of feminism. The emancipation of women has to have its place in the socio-political discussion and needs to be an integral part of contemporary debates.[22]

In advocating for a 'feminist Islam', scholars at that time set out to show how certain degrading practices that were incorporated into the Malekite[23] school of law were contrary to the spirit of Islam. Chapter 3 extends this idea by addressing the scholarly method of *maqasid*; that is, the method for exploring the spirit or meaning behind laws in a manner that differs from legalistic, formulaic interpretations and is employed today in the promotion of a third way, namely a new interpretation of Qur'anic scriptures that addresses the needs of a modern society.

A decade later, in the period 1949–52, the above-mentioned Allal al Fassi again pointed to gender-based inequality as an issue requiring special attention. In his *Autocritique* he lamented the failure of Moroccan/Muslim society with regard to the status of women. He wrote that a profound reform was needed that would place love at the centre of marriage, and demanded that husbands treat their wives as partners. According to al Fassi, the challenge included, 'liberating women from the perverse alienation imposed in the name of Islam'. He argued that Moroccan social reforms were necessary in preparation for independence from France since liberation from the colonial power should include liberation from domestic forms of oppression.[24] Alas, as history shows, this was not to be the case. Even today, Morocco has not been successful in eradicating some of the underlying causes that permit continued abuse – namely, poverty and illiteracy. With a 60 per cent illiteracy rate among women, a percentage significantly higher than in several much poorer African countries south of the Sahara, and an annual per capita income the equivalent of $4,050, women's rights in Morocco take on a dimension that extends beyond legal equality. Various writers have addressed the disappointment of women who actively participated in the struggle for independence but were subsequently relegated to a pre-colonial subservient status in the post-independence period.

Leila Abouzeid wrote in her novella *The Year of the Elephant* (1989) that liberation from French colonial occupiers did not go hand-in-glove with liberation for women. To the contrary, old-fashioned interpretations of Islam were invoked in an effort to frame a post-colonial national identity that would be distinctly different from the French protectorate period. Women came to bear the burden of this newly defined Muslim national identity. Abouzeid described how middle-class men cherished their newfound freedom and independence in the post-colonial period, whereas women were asked to revert to a subservient status and assume the role of 'good Muslim wife' in order to establish an authentic national identity based on Islam. In her autobiography *Return to Childhood: Memoir of a Modern Moroccan Woman* (1993), Abouzeid described her struggle within her own family as women fought for national independence on the one hand while at the same time seeking to carve out a new role for themselves. Though fluent in French, like most contemporary Moroccan authors Abouzeid wrote in Arabic, and was the first female Moroccan literary author whose books were translated into English. In her introduction to *The Year of the Elephant*, Elizabeth Warnock Fernea wrote of the protagonist Zahra:

> Zahra's experience clearly does not conform to that of most Western feminists. She is not a Western woman, but a Moroccan

woman, a Muslim woman who finds comfort in her religious faith ... One woman's experience becomes a metaphor for society, a view that has less to do with Western ideas of individualism than it does with Middle Eastern ideas of the value of the group.[25]

It is important to note that the term feminism has been in use since the time of the French Revolution of 1789. When speaking of feminism in North Africa, I am referring to a historic phenomenon that has been intermittently present there for nearly a century, and has addressed issues of gender inequality germane to the countries in that region.

Pioneer of Islamic feminism: Fatima Mernissi

Following in the footsteps of earlier male advocates for women's rights in Morocco is Fatima Mernissi, one of the contemporary initiators of what is now called 'Islamic feminism'. Mernissi is widely considered a pioneer of Muslim feminist scholarship. A French- and US-trained sociologist, she is quick to point out that a women's rights agenda in Morocco was first articulated by men, and that even today, a considerable number of men are actively engaged in gender rights endeavours. Mernissi is adamant that women's rights concerns must be embedded and cannot be achieved in isolation from larger economic, social, and political projects. Much like early Moroccan progressive thinkers, her concern with gender issues is grounded in an interest in broader societal change and development. Her books, which have been translated into more than 30 languages, are read worldwide, and are today considered classic texts. Some titles are: *Beyond the Veil: Male-Female Dynamics in Modern Muslim Societies* (1987); *The Veil and the Male Elite: A Feminist Interpretation of Women's Rights in Islam* (with Mary Jo Lakeland) (1992); *Dreams of Trespass: Tales of a Harem Girlhood* (1995); *Women's Rebellion and Islamic Memory* (1996); *The Forgotten Queens of Islam* (with Mary Jo Lakeland) (1997); *Scheherazade Goes West* (2001); and *Islam and Democracy: Fear of the Modern World* (2002).

Despite her international acclaim, Mernissi enjoys limited popularity in her home country of Morocco, where only a relatively small circle of intellectuals is familiar with her work. Invitations for public presentations come mostly from international organizations; consequently, her audiences usually include a sizable number of expatriate dignitaries and foreign exchange students who cherish the opportunity to hear such a renowned scholar up close. Since retiring from academia, Mernissi conducts her public appearances more as dialogues by requiring the audience to participate. She calls out questions and asks audience members to sit with her at the podium so as to create the traditional setting of a community meeting. With her quick wit and humour accentuating her flamboyant appearance in hot pink or purple tunics with matching turbans on her flaming red hair, her presentations are more like happenings than scholarly lectures.

Since Mernissi has not written about women's issues in years, I decided to visit her in her unassuming apartment in Rabat to learn about her current interests. There is no name nor any apartment number on the high-rise building where she lives, yet when her neighbours saw me, a foreigner, searching for the entrance, they immediately came up to ask if I was looking for Madame Mernissi and proceed to offer directions to her place. Given her achievements, Mernissi is remarkably unpretentious and accessible, though her assertiveness can at first be intimidating. She is adamant that she is no longer interested in women's rights issues, insisting that she said what she had to say decades ago and now has moved on. This *grande dame* of Muslim feminism describes herself as 'an intellectual nomad' who must move from one issue to the next. The question of women's rights formerly interested her as part of her focus on social change but for the past several years she has been researching the impact of satellite television, the Internet, and more recently social media on young people who grow up in authoritarian systems in the Arab world. Considering just how instrumental social media were in the North African and Middle Eastern uprisings in early 2011 shows yet again that Mernissi, in spite of her advanced age, has her hand on the pulse of the moment.

In addition to her scholarly endeavours, Mernissi supports young artists and organizes sessions with rural women weavers. Her spacious, bright living room is filled with contemporary local artwork. Tapestry is an ancient means of transmitting messages, so she feels she gets to understand the concerns of a largely voiceless segment of the population by learning about the worries they weave into carpets and blankets. In workshops with rural, often illiterate women, she focuses on art. When interviewed, Mernissi observed: 'It is not only by talking with these women that you learn what they think, it is by looking at what they weave, what they paint, the songs they sing that you understand them.' Mernissi said she frequently strolls through rural *souks*, weekly outdoor markets, to look at changes in the design and colours of the wares women bring as a means of ascertaining what is occupying their minds at a given time. In so doing, she has discovered local artists of considerable talent and has used her stature to promote their work.

Mernissi's interaction with local artisans has inspired her to design her own clothes and jewellery and reject factory-made outfits. She pointed out that making garments and crafting jewellery are the Moroccan way; they are time-honoured, collective, and creative activities. Indeed, she finds repulsive the widespread enchantment of the Moroccan upper and middle classes with Western designer clothing and accessories. As an independent woman, she refuses to adhere to the dictums of foreign fashion designers, no matter how famous. Mernissi sees her choices as a stab at what she called the obsession of elite Moroccan women with high-end European labels, which to her are an indication that such purportedly emancipated women remain 'voluntarily slavishly linked to the West'. In fact, Mernissi believes that one of the biggest challenges for Moroccans is to become genuinely independent:

> The emergence of the individual is one of the single most important trends that have become apparent in the past decades. But people here have to get used to being individuals and being treated as such. Because of our authoritarian culture, we are not used to thinking for ourselves. For substantial change to take root, we need to reflect on what it is we want and not just criticize what is.

Mernissi cites this groupthink mentality as one of the reasons she is no longer interested in discussions about women's rights. She sees people on most sides of the spectrum, secular feminists and Islamists alike, as reiterating positions already articulated elsewhere without developing authentic new ideas.

Given Morocco's history of bringing people from diverse backgrounds together, Mernissi is hopeful that women's rights advocates in her country will in time join ranks and devise a plan that serves all its citizens. She refers to the fact that throughout the Maghreb,[26] various Amazigh (Berber) ethnic groups and Arabs have mixed for more than a thousand years, creating a distinct Maghrebi culture that differs from predominantly Arab countries. In her usual polemic manner, Mernissi provocatively asserted:

> Syrians and people from Arab states of the Persian Gulf are strangers to me; I don't feel Arab in the same way Middle Easterners do. The only thing we have sort of in common is language and religion and not even that completely.

Indeed, the Moroccan Arabic, *derjea*, is a distinct Arab dialect that draws heavily on various Tamazight[27] languages and French and is not easily understood beyond the Maghreb. Islam in Morocco is heavily influenced by Sufism, the mystical and less dogmatic branch of Islam. Furthermore, indigenous Imazighen (Berber) communities have in the course of history adopted Judaism, Christianity, and Islam.

Reluctantly returning to the issue of feminism, Mernissi said she left the scholarly study of women's rights long ago:

> I even find the current term 'gender' ridiculous. It does not make sense to ordinary people whose lives we say we want to improve. These terms enslave people. When I wrote about women and their rights in the Muslim world, I found that historically the greatest feminists among Muslims were men. Labels are meaningless to me; I find them divisive. It sets intellectuals apart from the masses whose rights they say they advocate. I wrote about Islamic feminism thirty years ago. It has become fashionable now but it no longer interests me. I don't keep up with trends.

Fatima Mernissi, who recently changed the spelling of her first name to Fatema in order to be consistent with a Moroccan pronunciation, is one of the first authors of what now is referred to as 'Islamic feminist texts'. Despite no longer conducting research in this field, she naturally is pleased when people offer her books that are stimulated by her work. To prove the point, in one of my meetings with her, she hauled a cardboard box into her living room, filled with books on women's rights in the Muslim world. The books were either dedicated to her, credited her as inspiring the work, or extensively cited her. Almost weekly, a new addition arrives in the mail. She claimed not to have read any of them, adding: 'The academic world is too narrow for me; I cannot focus on one theme forever. I need to move, I need to think about new topics, fresh ideas.'

Not surprisingly, then, rather than answering my questions, Mernissi steered our conversation to issues currently of interest to her. She explained why she enjoys talking about Sufism, the mystical dimension of Islam with deep roots in Morocco:

> In Sufism you learn about yourself by exploring that which is different. The same applies to academic inquiry. If you stay with the same subject too long, it is no longer unfamiliar and therefore does not teach you much anymore. You are not really expanding but get caught up in ever more details regardless of their importance. To me that is not appealing. This is why I have moved my interest from feminism to psychoanalysis[28] to discussing art and currently the influence of the new communication technologies, satellite TV, and social media on our youth. What interests me here is the absence of boundaries in cyberspace. I am always interested in moving beyond boundaries, crossing frontiers. Social media allow for the breaking down of barriers in ways I did not imagine possible in my younger years.

Mernissi likes to relate one of her favourite Sufi maxims, which is that a truly wise person learns from the wanderer, from the stranger who passes through your land. Thus, she sees no conflict between her Moroccan Muslim identity and her interest in ideas imported from abroad.

Asserting this particular aspect of the Sufi tradition puts Mernissi yet again at odds with contemporary gender-related discourse which is, to put it simply, either anti-Western and Islamist or secular and pro-Western. In keeping with her groundbreaking academic track record, Mernissi continuously seeks to explore emerging changes before they become manifest. She feels that the surfacing of a third way, a topic explored in Chapter 3, is an anticipated development in Morocco whose time has come. Still, now that women's rights debates have moved to the forefront in Morocco, she says she prefers to leave this argument to a younger generation:

> I could be the mother – grandmother even – of the people who are discussing women's rights nowadays. They think they are proclaiming a new paradigm, are proud of their novel ideas. I had these debates inside my head a long time ago and have written about various changing approaches to women's rights. That is as much as I have to say about this.

With this comment, she picked up her delicate gold-rimmed glass and took a sip of strong, sweet mint tea, indicating that the discussion on this topic was over.

As with most pioneers, Mernissi's work caused controversy when it first appeared, especially among fellow Moroccan scholars. It is certainly possible that envy at her rapid international success played a role in the animosity she faced, particularly from her male peers. Much of the scholarly criticism concerned her assertion that the Qur'an needs to be historicized. Though this contention is accepted today (and discussed further in Chapter 3), at the time of Mernissi's writing this idea was controversial. Though she does not deny the divine origin of the Qur'an, Mernissi has emphasized its human dimension, most evident in the infamous 'Satanic verses' (53:19–23),[29] which can be interpreted as indicating that the Prophet momentarily acknowledged the existence of female goddesses of the Quraysh ethnic group, a statement he later retracted. To Mernissi, this is indicative of the Prophet's own admitted 'humanness' and definite evidence that he made no claim to being divine. Mernissi proposed that the Qur'anic revelation has to be understood in relation to the specific historic and geographical context in which it was conceived, and that in a modern context it requires a fresh look in order to understand its meaning and application to changing times.

One of Mernissi's early critics, Anouar Majid, accused her of 'desacralizing the Qur'an by reducing it to a historic document'. In turn, Raja Rhouni called Majid's critique of Mernissi a prime example of 'authoritarian discourse' in Moroccan academia.[30] In fact, Rhouni highlighted passages in Majid's criticism in which he seemed to have appointed himself judge over which interpretations are and are not Islamic. Thus, Rhouni argued, while Majid gave himself the right to interpretation, he refused to concede this to his female colleague Mernissi. Today, of course, reading the Qur'an in its historical context is a common practice that no longer incites contentious debates in scholarly circles. Interestingly, some of Mernissi's former critics have since adopted similar methods and one of Majid's own books explores the necessity of debate and dissent among Muslims.[31]

Rhouni, a young Moroccan academic, has provided the first comprehensive analysis of Mernissi's complete works. She argued that inconsistencies in Mernissi's positions – another point of contention for Mernissi's critics – are due to the exploratory and innovative nature of her work. Because Mernissi was a pioneer in the field of Muslim feminist scholarship, she covered new ground and experimented with different approaches and paradigms. Rhouni has suggested that Mernissi's intellectual inquisitiveness led her at times to embrace secularism and with it Western feminism, and at other times to delve into sacred scriptures and historical examples of female Muslim leaders as a means of finding a basis for gender equality within an Islamic context. Mernissi's research also reflects academic trends of the times in which they were written. What others have called contradictory or conflicting conclusions in Mernissi's research, Rhouni has taken as the expected evolution of an emerging scholarship.

Rhouni also examined a neglected aspect of Mernissi's scholarly output, namely her research on poor rural and urban women who constitute the majority of Morocco's female population. Prior to Mernissi's investigation, this group had not been the subject of Moroccan scholarly analysis. By the same token, until recently government programmes routinely excluded these women, who are perceived as not playing a vital part in the economic progress of the country. Early on, Mernissi identified their exclusion as an essential flaw in the modernizing agenda, the focus of which was expanding the rights of an already privileged urban elite rather than bringing the large masses of illiterate and poor women into the mainstream.

Support for Mernissi's assessment of this situation came from unlikely circles: Islamists took up this very argument in criticizing the Personal Status Code reform of 2004, contending that the law reform endowed well-to-do urban women with rights while rural and poor women remained disenfranchised. Illiterate and without legal representation, such women remained subject to ancient forms of adjudication. The exclusion of a sizable segment of the female population from Morocco's nation-building project has been a consistent grievance of some Islamists, especially those belonging to Al Adl wa Ihsane (the Justice and Charity movement). It is not surprising, then, that Mernissi was one of the first observers of an emerging Islamic feminism in Morocco. Writing in the last of her trilogy on Islam and gender equality, *Islam and Democracy*, she noted:

> What we are seeing today is a claim by women to their right to God and the historical tradition. This takes various forms. There are women who are active within the fundamentalist movements and those who work on a reinterpretation of the Muslim heritage as a necessary ingredient to our modernity. Our liberation will come through a rereading of our past and a re-appropriation of all that has structured our civilization.[32]

Mernissi asserted that the umbrella term Islamic feminism encompasses different actors with differing agendas and includes even those who reject this designation. Rhouni observed that Mernissi employed Islamic feminism as an analytical term that includes the ideas of intellectuals like her (those who do not support the project of an Islamist state) as well as those who argue from a position of faith and others who use it in recognition of the need to contextualize Islamic gender norms. Defined in this way, Islamic feminism is not a coherent theory that provides the basis for a plan of action but is an approach that includes the differing conceptions of Muslim women in various Muslim-majority countries, as well as those in the West who advocate for women's rights based on a shared religious heritage.

Regardless of how fellow Moroccans perceive the work of Fatima Mernissi, she has inspired and influenced the discourse on gender in this North African country and the larger Muslim world like few other figures before or after her. Having her books published in English gave Mernissi an advantage over other scholars, such as Farida Bennani, who has worked on similar themes for almost as long as Mernissi, but has published only in Arabic. Because Bennani's books have not been translated into French or English, her considerable scholarly output has been inaccessible to most Western audiences.

Though Mernissi sees gender equality as part of necessary broader social transformations in Morocco, like anyone else she could not have foreseen that the women's rights agenda in Morocco would benefit from national and international events that had nothing to do with women.

The war on terrorism and women's rights

In 1777, Morocco was the first country to recognize the United States, and since then the two countries have maintained a strong relationship. Morocco was one of the first Arab countries to support the US global war on terrorism in the aftermath of the 11 September 2001 attacks in New York City. Morocco itself has not been impervious to terrorism. On 16 May 2003, suicide bombings rocked Casablanca, the economic centre and largest city in the country. For Moroccans, these murderous attacks were traumatic. Members of the Salafia Jihadia, a self-proclaimed Islamist extremist fringe group with links to Al Qaeda, killed 43 people in bright daylight. In April of 2011 the same group attacked a well-known tourist restaurant in Marrakesh, killing 17 people. As a moderate Muslim-majority country, Morocco had felt immune to such attacks, and in the wake of this home-grown terrorism, Morocco aligned itself even closer with the United States. Until the attacks in Casablanca, Moroccan Islamism was represented by peaceful voices that often opposed government policies, in the case of the Justice and Charity movement, even speaking out against the institution of the monarchy. Violence has not been part of the agenda of Moroccan Islamists; instead, one of their main goals has been controlling public morals. Yet after the terrorist attacks in 2003, Moroccan Islamists were keen to establish their distance from the criminal elements that had wreaked havoc in the name of religion, and temporarily stood united behind the king and the government.

The bombings coincided with King Mohammed VI's finalizing of a major reform of the *moudawana* (the Personal Status Code in Moroccan law) that would significantly elevate the status of women. Until then, the Islamist political party and the largest Islamist movement had opposed the reform. The 2003 terrorist attacks resulted in a pervasive climate of fear, one that temporarily drew people closer even across ideological or religious divides, much as happened in the United States following the attack on the World Trade Center in New York in 2001. In an effort to demonstrate loyalty to their country and affirm their law-abiding nature, Islamists ceased their critique of the monarch's reform plans. In so doing, Islamists wanted to emphasize their categorical rejection of violence and confirm their distance from criminal groups that carry out deadly attacks in the name of Islam. Thus, the actions of some of Morocco's own misguided sons created a sense of national unity and silenced internal dissent. Seizing the moment, the king used this climate of national solidarity to push through the Personal Status Code reform. As was to be expected, the alliance of peaceful Islamist groups with the king's Personal Status reform plans did not last long, and soon after the new *moudawana* (family code) was announced they went on the offensive again, ironically claiming this time that the changes did not go far enough.

It is within this context that the women's rights agenda in Morocco received a big push forward and benefitted from otherwise tragic events. The 2004 Personal Status Code revision marked a turning point in modern Moroccan history nearly a century after it was first suggested.

Changing laws, changing minds:
The Personal Status Code reform

Because the family is essential to every society, each country has specific laws pertaining to this unit. No country allows individual citizens to decide for themselves what constitutes a family and which laws should govern it. Thus, to the extent that the state intervenes to protect and grant rights to each member of the family unit, the family is in fact a politicized entity. For example, there are laws that protect the weakest members of a family by making severe child abuse and exploitation a crime. As Olivier Roy argued, 'law is first and foremost an expression of will: positive law, the law of the state, does not need to reflect any supposed natural morality; it is foundational, just as divine will is creative'.[33]

Laws pertaining to the family are closely linked to religious beliefs. In the West, based on Judeo-Christian norms, marriage is defined as a union between one man and one woman. In predominantly Muslim societies, on the other hand, a man may marry up to four wives. A legal age for marriage is set to ensure the protection of minors, though in most countries the legal age for marriage historically has been lower for girls than for men. Inasmuch as the family is the smallest unit of society, transformations that occur within it will by extension affect the society and nation at large. Further, when laws pertaining to the family change, the conception of what constitutes a family changes. According to Malika Benradi, this shift can result in 'a profound crisis' within the heart of society.[34]

Conflicts over legal reform result in part from the distinction between religious and secular laws. While religious laws pertain to the upholding of particular standards for a community and are designed to ensure its well-being, modern secular laws are concerned with the rights of individual citizens. Weighing the importance of community welfare against the importance of individual rights requires a complex balancing act. This is especially the case in previously colonized countries that still today often have a mixture of traditional, religious, and modern Western laws. To complicate matters even more, these laws can sometimes be contradictory. Newly independent nations faced the challenge of merging, combining, and creating a legal system but often-differing sets of laws were just kept in place. As noted in the United Nations Development Programme's (2004) Human Development Report:

> The colonial imprint can be marked. Indeed, it is often difficult to determine which legal processes are genuinely traditional and which can be seen as a hybrid by-product of colonial manipulation and control. An added complication in separating authentic from imposed practices is that colonial rule and its 'civilizing mission' unilaterally claimed responsibility for introducing modern values, beliefs, and institutions to the colonies.[35]

While Morocco's present criminal and civil law is based primarily on French regulations, the Personal Status Code, which concerns family law, is based on Islamic religious law, creating two sets of laws that are at times in conflict with one another. To the extent that family law is a reflection of a country's culture, it is as much a cultural institution as a legal norm.[36] In addition, since the concept of the family as defined in family law forms the basis for women's private, and, by extension, public roles, it is central to society. Thus, changes to family law inevitably result in larger societal transformations.[37]

In Morocco, as in many Muslim-majority countries, Islamic jurisprudence emerged within a context of collective identity in which the extended family was the norm. A traditional extended family is a system of kinship across generations and consists of members beyond the conjugal family. Members are responsible for each other, especially male for female ones and the young for the elderly. Obligations to each other – financial and otherwise – are clearly delineated. Family law primarily outlined the responsibilities of male relatives to female ones. While this system ensured social cohesion in times past, in today's society, where the nuclear family has largely replaced the extended family in Morocco, what were once responsibilities have turned into claims or rights, such as a provision dictating that males inherit twice that of female members of a family. The purpose of privileging male inheritance was linked to their financial obligation for their female relatives. The socio-cultural shift from extended to nuclear families, then, made evident the need for laws that reflect modern realities.

In order to gain a broader perspective on possible detrimental consequences of changes to the Personal Status Code in Morocco, we can look at debates in the United States and Europe about the legalization of same-sex marriage. Both advocates and opponents acknowledge that changes in law will ultimately lead to an altered perception of what constitutes a marriage as well as a family. Moral and religious considerations weigh heavily on such debates, as do fears of weakening or endangering the cornerstone of civilization. Nevertheless, none of the countries that have legalized same-sex marriages – Spain, the Netherlands, Luxembourg, South Africa – has thus far experienced a major social breakdown.

One noteworthy difference exists between changes to marriage laws in the West and the changes to family law in Morocco. The Personal Status Code reform affects all members of society rather than granting rights to one particular minority. Further, unlike in the West, where family law is part of civil law, in Morocco, as in the Muslim world and Israel, family law is a category unto its own that is based on religious tenets. This religious component makes the stakes higher and the emotions, arguments, and debates about changes to the Personal Status Code even more vigorous than those about gay marriage in the West. In such a case, differing worldviews clash, with more religiously inclined people on one side, and more secularly minded ones on the other. Of course, even where family law is not rooted in religion but is secular, vehement disagreement exists when it comes to matters such as marriage and family. As legal scholar and anthropologist Lawrence Rosen put it:

> Though couched as statements of fact, legal discussions are, quite often, really creators of facts. Like religion, law is kind of a metasystem, which creates order in a universe that is often experienced in a more disorderly way.[38]

In Morocco, because laws governing the family are based on *shari'a*, or religious law, legal reform has serious religious implications as well.

If the Qur'an allows for polygamy, how can this practice be banned without a new, possibly controversial, interpretation of the scriptures? Issues surrounding practices such as polygamy or inheritance laws have religious significance as well as social importance and cannot be debated without acknowledging each of these components. In fact, Morocco's Personal Status Code reform required a religious approach as much as a legal one, since the premise *Islam din wa dawla* (Islam is religion and state) applies most closely to family law.

Beginning in 2000, Morocco's King Mohammed VI has advanced an agenda that seeks to reduce the contradictions between secularly based and religion-based laws. His efforts make the Personal Status Code reforms a social change project with far-reaching consequences. When adult members of a family, male and female alike, are legal equals, the conjugal relationship becomes the smallest unit of society in which democracy is constructed. In effect, the revised 2004 *moudawana* (family law) has changed the family from a hierarchical institution presided over by a man to a horizontal union between two equals. Though to date there have been no substantive studies on the impact of the law reform on education, employment, or level of political activity among women, this major modification can be expected to empower women to become more involved in political, economic, and religious life beyond the home. The reform also paves the way for children, differently abled, or other non-conformist members of the family to be treated with greater consideration. In a speech announcing the reform, the king explained the long-term consequences for his society in this way:

> We confirm our explicit will to consolidate major advances, embodied in the family code and which comprise of rights and obligations. These are not only founded on the principle of equality between men and women, but are conceived essentially to preserve family cohesion and to protect the family's authentic national identity.[39]

The 2004 Personal Status Code reform has informed public discourse, invigorated both the secular and various religious factions in

Morocco, and formed the basis for much of the public discourse concerning the status of women. Since the passing of the reform, a new dynamic between seemingly opposing forces has been stimulated. On the one side is King Mohammed VI – and by extension the government – intent on modernizing and, to a certain degree, secularizing the country, using women's rights as the battle cry. In this, secular feminist associations support the monarch. On the other side are male and female Islamists who believe that social change needs to be based on religious premises and achieved by way of cultural renewal and stricter religious observance. In broad terms, Islamists generally oppose reforms that are seen as copying Western models of emancipation and do not take the local context into consideration. They decry the king's motives as an effort to endear himself to the West in order to consolidate his power by securing international support. They charge that women, then, are being instrumentalized as tools of the State.

In Morocco, most of those who refer to themselves as Islamist or Islamic feminists (many activists in Morocco use the terms interchangeably) are not intent on rolling back the clock as it were, but on actively charging forward in an effort to identify a means by which women can gain their rights – and assume previously unheard of responsibilities within the family and beyond – while maintaining their spiritual integrity and religious identity. In fact, neither the label 'feminist' nor 'Islamist' describes activist women in Morocco very well. Both terms are connotatively laden, one infused with notions of Western supremacy, the other with religious dogmatism. Moreover, neither side is homogenous. Islamists disagree with each other over the correct interpretation of their sacred scriptures and the practical implications of these teachings. Though secular or liberal feminists share a similar agenda, they are splintered into dozens of associations. The forceful women who lead these non-governmental organizations (NGOs) are often in personal disagreement with each other, and their organizations rarely embody open, democratic structures. As Eddouada observed, patriarchal or authoritarian systems not only survive, but also are perpetuated within women's associations.[40] In all, much time and ink is spent discussing the meanings of terms like feminist or Islamist rather than addressing the actual concerns of women.

A royal tussle over reform

The one issue on which all non-Islamist women's rights activists in Morocco united was the Personal Status Code reform. 'Non-Islamist' includes secular women's rights advocates as well as pious women who nonetheless do not want religion to be the basis for law. A look back at the development of the 2004 *moudawana*, or family law reform, sheds light on the particular political and gender dynamics in this North African kingdom.

In the early 1990s, the Union de l'action féminine (UAF), or the Union for Feminine Action, a prominent Moroccan women's advocacy association, collected a million signatures for a petition urging the reform of the *moudawana*. In addition, they staged mock trials and rallies with the goal of starting a process of 'secularization' of women's rights issues. Various Islamist organizations and conservative thinkers opposed this activism and some issued a *fatwa* (a religious pronouncement by a scholar), charging feminists with apostasy. Al Islah wa a-Tawhid, the Mouvement unité et réforme (MUR), or the Unity and Reform Movement, out of which the Parti de la Justice et du Développement (PJD), or the Islamist Party of Justice and Development, eventually evolved, expressed grave reservations concerning *moudawana* reform. The criticism went so far as to decry changes to the Personal Status Code as a 'global Christian project', intent on undermining the 'Muslim fortress' as enshrined in divinely revealed family law. This debate occurred in Morocco before American political scientist Samuel Huntington wrote his landmark 1993 article *The Clash of Civilizations*,[41] and years before the publication of his book of the same title, in which he proposed that cultural and religious identities would be the primary source of conflict in the post-Cold War era.

In the midst of the contentious discourse on *moudawana* reform, the late King Hassan II, who ruled from 1961 until his death in 1999, who generally was not known to be particularly mindful of his subjects' opinions or demands, responded to the UAF's rallying cry and referred the matter to a council of religious leaders. After all, the UAF activists were highly educated middle- and upper-class women, some of whom were part of the Moroccan elite surrounding the monarch. In

1993, the king announced limited reforms to the *moudawana*. In this way, Hassan II assumed his customary role of keeping the peace and ensuring order in his North African kingdom by taking the lead on a divisive issue that was poised to cause internal strife. In his capacity as head of state and supreme religious leader, Hassan II made a shrewd move and spearheaded a limited reform of the Personal Status Code himself, thereby taking the wind out of the sails of both secular women's advocacy groups and Islamists, and diffusing the rising tension in the country.

As Moroccan sociologist and novelist Abdelkebir Khatibi has argued, external factors often play an unacknowledged yet major role in domestic decision-making.[42] Such was the case in Morocco, where Hassan II was known for brutally cracking down on political opposition but at the same time cultivating a good standing within the Western international community. The matter of timing was pertinent as well. His announcement to take charge of the Personal Status Code reform just preceded publication of a 1995 United Nations Human Development Report that ranked Morocco 117th out 147 surveyed countries. The damaging UN Report, coupled with a heavily indebted economy, made it necessary for the king to generate some goodwill in the international arena. It became expedient, then, for Hassan II to give the appearance of moving forward with a women's rights agenda. After ascending to the throne following his father's death in 1999, the young King Mohammed VI appointed yet another Personal Status Code commission. Aware of the rising influence of Islamism, the new king charged the commission with checking each article of the proposed reform against the Qur'an. If the scholars chosen for the task found justification for the changes in the sacred text, they were accepted. Certainly because members of the commission were handpicked, they were loath to find fault with the king's intended interpretations. Appalled by this blatant use of religion for political purposes, Islamists in 2000 activated half a million people to march through the streets of Morocco's biggest city, Casablanca, in protest against the intended reform. At the same time, smaller demonstrations in favour of the reform were organized in the capital city of Rabat. The large outpouring of public opinion was a new phenomenon in Morocco, and interestingly it was over the question of women's rights that the country had erupted. Of course, neither of the mass demonstrations was an actual spontaneous outburst, but instead carefully organized and orchestrated by both sides for maximum effect. In this way, Islamists and reformists demonstrated their clout in mobilizing people for their respective causes.

Aware of the male-centered nature of Moroccan society, King Mohammed VI described the legal reforms not as granting women more rights but instead reflecting the 'true nature of family law', meaning that the new laws pertained to all members of a family, including father, mother, and children. The following are some of the key aspects of these reforms to the Personal Status Code:[43]

1. Marriage age: The legal age of marriage for girls was raised from 15 to 18 and now is the same as for men.
2. Polygamy: This practice, permitted by the Qur'an, was severely restricted. The ruling of a judge is required to allow a husband to take a second or third wife and significant reasons must be offered in order to do so. Women are given a say in their husband's decision to marry a second wife. By statute, 'Women have the right to impose a condition in the marriage contract preventing the husband from taking a second wife. If there were no conditions, the first wife should be summoned to secure her consent. The second wife should be informed that the husband was married to another woman and her consent should be obtained, and the first wife should be given the right to demand a divorce.'
3. Repudiation: The Islamic practice of *talaq*, the right of a man to single-handedly repudiate his wife, was outlawed. This practice did not guarantee financial support for the repudiated woman and her children. The 2004 law stipulated that a court must grant divorce: 'A new procedure for divorce has been established, requiring the court's prior authorization. Divorce cannot be registered until all money owed to the wife and the children has been paid in full by the husband.' The law does state, however: 'Divorce is the husband's prerogative but the wife may avail herself of this prerogative.'

4. Divorce: The wife was granted the right to ask for a divorce. Before, a judge would not accept a request for divorce by a woman unless she could present a case of 'suffering prejudice' and witnesses. Now a woman's request for a divorce is considered on its own merits without requiring witnesses.

5. Obedience: Previously, a woman's obedience to her husband was legally required. This provision was stricken from the Personal Status Code.

6. Inheritance: Whereas in the past inheritance was patrilineal, the new law gives 'the granddaughter and the grandson on the mother's side the right to inherit from their grandfather, as part of the legacy, just like the son's children'.

7. Guardianship: The wife no longer needs permission from a guardian (*wali*) in order to marry, which was required by the old law.

8. Civil marriages: Marriages entered into outside of Morocco are now recognized, provided two of the witnesses to the marriage are Muslims.

9. Sharing of assets: Spouses may enter into a pre-nuptial agreement before marriage in order to ensure a fair sharing of acquired assets.

10. Child custody: In case of divorce, guardianship of children goes first to the mother, next to the father, next to the maternal grandmother, or otherwise is decided by a court. Appropriate housing and child support must be guaranteed.

11. Children outside of marriage: The rights of children will be safeguarded in case the parents were not married. Before, children born out of wedlock did not have to be recognized by the father, hence the mother could not expect or claim child support.

The perils of legal reform

Though the Personal Status Code reform was a watershed event, in the years since its enactment there have been numerous and repeated complaints about a lack of implementation. Vague on certain points, the law accords judges significant discretion. Statistics show that judges routinely grant exemptions to the provision outlawing polygamy and to the prohibition against marriage for girls under the age of 18. Likewise, court records of divorce proceedings, particularly in smaller towns, indicate that men and women seeking separation are frequently unclear about legal provisions, leaving judges with the power to decide most cases. Further, because the training of judges takes time, most current judges continue to utilize the old law and are slow to implement the new one.

In fact, dissatisfaction with the law reform may be due more to its uneven application than to the law itself. As the 2004 law vests judges with considerable discretion, its implementation can best be described as irregular. According to Transparency International, an international NGO that collects data on corruption in order to raise public awareness, the Moroccan judiciary is among the most corrupt segments of society, even ahead of the police and health care services. Their 2008 report states:

> Corruption is prevalent and widespread in the MENA (Middle East North African) countries, manifesting itself most frequently in the shape of both petty and grand corruption. Here, corruption is marked strongly by the unique style of governance found throughout the region; it is deeply rooted in the political infrastructure of the state (mainly military dictatorships, totalitarian regimes or monarchies) and the institutional infrastructure of the public sector (typically very large, overstaffed with low salaries); and develops as a result of the relatively limited opportunities for public participation. Several other factors that contribute to providing opportunities for corruption and encourage limited transparency in the region include regional and/or national insecurities, the prevalence of conflict and heavy dependence on oil revenues.[44] All countries exhibit weaknesses in terms of accountability and access to civil and political rights, and political participation is less advanced in the Arab world than in other developing regions. Not a single country in the region figures in the top half of the world in terms of public accountability, as

measured in terms of access to information or holding leaders accountable for their actions.[45]

Those who have attended family court sessions report that less educated Moroccans are generally ill informed about the new family law, which leaves judges to rule in accord with their own interpretations. In many cases judges decide in favour of men or those who offer the judge an incentive, financial or otherwise. Unofficial transcripts also reveal an astonishing level of contempt for those who appear before the court. Judges are on record for having called women 'donkeys' (the quintessential insult in Moroccan Arabic) when asking for divorce settlements. Bringing divorce proceedings to court is a relatively novel occurrence; previously, domestic conflicts were settled out of court with male guardians convening to discuss divorce arrangements. For instance, the *wali* (most often the father of the wife) would negotiate with the soon-to-be ex-husband and his relatives to assure that his daughter was provided for after a divorce, an arrangement that was in his own best interest, as otherwise he would have to assume financial responsibility for his divorced daughter and her children. Because the reform did away with the community-centred approach to settling divorce and now requires ruling by a judge who is not personally affected by the outcome, it is understandable that some people feel the old system offered them a better deal than the one provided under the new law.

In rural areas in particular, marrying off a daughter at a young age often is the only way for her to be taken care of if the parents are poor. Some have argued that raising the marriage age has increased the problem of *petites bonnes*, underpaid domestic workers, rather than alleviated it, as poor families now have to send their less-educated or uneducated daughters to work as domestics – and expose them to the injustices or cruelties associated with this job – until they reach the age of 18 and can get married. Other options for getting around the law are to forge a birth certificate, use the birth certificate of an older sister, or bribe a court so as to obtain an exception. Hence, in Morocco, guaranteeing women certain rights without at the same time putting in place an infrastructure that offers women genuine educational and professional opportunities has not addressed underlying problems that affect large segments of the population – and may even exacerbate these problems.

Some, like Fouzia Assouli, head of the Ligue Démocratique pour les Droits de la Femme au Maroc (LDDF), or Morocco's Democratic League for Women's Rights, have levelled the criticism that important issues are not addressed in the law reform, such as children's legal representation, which remains the exclusive right of men. Even when a mother is granted custody, she can legally represent her children only after the father's death or in case of 'legal incompetence'. Another controversial issue is domestic violence, which is not addressed at all in the 2004 Personal Status Code. At the time of this writing, vigorous debates on bills that would render domestic violence a crime and criminalize sexual harassment are occurring in Morocco. In a country where the beating of wives by husbands is habitually tolerated and where cat-calls on the street and sexual innuendo are *de rigueur*, laws in and of themselves can't be expected to eliminate such practices. For such change to happen, broader cultural and social shifts must occur that render such activities unacceptable.

Morocco is a place with a long history where most change comes slowly. It is therefore difficult to assess fully the merits of family law reform only five or six years after its pronouncement. Historically, monarchs have come to rely on their subjects' patience. This may explain why, after being on the throne for ten years, King Mohammed VI is still referred to as the 'new' king. (Ten years, it should be noted, is longer than any president can serve in office in the United States.) On the tenth anniversary of his ascension to the throne, in the summer of 2009, Moroccans were asked to evaluate the king's performance using a survey authorized by a French daily newspaper and a Moroccan weekly magazine. The survey revealed that Moroccans generally were pleased with their monarch. Of those surveyed, 91 per cent said they noticed positive changes in their immediate environment, such as access to schools and hospitals, and an improvement of the road and highway system. Respondents overwhelmingly registered disappointment in the failure of the monarchy to significantly reduce poverty, however. And on one issue the country was divided: women. One in two people surveyed felt the king had gone too far in 'liberating women'. They disapproved of abolishing the system of *wali* (guardian), whose consent was not needed in the new system for a woman to marry. Half of the respondents also said they did not like the right of women to initiate divorce and the difficulties imposed for polygamy. Only 16 per cent of men and women said that women needed more rights. Unfortunately, the survey results did not offer a breakdown as to the difference in responses by men and women.

It should be noted here that polls and surveys are not a common feature in Morocco; hence, those surveyed may not have fully believed that their privacy would be respected and their names would not be revealed. It is therefore possible that some respondents did not provide honest answers but said what they believed the surveyor wanted to hear or what they believed to be the most acceptable answer. Because Islamism enjoys growing popularity in Morocco, responding in line with well-publicized Islamist positions can mean that those surveyed were simply following a trend. Nevertheless, despite its limitations, the survey results are an indication of just how unsettling change can be. The 2004 Personal Status Code reform set in motion social transformations that those who have lived in a patriarchal society for centuries may find difficult.

While the results of the survey showed general approval for M6, as he is sometimes fondly referred to, his majesty King Mohammed VI was not amused by the outcome. Despite the king's overall modernizing agenda and his commitment to gender equality, he remains an autocratic leader with limited tolerance for critique of his actions.[46] In response to the survey, the palace banned the weekly news journal *Tel Quel* that had published the results. Its Arabic version, *Nichane*, was also confiscated before copies could hit the newsstands. The issue of the French daily *Le Monde*, which had co-sponsored the survey, also was banned. *Le Monde* quoted the Minister of the Interior, Chakib Benmoussa, as saying: 'The monarchy may not be questioned, not even by means of a survey or a poll.'[47] An article in *Le Monde* also pointed out that limiting press freedom in such drastic manner was commonly associated with Morocco's neighbours, led by then-President Zine El Abidine Ben Ali of Tunisia and Abdelaziz Bouteflika of Algeria, both of whom routinely cracked down on freedom of the press. The heavy-handedness with which the palace responded to an attempt to gauge public opinion was a stark reminder that the authority of the king is not to be questioned in Morocco, even bent as he may be on modernization.

Morocco is in a state of transition. Just as with every individual or nation experiencing a major transformation, there is much ambiguity, complexity, and inconsistency in what goes on there. Apprehension and confusion are expected and are unavoidable components of change. Equally understandable are fears of impending chaos if old structures are altered but not yet replaced by new ones. Though Morocco's government has taken steps to address some of the most pertinent issues associated with women's rights, they have been met with resistance. Such is the case not only with regard to the Personal Status Code reform, but also with the plan to include women in national development.

Women in national development

As mentioned above, as the Personal Status Code reform came into effect, the government drew up a plan that would pave the way for women's inclusion in the larger effort to stimulate national development. In 2007, a new Ministère du Développement Social de la famille et de la solidarité au Maroc, or Ministry of Family, Social Development and Solidarity, was established along with a national plan for the integration of women in national development, *Le plan national de l'intégration de la femme au développement*, also known as PANIFD. The new plan was a reconsideration of one originally drawn up in 1998, in which legislators failed to include poor, rural, and illiterate women in national development. PANIFD corrected these omissions by outlining four primary objectives:

1. Education
2. Women's integration in economic development
3. Strengthening women's legal and political rights
4. Improvements in women's reproductive health

Human rights and women's associations as well as leading community members supported the plan as a viable step for the participation of women from all backgrounds in national development. Some Islamists, on the other hand, again voiced outspoken opposition, claiming that such a plan was a 'blatant attack on Islam'. They viewed the emphasis on women's insertion into the work force as diminishing their divinely ordained role as mother and homemaker. Some Islamists claimed that the very title of the plan implied that women had previously been left out of the development process. Such an assumption, according to certain Islamist critics of the plan, was based on a specific understanding of gender and development, namely that development occurs in the public domain and is primarily defined by organizations such as the United Nations as an economic process in which women do not participate sufficiently. These critics argued that such a plan considers women who take care of the home and raise children as not contributing to national development. To these Islamists, such an understanding degrades or demeans the role and function of motherhood and homemaking, which, in their view, are the actual cornerstones of national development.

Most vocal in rejecting the plan for the integration of women in national development was the Islamist movement known as Al Islah wa a-Tawhid (the Unity and Reform Movement). Not surprisingly, this movement also had strongly opposed the family law reform as well. Al Islah wa a-Tawhid charged that in accordance with Islamic tenets, a woman is not supposed to contribute financially to a household, and by extension, to economic development. The plan, they claimed, undermined the basic Islamic conception of gender complementarity based on paternity and maternity. In their version of Islam, gender roles are primarily determined by their function within the family. Thus, the father would assume the financial obligation for the household and the mother would be responsible for domestic affairs, such as the raising of children and household matters. Since both of these tasks are seen as necessary in raising a family, and because men are excluded from childbirth and child rearing, women are dispensed from economic responsibilities. From this perspective, challenges to basic gender roles represented a neo-colonial Western project aimed at undermining the Muslim religious and cultural identity.

According to their conception of gender roles, those in the Al Islah wa a-Tawhid movement have argued that women in Morocco have never been excluded from national development, but play an integral part in assuming their roles as wives and mothers and building families that form the basic unit of the nation. Some Islamists feel that core Muslim values are undermined if women are seen as a human resource for economic development. Though not all Islamists shared the Al Islah wa a-Tawhid viewpoint in its entirety, many echoed the deep-seated scepticism of Western norms, which in the past were imposed through colonial occupation. Today, it is in the name of modernization that Western norms are inserted once more, and Islamists see it as a neo-colonial or imperialist ploy. Because the plan for national development was written by Moroccan government officials in largely Western terminology and used Western concepts of gender, Islamists saw it as a further attempt by the Moroccan government to ingratiate itself to the West and discount a genuine Moroccan approach to national development and the role of women in that development. For Al Islah wa a-Tawhid, individual agency and choice is not a goal in itself; rather, by definition women are meant to become wives and mothers. There is a prophetic tradition according to which a person who marries fulfils half of his duty as a Muslim.[48]

Another source of contention was the king's appointment of Nouzha Skalli as Minister of Family, Social Development, and Solidarity in Morocco. Skalli is a founding member of the feminist Association Démocratique des Femmes du Maroc (ADFM), or Democratic Association of Moroccan Women, and in appointing her the king confirmed his 'modernist' (read: Western) stance on women's issues, a choice that angered Islamists. Indeed, the plan for integrating women in national development was supported most notably by ADFM, an organization that receives much of its funding from the European Union and other Western sources. ADFM has been active in Morocco since 1985 and operates under the motto: 'Together for Equality and Dignity and with the Goal of promoting Women's and Human Rights.' Mostly staffed by volunteers, including Europeans and Americans, it is one of the largest, best-funded, and best-organized women's organizations in Morocco, as well as the most secular and overtly pro-Western of all located there. Thus, with the appointment of ADFM's leader to a high government position, the king sent an unmistakable signal.

Modern traditions or traditionally modern

Regardless of concerns that are particular to Islamists, modernity, and how to approach it, is indeed a problematic issue. In Morocco, the conflict between modernity and tradition stems from the abiding belief that modernization is an intrinsically Western phenomenon. The difficult historical relationship of the previously colonized world with its colonizers poses challenges to concepts imported from the West. Scepticism towards and resistance to Western notions of modernization in Morocco are not only understandable but are an essential component of a healthy debate.

In global South countries, globalization is often seen as a one-way street in which the West steamrolls over the rest of the world. For this reason alone Islamist concerns cannot be dismissed as simply retrograde or obscurantist; they do in fact give voice to a genuine and widespread fear of domination by the West. The economic, military, and political power of Western nations throughout the world cannot be ignored, posing a dilemma for states that remain economically indebted and dependent. Certainly, Islamists in Morocco appreciate Western inventions – from electricity to refrigerators, cars, trains, television, telephones, computers, and the Internet. Moroccans also benefit from advances in modern medicine and science. Few advocate abandoning these in the name of an authentic cultural or religious identity. Even the most fundamentalist Islamists use the Internet and social media to propagate their messages; nevertheless, they seek a way to validate their own heritage.

King Mohammed VI, meanwhile, is straddling the religious, cultural, and secular realms of his country with his dual approach to the issue of women: reforming religion-based family law while outlining a plan that includes women in national economic development. These projects have marked a general shift in the government's policy on gender. They also have coincided with another royal initiative, namely a quota for female elected officials. Even further, the king's modernist agenda has been extended to the religious sphere. In 2006, the Ministry of Religious Affairs recruited the first group of future female religious leaders, called *murchidates* (guides). Apart from leading prayers in a mosque, their function is essentially the same as that of *imam*. While the training of such female religious leaders received mixed reactions in most Muslim countries, in the West it was hailed as an important step toward modernization in Morocco. The monarch was, in effect, taking the lead on several fronts: law, civil society, and religion.

In sum, the Moroccan government advanced three landmark initiatives – the Personal Status Code reform, the inclusion of women in national development, and the training of female religious leaders (an issue addressed later in this book) – as integral aspects of a democratization and modernizing process. These government projects were in no small measure a response to demands from a homegrown women's movement as well as the opposition of Islamists, groups that have energized the debate about women's rights in Morocco. Their struggle suggests that ultimately, the key to the success of gender equality is to construct the argument for reform in a culturally authentic language.

As stated at the outset, when it comes to changing the status of women, virulent discussions on religion, culture, and identity ensue. Women bear the burden, or are the scapegoats, depending on one's point of view, in all manner of discussions unrelated to gender. They can, as we have seen, also become the inadvertent beneficiaries of terrible global events.

A view from a train

Apart from the discourses of official government entities, secular women's rights associations, and Islamists, a lively debate exists among ordinary Moroccans concerning the status and rights of women. People engage in animated discussions almost everywhere, all the time. More recently, these discussions have revolved around the massive transformations underway in several North African and Middle Eastern countries. Even among strangers there are no off-limits topics. Anyone who rides the train, especially in crowded second-class compartments, or travels in a *grand taxi* (usually an old Mercedes sedan that serves as a form of public transport between cities and carries up to six passengers) will witness heated arguments about the *moudawana*, the role of women, Islam, Islamism, and so on. During longer journeys, unrelated passengers often start lengthy conversations to pass the time. A five-and-a-half-hour train ride from the capital city of Rabat to the northern port city of Tangier will offer a glimpse into quite a spectrum of arguments. The description of one such journey best illustrates this point.

Soon after the train pulls out of the station in Rabat, passengers settle into their compartments and begin chatting amicably about the weather, family, and soccer. The conversation takes a sharp turn once a young veiled woman enters at one of the later stops. When the conductor checks tickets, she produces a document that attests to her status as a chaumeur diplômé, *meaning an unemployed person with a university degree, entitling her to a reduced fare. The other passengers raise their eyebrows and exchange displeased looks. Aware of these glances, the young woman announces that she has a graduate degree in mathematics but is unemployed due to her headscarf. Without being asked, she continues to expound on her views about religion and proclaims that Islam is the essence of her life as it should be for all Muslims. She is interrupted by another female passenger who asks if she has looked for a job in the private sector, has ever tried to start her own business, or find work in an area unrelated to her field of study. The veiled woman insists that she seeks a government job and that her expertise is in alternative energy research – more specifically, calculating the rate at which the panes of windmills move given the airflow in a certain region of the country. To prove her point, she pulls out a folder filled with mathematical equations and depictions of windmills. She explains that there are no private sector jobs that require her specialized skills. Once more she points out that she is the victim of discrimination in the job market because of her overt religious devotion. Before she can finish her sentence, the other passengers erupt with a barrage of exclamations and accusations, one after another, and sometimes in unison, telling her that her* hijab *has little to do with her unemployment. They chide her for wanting to make a political statement with her headscarf and that people with many fewer qualifications manage to find some sort of work. The discussion gets increasingly animated; voices are raised so that anyone entering the compartment at this point might think they had come upon a quarrelling group of old friends or family members. A female passenger with a short-cropped fashionable hairdo takes a little Qur'an from her purse and waives it wildly in the air. 'See we are all Muslims,' she says, 'you are not a better Muslim than me. Only God knows.' Another passenger wants*

*to know what she does with her time given that she is unemployed. With pride
in her eyes, she produces a slide show on her laptop that she passes around. It
shows her in the front row of demonstrations in Rabat and Casablanca. 'Look
here we are protesting the injustice of the system. We are educated and now we
don't have jobs.'* [49] *To emphasize the depth of her commitment, she adds: 'I am
an Islamist; we fight for our God-given rights. Any self-respecting Moroccan
should be on our side.' A discussion ensues that the widespread problem of
unemployment has nothing do with the level of religiosity or the veil. But, most
agree, it does not help to proclaim one's own religious convictions as superior
to those of others. Undeterred, her reddening cheeks contrasting with her beige
embroidered headscarf, she pulls out another trump card: she proclaims that the
Personal Status Code reform shows that the king has strayed from the path of
Islam and, therefore, the country is doomed. The other women burst out shout-
ing that the passage of the new Personal Status Code has improved the status
of women, and that eventually women will have the same opportunities as
men. The men chime in and say that people can disagree about the merits of the
moudawana reform. Above all, her fellow passengers resent that young, unemployed university graduates now get special privileges that were not accorded to
them when they were young and looking for work. With a temperament common throughout the Mediterranean region, all the men and women talk loudly
and at the same time, each one trying to score a point by speaking at a higher
volume than the person sitting next to them. The rattling of the train adds a
certain rhythm as all passengers rock back and forth in unison. Eventually,
someone passes a box of homemade cookies around, tempers calm, and the eight
passengers compliment the baker and turn to less contentious subjects.*

*At the next station, some get out and new passengers enter. One of the new
arrivals is a young man wearing headphones connected to an iPod. A middle-
aged traveller asks him what he is listening to. The young man answers:
'Moroccan rap.' This turns out to be a subject on which every passenger has an
opinion too. As expected, each of the travellers over the age of 40 is sure that
rap is bad and polluting young minds with uncouth lyrics. The boy protests.
He too has a trump card: did his fellow passengers know that there are now
even female Moroccan rap groups that have very patriotic lyrics? Has anyone
in the compartment heard of Tigresse Flow, Fatie Show and Bnaat Rabat?
Only one had, vaguely.* [50] *The young man continues to explain that these girl
bands are successful because of their clean lyrics and that they want to produce*

music that all generations can enjoy without feeling embarrassed or ashamed when listening to their words. He hands his headphones to the man sitting across from him, who, not showing any of the anticipated enjoyment on his face, passes them on to the next person within seconds. The veiled woman declines to pay this type of music any attention. Soon everyone else has had their share of listening to home grown hip-hop and is ready to announce their assessment of the just heard. Though the music they heard was performed by male rappers (since the female bands have not yet made any albums but perform mostly at open-air concerts) all the passengers are unanimous in arguing that what they heard proved their point, and that female hip-hop could not possibly have any more redeeming qualities – if anything, it must be worse. Though the self-proclaimed Islamist woman with the headscarf had isolated herself earlier with her inflammatory rhetoric, it was now the young rap fan who earned the scorn of his fellow passengers. All the men and women in the compartment, including the Islamist, found a new topic on which all but one person agreed: the degradation of morality among the youth. Only this time around it was the young rap fan who found himself singled out.

Certainly, the female rappers admired by the young man are at the forefront of the outer limits of what is culturally acceptable in Morocco, even though by Western standards their attire and public appearances are modest. They push the boundaries of female empowerment to new levels. Performing mostly at music festivals, they are not widely known, since French and American hip-hop music dominates the local music scene. Though male Moroccan bands have enjoyed some degree of popularity in the country, the young, female rappers are seen as such a novelty and so on-the-edge that only a few hardcore fans listen to their music. Thus, even in the midst of the rising popularity of religious performance, and a forceful royal agenda of promoting women's empowerment, there are fringe phenomena that are part of the larger tapestry of the Moroccan cultural landscape. Back to our journey on the train.

After having covered all the important topics of the day: Islamism, unemployment, the decadence of the up-and-coming generation, the train nears its final destination around midnight. The conversation now turns to the more imminent task at hand – that is, to obtain transport to their respective final destinations, since the train station is a little out of town. The women, veiled or unveiled, young or mature, agree that it is safer to share a taxi unless they are met at the station by a relative. Despite earlier vehement disputes and disagreements, everyone makes sure that there is appropriate transportation for all. As the whistle blows and passengers scramble to collect their bags from the overhead bins, they wave at each other, and, with the customary 'B'salama' (go in peace), bid each other farewell.

From the throne to the gathering places of pioneering intellectuals, feminists, or Islamic activists, to the homes of families, to the locations where everyday people come together, the role of women is eagerly discussed at all levels in Morocco. In Morocco, questions about women's rights are met with no shortage of opinions and nor are people hesitant to express their views. This topic, after all, evokes deeply personal vested interests, as it has throughout history. In North Africa, neither religious scholars, politicians, nor savants have been able to provide easy solutions to this most basic challenge: that is, to create equality between two different kinds of human beings who thoroughly depend on each other.

CHAPTER 2

FEMINISM AND ITS DISCONTENTS

Some Moroccan activists categorically reject feminism because it is a Western concept. They argue that feminism in this North African kingdom is going too far while others say it has not yet fully arrived. They argue that feminism is not suitable for the country. Across the board, frustration with the West runs deep, with causes ranging from the Crusades and the early days of French colonization to more recent stereotyping of Muslims, especially in the aftermath of the 11 September 2001 terrorist attacks on the World Trade Center in New York City. Increasingly, Muslims perceive the global war on terrorism lead by the United States as a war against Islam. Further, Muslim women in particular have for centuries been a focus in Western discourses on Islam. Leila Ahmed writes in her comprehensive work *Women and Gender in Islam*:

> The peculiar practices of Islam with respect to women had always formed part of the Western narrative of the quintessential otherness and inferiority of Islam. A detailed history of Western representations of women in Islam and of the sources of Western ideas on the subject has yet to be written, but broadly speaking it may be said that prior to the seventeenth century, Western ideas about Islam derived from the tales of travellers and crusaders, augmented by the deductions of clerics from their readings of poorly understood Arabic texts.[1]

Ahmed has argued that Western views about Muslim women have remained largely unchanged throughout the centuries. Even feminism was introduced in a colonial context to justify Western dominance in the Muslim world. The Western sense of superiority during colonial times was in part expressed by pointing out how poorly women were treated in Muslim-majority countries and that the colonial presence was needed to alleviate the lot of women. As Ahmed explained,

> Broadly speaking, the thesis of the discourse on Islam blending a colonialism committed to male dominance with feminism – the thesis of the new colonial discourse of Islam centered on women – was that Islam was innately and immutably oppressive to women, that the veil and the segregation epitomized that oppression, and that these customs were the fundamental reasons for the general and comprehensive backwardness of Islamic societies.[2]

During the colonial period in Morocco, women in European countries did not enjoy equal rights; therefore, the premise of liberating Muslim women from male dominance had little credibility. Though France proclaimed that it had to 'civilize' the indigenous Moroccan peoples, French women themselves at the time were not emancipated. Thus, Moroccan suspicions of Western feminism, past and present, are not entirely unfounded. Western portrayals of Muslim women as victims, as submissive and oppressed second-class citizens, anger Moroccan activists who are dedicated to improving the status of women. They feel that even warranted criticism of the status of women in their country puts their entire culture and way of life under attack. Further, they have noted that few in the West differentiate between the status of women in one Muslim-majority country and another; Muslim women are lumped together in one homogeneous, voiceless mass. Some female activists even say they hesitate to attend international gatherings because they are treated as objects of pity and are routinely put on the defensive.

Yet, many Western feminists, aware of their culturally biased approach toward women of the global South in general, and Muslim women in particular, have in recent years begun to think in terms of concepts such as post-colonial feminism and transnational feminism in order to propagate the universal aspirations of feminism. For the first time in more than 30 years, the *Feminist Review* addressed the issue of religion and spirituality in its March 2011 issue.[3] In the introduction, Lyn Thomas and Avtar Brah wrote about the 'strong historical relationship between many (and especially Western) feminisms and secularism, as well as the new visibility of religion in the contemporary world.[4] The authors observed that it is now 'vital to interrogate earlier feminist certainties about the alliance between feminism and secularism, without losing the capacity to critique religious practices that oppress women'.[5] Furthermore, Kristin Aune observed:

> In the twenty-first century, feminist engagement with religion is undergoing considerable transformation. In the last few decades, since the rebirth of the women's movement in the 1960s and 1970s, many academic feminists have paid little attention to religion. It was not until the 1980s that feminist literature on religion, often produced by feminists with spiritual and religious commitments, appeared in significant quantity. Into the 1990s and beyond, scholars began addressing the thorny question 'why, given that religions often define and restrict women's roles, are women religious?'[6]

Such new understandings take into account women's diverse histories and cultural differences, while at the same time emphasizing common goals that are shared across cultural, religious, and social divides. Still, this transnational and post-colonial feminism has not cast aside all doubt in Morocco that feminism is a neo-colonial project. Some women's rights activists suspect feminism to be a Trojan horse, carrying with it the seeds of destruction of Moroccan identity. Today, more than 50 years after Morocco gained its independence from France, the rejection of feminism as a colonial holdover is frequently based on misguided notions of what feminism – and by extension the West – stands for.

In fact, as discussed in the previous chapter, those who reject feminism as a purely foreign import are oblivious of Morocco's own home-grown feminism in the early part of the twentieth century. Often, this rejection reflects a view of feminism as synonymous with secular society and void of moral or religious values. Increased rights for women are seen as responsible for an absence or decline in moral standards, since in the West – so some assume – women do as they please, sexual promiscuity is rampant, and divorce is common. Gender equality, then, is believed even by educated Moroccan men and women to lead invariably to more frequent marriage break-ups when women destroy families in pursuit of their own professional or personal advancement. Of course, such opinions reflect the deeply held belief in Morocco that the responsibility for keeping a marriage and family together lies disproportionately with women, a sexist attitude that is sometimes even held by women's rights advocates. Until the Personal Status Code reform in 2004, men had a unilateral right to initiate divorce, and women who sought to divorce their husbands faced severe legal restrictions. Obviously, when women have limited rights to file for divorce, they tend to stay in a marriage. Closer to the real issue may be an unspoken fear that if women were to be given the same rights as men and could do some of the same things men do, society would fall apart. This is a point worth pondering.

The position that gender equality inevitably leads to moral decline in the West is not without foundation, however. American or European television shows with blatant sexual themes such as *Baywatch, Desperate Housewives, Sex and the City*, and many of those on MTV, for example, provide a main window to Western society for many Moroccans. Western fashion magazines routinely parade women as scantily clad sex symbols and pronounce hedonism and consumerism as the ultimate gates to well-being. People unaccustomed to such messages and images are understandably concerned that Western gender norms may contribute to moral decline. With their distorted images of women, popular Western mass media send mixed messages around the world. Shows about women living ordinary lives do not make for export-worthy television viewing. The effects of television shows as a cultural export have yet to be sufficiently studied. Nevertheless, though the misogynistic lyrics of rap music are often blamed for poisoning young people's minds, television shows reach much larger audiences and have a more sustained impact worldwide since they are watched by young and old, rich and poor, men and women. The images of women in popular Western television pro-grammes, which appear on small screens even in remote areas without electricity where TVs must be powered by generators, can be bewil-dering and cause a false perception of what gender equality means for women in the West.

Misunderstandings prevail, and not only on the popular level. Scholars and political activists in Morocco whose views are not informed primarily by Western popular culture frequently have a lim-ited understanding of feminism as well. Western feminism is rarely understood as a movement that seeks to end inequality based on gen-der and one that includes women of all social classes, races, ethnicities, and religions. Indeed, Western middle-class feminists have not always displayed much sensitivity to women's rights agendas that were dif-ferent from their own. Certainly, religious or spiritual concerns have not been a focus in Western feminism and issues of social class or race have been included only in the last two decades. bell hooks is one of the most prolific advocates of a more inclusive third-wave feminism, a subject hooks has explored since the 1980s. Misunderstandings aside, feminism is an issue of public interest in Morocco. Not confined to scholarly debates in the ivory tower, feminist concerns appear in glossy popular Moroccan women's magazines that specialize in fashion and advice columns. Following pages with colourful photos appear in-depth interviews with academic and legal experts on women's rights. French feminist Elisabeth Badinter, known for her criticism of contemporary Western feminism, was interviewed at length in *Femmes du Maroc* (Women of Morocco)[7] about the debate over the Muslim headscarf in France, for example. In the interview, Badinter said that this debate has brought together peculiar alliances, such as that between radical leftwing feminists and conservative Muslims, because both groups are outspoken critics of the 2004 ban on ostentatious religious symbols in public schools in France and more recently the ban on the full-face veil in that country. Badinter also discussed her fear that in the name of multiculturalism practices get supported that run counter to Western ideals of individual choice and freedom. Badinter, an author of several groundbreaking books, argued that young girls who wear the veil are often coerced to do so by their families and do not choose this practice of their own free will.[8]

The same issue of *Femmes du Maroc* presented various sides of the headscarf controversy using lengthy interviews with renowned international scholars, rather than easy-to-read, sound-bite-like comments. American feminist Judith Butler has made the point that Western discourse needs to include the objectives of 'oriental women' who chose to wear the veil: 'Acts of resistance need to be translated from one context to another. It concerns a battle of ideas and reversal of performance of representations.' Butler's approach to the issue of the Muslim headscarf is more theoretical than Badinter's, perhaps because the wearing of the headscarf is not a controversial issue in the United States nor does it occupy discussions in Congress. Further, it is fair to say that few fashion magazines in the United States carry scholarly articles that weigh in on the relative merits of transnational feminism. Conversely, the Moroccan popular press, in presenting such articles, helps to spread an awareness of feminism in a global context among Moroccan women.

By all accounts, among women in the West there are as great a variety of attitudes and understandings about feminism as among women in Muslim-majority countries. How often does one hear expressions such as, 'I am not a feminist but …' or, 'I am a feminist, but let me clarify what I mean …'? The term feminism actually has taken on a negative connotation in the United States. Gender communication scholar Julia Wood has asserted that the popular media have promoted this negative slant on feminism since the 1970s, as if the proponents of women's rights are a homogenous group of men-hating radicals. Toril Moi wrote that feminism has become the F-word; the very word feminism has become toxic in large parts of American culture. According to Moi, this attitude has evolved because 'so much feminist work today produces tediously predictable lines of argument'.[9] Some scholars have expanded the feminist platform and developed a more nuanced, inclusive approach to feminism that addresses criticisms of the so-called 'second-wave' feminists of the 1960s and 1970s. In 2000, prolific North American scholar bell hooks defined feminism as a movement 'to end sexism, sexist exploitation, and oppression'. She recognized that most people 'do not understand sexism, or if they do, they think it is not a problem. Masses of people think that feminism is always and only about women seeking to be equal to men. And a huge majority think that feminism is anti-male'.[10]

hooks observed that Western feminism has often been an exclusive white, middle-class phenomenon that does not take into consideration the concerns of poor, socially disenfranchised, less-educated, or ethnic minority groups. To truly be a feminist, according to hooks, one must identify oppression or discrimination wherever it occurs. Even when focusing on women's rights, the lens of gender should be employed to examine other forms of inequality even if they extend beyond issues directly related to women. In a plea for what she calls 'visionary feminism', hooks called for a feminist imagination rooted in concrete reality while at the same time conjuring possibilities beyond that reality. This 'concrete reality', she argued, must take into account differences not only between social classes or ethnicities, but also between continents and countries. In spite of misconceptions about the goals of feminism, one contribution of feminist theory that has been accepted worldwide concerns the differentiation between gender and sex. Feminist theory has advanced the notion that gender is socially constructed while sex is biology. The implication of this idea is that gender roles are not biologically determined but are a matter of negotiation, social convention, and religious interpretation. In Morocco, even religiously oriented women's rights activists have used this understanding of gender as a basis for their re-interpretations of sacred texts.

In the West, secularism and feminism fit hand-in-glove. The fact that women's rights in Europe and the United States were achieved in the secular sphere leads some to believe that Western secular society means the disappearance of religion and a moral void. In Morocco, a country that knows no separation of religion and the state, where the king holds the dual role of head of state and highest religious authority, it may be hard to envision that religion can be a personal, private matter. However, the founding principle of secular societies – that is, the separation of church and state – is not intended to eradicate religion but to restrict or prohibit the imposition of religious dogmas on a citizenry. This idea actually is close to the hearts of some Moroccans, especially members of certain Islamist movements who feel restricted in their activities by state-imposed Islam. The example of a secular society that Moroccans are most familiar with, however, is France, where the concept of *laïcité* was introduced in 1905 with the explicit purpose of keeping at bay the influence of the Catholic Church in matters of state. Because of the continued close relationship between Morocco and France, the French model has largely shaped Moroccans' understanding of secularism. From a historical point of view, France can be seen as an exception because it is the only democracy that has fought religion in order to impose a state-enforced secularism. As Olivier Roy explained:

> In France, *laïcité* is an exacerbated, politicized, and ideological form of Western secularism that has developed on two levels:
>
> 1. A very strict separation of church and state, against the backdrop of a political conflict between the state and the Catholic Church that resulted in a law regulating very strictly the presence of religion in the public sphere (1905). This is what I call legal *laïcité*.
>
> 2. An ideological and philosophical interpretation of *laïcité* that claims to provide a value system common to all citizens by expelling religion into the private sphere. I call this ideological *laïcité*: today, it leads the majority of the secular Left to strike an alliance with the Christian Right against Islam.[11]

It is understandable that a Muslim country would zero in on the aspect of secularism that in contemporary discourse in Europe is invoked most often with regard to Islam: the 2004 ban on the Muslim headscarf for girls attending public schools in France, a ban that was justified by the principles of *laïcité*. In addition, Moroccans see the French controversy surrounding the opening of *halal* fast-food restaurants (which adhere to Muslim dietary laws) as yet another indication that secularism means restricting Muslim presence and influence in the public sphere. This view is not without justification, since kosher restaurants have been part of the French culinary scene for decades without raising an eyebrow. Yet, it is Muslim women in particular who occupy a central place in Europe's often-contentious discussions on Islam. The French government's 2011 legislation banning the full-face veil (*niqab*), attire that only leaves a small slit for the eyes, applies to no more than 2,000 women out of a Muslim population of approximately six million in France.[12] Even though most Moroccans reject the *niqab* as a foreign, non-Moroccan custom, and look with concern at Moroccan women who are covered in this way, they consider an outright ban in France as an affront against Muslims generally. In the United States, the situation is somewhat different, as religious freedom is a strongly defended principle and secularism is understood as protecting the right to diverse religious expressions.

Feminism and secularism are just two aspects of larger misperceptions in the global North as much as in the global South. The narrow understanding of the Muslim world of many in the West is mirrored by those in the Muslim world who have an equally reductionist view of the West. Islamists, especially those who have not been exposed to different ideas and have not explored worldviews other than their own, express opposition to feminist ideas. They often reiterate that feminism and the absence of religious values are inseparable and therefore not applicable to Morocco. The limited grasp and misunderstandings of feminism and secularism on both sides of the Mediterranean and Atlantic is a hindrance for women's rights activists who aim to address the complex problems of women in the twenty-first century.

Transnational discourse is always problematic because it is difficult to understand a society to which one does not belong. There is an important difference between studying a society or culture and being part of it. For example, for most Moroccans, the seeming ease with which Americans change religious denominations or religions altogether is incomprehensible. Throughout North Africa, religion is an integral a part of identity akin to skin colour. Neither can or should be changed, most Moroccans would say. On the other hand, for Americans in particular, it is hard to grasp the lasting impact of the colonial legacy in formerly occupied countries, so they often brush it aside as a phenomenon of a distant past. Yet, the enduring effects of a system such as that imposed by France in its colonies can be profound, even if they are hard to quantify. The term *'mission civilatrice'*, or 'civilizing mission', was used by the French to rationalize their colonization of other countries, and it meant a spreading of Western/Christian norms and values in areas under their control, replacing local culture and religion that were, by definition, 'uncivilized'. According to this rationale, Muslim countries like Morocco were backward and culturally inferior, and their conquest was to be a blessing for those conquered.

For Americans, whose national identity is grounded in the history of a break from a foreign yoke, it is hard to understand what it means to have one's political, economic, and legal systems forcefully replaced by an occupying power. Viewed in this context, the transport of the ambitions of feminism from one location to another is fraught with complications. Though feminists in the East and in the West argue that women's rights are universal, claims to universalism are often understood in North Africa as synonymous with Western norms. After all, the 1948 Universal Declaration of Human Rights, which was signed by United Nations General Assembly in Paris in the aftermath of World War II and the Holocaust, was based on the Bill of Rights in the United States, the Bill of Rights in England, and the Declaration of the Rights of Man and of the Citizen in France — all Western countries with a Judeo-Christian heritage. The concept of universal values is a product of the Age of Enlightenment, a European phenomenon of the eighteenth century that placed reason as the source of legitimacy and authority over religious faith. Islamists in general insist that the message of the Qur'an, revealed more than a thousand years ago, is universal and therefore no new claims to universalism based on Western norms are needed. Mohammed is believed to be the last prophet and one whose message is intended for the entire world: 'We have sent you only as a bearer of good tidings and admonisher for all mankind; yet most people do not understand' (34:28).

Exposing oneself openly and honestly to another civilization is an important endeavour when aspiring to a genuine transnational perspective. The goal lies not only in attempts to understand 'the other'. Rather, a transnational perspective requires that one engage in an enriching process leading to a re-imagining of one's own identity. Educated Moroccans frequently have many opportunities to engage in such a process. Moroccans have been exposed to other cultures throughout history, and in the past century French and Spanish cultures in particular. Today 10 per cent of the Moroccan population study or work abroad and therefore are immersed in cultures different from theirs on a daily basis. In foreign settings, transnational discourse is a matter of survival; negotiating one's own customs with the prevailing norms of a host country becomes the means by which one creates newly emerging and multiple identities. As well, Moroccans residing abroad exercise influence in their country of origin not only by transferring funds there but also by bringing back new ideas, among them an altered understanding of gender relations. Consequently, Morocco finds itself in the position of contributing to the articulation of a global feminist perspective in the twenty-first century. In fact, Islamic feminism may at least in part have inspired the recent appearance of a number of texts and websites on 'Christian feminism'.[13]

Feminism in the West is grounded in a common understanding of the rights and freedoms of individuals. Most Western societies cherish the idea that the seat of moral authority resides in the individual, and that individuals can and need to be entrusted to make decisions and choices about their lives. In Morocco, by contrast, moral authority is understood as vested not in the individual but external to the self. The level of expectation of support from the community, society, or the state also differs in the West and in Muslim-majority countries like Morocco. In the West, individual agency is accepted and even expected. Thus, individualism has as much to do with expectations of personal responsibility and self-sufficiency as it has to do with rights. A diminished role of community in a person's life is an inevitable outcome of individualism, but not necessarily one that is happily envisioned in Morocco, where there is an emphasis on community caretaking of those in need. This sense of a collective identity associated with so-called traditional societies offers a sense of security to those who conform, yet can be threateningly restrictive for those who deviate from generally accepted norms. Thus, in the context of collectivist, traditional cultures, women's rights mean accepting a diminished dependence – economic and otherwise – on men.

In Morocco, families hold no expectation that a professional woman will contribute her earnings to the household. According to Islamic law, a woman's earnings and inherited wealth are her own, and she is legally not required to share her assets for the maintenance of her family. Providing for the family is a man's responsibility, legally as much as culturally. Nowadays, women occasionally have higher-paying jobs than their husbands or a husband is unemployed while his wife earns wages. Even in these cases, Islamic law does not require that a woman support her family. This law was conceived so that in case of divorce or death a woman can rely on her assets to provide for herself and her children, and it has served to ensure social stability. Some Islamists are adamant that a women's rights agenda cannot include a reform that changes this system so that women must contribute financially to a household. In fact, many Moroccan women are wary of giving up this distinct privilege accorded to them by religious law. Further, the fact that these financial regulations are rooted in religion creates a strong resistance against changing them. Secular Moroccan feminists, however, agree that in exchange for rights, responsibilities need to be part of gender equality, including a provision that wage-earning women need to contribute financially to their families. For secular feminists, most of whom are highly educated middle- or upper-middle-class women, such a provision would not mean undue hardship. For less-educated or lower-class women who work menial jobs with low salaries and no job security, however, their inheritance or savings from income may be the safety net they need should they end up divorced or widowed.

Feminist discourse in Morocco must take the religious dimension of women's lives and their larger culture into consideration. Islamist women's rights advocacy is not in opposition to the activism of feminists from societies grounded in Judeo-Christian traditions. Islamist activists wrestle with the values of Western secularism, not with the dominant Western religions themselves. In fact, it is in the quest to define modernity within a Muslim context that Moroccan feminists address concerns that are different from those in the West. Pertinent examples are polygamy laws and inheritance laws that privilege male over female heirs; such laws are of no concern in Western gender discourse.

Islamist women's rights activists argue that the Muslim world has to generate its own dialogue to address the specific problems that arise out of an Islamic socio-cultural context. Simply copying or adopting Western feminism misses the point of authentic emancipation.

Secular feminists in Morocco disagree with Islamist feminists, however, instead believing that the Western model is based on universal values, such as those espoused in the International Declaration of Human Rights or the United Nations Convention on the Elimination of all Forms of Discrimination against Women (CEDAW). They reject the notion that 'universal' is merely synonymous with Western norms. They also point to the fact that Arab and Muslim countries participated in developing the CEDAW, and so reject the notion that this international convention is a purely Western creation. One refrain reiterated by secular feminists in Morocco is best summarized in what one gender rights activist told me:

> Here we are all Muslims. But we don't use religion to advocate for change because women's rights are universal and are not specific to one culture or religion. Religion has no place in the discussion on women's rights because it treats them as culturally relative.

Secular feminists in Morocco further insist that they are not 'bad Muslims' because they want to exclude religion from their gender rights agenda. For them, it is counterproductive to develop a Moroccan model based on Islam because doing so would diminish the global nature of individual rights, freedoms, and responsibilities. They believe that Moroccans need not become 'less religious' in embracing gender equality but should leave religion to individual choice and not use it as the basis for legislation. Furthermore, they argue, not all Moroccans practise Islam in the exactly same way; therefore, it is futile to wait or even strive for religious consensus. Secular activists also point out that all monotheistic religions are patriarchal and have been used as the basis for male domination: God is male, Biblical prophets and those mentioned in the Qur'an are mostly male, Prophet Mohammed is male, the Messiah is male, and exegesis has been a male domain for centuries. They view a discourse within a religious framework as either a dead-end street or a sure recipe for serious conflict.

Secular women's associations in Morocco and throughout North Africa benefit from significant financial support from the European Union and the United States. In addition, constant flows of American and European volunteers donate countless hours to research or office work. Even the premises occupied by such associations as l'Association Démocratique des Femmes du Maroc (ADFM), or the Democratic Association of Women in Morocco, are often generously supported by the European Union or other Western sponsors. While this support can be seen as a commendable act of transnational collaboration, American anthropologist and gender studies scholar Lila Abu-Lughod has expressed scepticism about such East-West collaboration: 'The plight of "Muslim women" has long occupied a special place in Western political imagination, whether in colonial officials' dedication to saving them from barbaric practices or development projects devoted to empowering them.'[14] Over the past decades, women's rights advocates have come to be framed as universal human rights, primarily through a series of large-scale international human rights conferences and the efforts of mostly secular feminist activists. In response, Abu-Lughod asked a pertinent question: 'What are the regional consequences of the new internationalism of women's rights? Must this new transnationalism dictate the language in which rights are framed today?'[15]

When French colonial control of Morocco gave way to new foreign influences in a seemingly seamless manner, it allowed the country little time to formulate a complete, authentic post-colonial narrative. From colonialism to globalization, the West has come in and out of the African continent as through a revolving door. To acknowledge the weight of internationalism on local discourses, however, is not to denigrate European accomplishments in its former territories. European occupation brought with it the establishment of infrastructures that benefitted the local population, such as railways and road systems, modern educational institutions, and hospitals and health care facilities. Thus, the Western presence forced into motion a process of modernization in which Moroccans themselves had little say but which did indeed improve the quality of people's lives.

Today Moroccans enjoy the same telecommunications technologies as the West, providing them with near unlimited access to information. Cell phones do not depend on cumbersome landlines, thus allowing the rural population, which frequently does not have access to sufficient public infrastructure, to utilize modern communication technologies. Private industry has sidestepped government procedures and made it possible for a large segment of the population to partake in conveniences that were until recently only available to the urban middle class. With communication technologies penetrating the shantytowns and the hinterlands, new ideas and opportunities have spread, and advances in science and technology have become adapted to meet local needs. In rural outdoor markets, vendors can be seen standing in the mud, cell phone in hand, negotiating the price and sale of live sheep to customers on the other side of the country. Such instantaneous cross-country sales and communication with people in various parts of the country would have been impossible a decade ago. Just as importantly, these changes in the marketplace are mirrored in larger societal transformations underway in Morocco.

Social stability and the role of women

Regardless of the long-term benefits of the diffusion of technological capacities, change always involves uncertainty. When one is faced with the possibility of social rupture, religion can offer the refuge of stability. References to religious tenets have historically regulated women's status in Morocco; consequently, many women have come to accept their disadvantaged situations as being in accordance with divine providence. Some women view emancipation as going against God's will, even if it offers prospects for a better situation. Hence, for women's rights to be seen as widely acceptable and worth fighting for, they have to be considered as being in keeping with religious beliefs. The continuance of gender norms based on centuries of inculcation provides a measure of stability and assurance for many people. Moreover, the belief that such an order is in line with divine design offers a deep sense of purpose.

In a place like Morocco, where religion plays a highly important role and is one of the main components of people's identity, it makes little sense to move the discussion of women's rights beyond the religious sphere and into a secular context. A point that is not always clearly understood in this North African country is that legal equality does not prevent women from assuming a subservient role to their husbands if they so choose. Legal equality merely means that submission cannot legally be enforced and that women are free to change their minds about their own roles and behaviour. Especially at a time when the West's preoccupation with the Muslim world revolves to a great extent around women's rights issues, Muslims have to re-appropriate the debate, make it their own, and make it relevant to their specific religious and cultural contexts. However, secular feminists in Morocco deride such attempts as futile, insisting that gender equality is common sense in a modern era and, therefore, does not require any theological justifications. Nevertheless, as the debates about gay marriage and abortion in the United States indicate, religious convictions are deeply rooted and play a significant role in public debate even in modern, Western, secular societies.

The lessons of the marketplace

Despite theoretical divergences between secular and Islamist women's rights advocates in Morocco, the shared reality of daily life there points to common bonds that transcend such differences. A few examples should serve to illustrate these commonalities.

Any visitor to Morocco will notice that a large clock adorns every office, train station, airport, store, classroom, restaurant, coffee shop, and most private homes. Rarely do any of these big clocks show the actual time even when ticking. In fact, many don't work at all, but are mere decorative items. Yet clocks are prominently displayed everywhere. As their function in Morocco is often decorative they possibly epitomize a different understanding of time.

Another aspect of daily Moroccan life that is baffling to most Westerners is street traffic. Traffic lights, designated lanes, and one-way streets are all understood as suggestions to be followed if deemed appropriate. Honking and yelling are the prime modes of communication between drivers. Policemen and increasingly policewomen stand in the middle of many intersections and perpetually blow a whistle in an attempt to outdo the honking and yelling. The exact purpose of all that ear-splitting whistling is clear only to those in the know. The seeming chaos of Moroccan traffic is bewildering to foreigners from the West; however, the accident rate in urban areas is not significantly higher than in places where drivers adhere to traffic rules. Traffic in Morocco moves noisily, yet, in its own manner, smoothly. Neither the absence of the dictates of time nor the loose nature of traffic rules impedes people from conducting business. Life has its own rhythm and Moroccans move in accordance with this rhythm without needing accurate timepieces or strict adherence to traffic rules.

A distinguishing feature of Moroccan society concerns the nature of organized meetings – be they at schools, universities, gymnasiums, or any other venue: meetings rarely start at the announced time but begin when the person in charge arrives. Once the leader of a meeting appears, attendees begin to show up within minutes, seemingly out of nowhere. People are connected with each other in such a way that word gets around quickly. Thus, it is not time-based rules that make people appear at a meeting; its signal is the presence of the person with authority. Life is based on people and relationships in Morocco; anthropologist Hildred Geertz called this set of values 'person-centered ethics'.[16] Though Geertz used this term to describe family and kinship interactions, it applies to Moroccan society at large.

The Moroccan marketplace provides another opportunity for Westerners to re-evaluate their own norms. The seeming disorder in a Moroccan market can be as disconcerting as the street traffic. In the crowded, narrow alleys between stalls or shops, men and women push and shove and rub against each other; at peak times there often is less than a hair-width of space between people. (I have seen Americans seized by panic attacks in the market because they could not tolerate such a stifling absence of private space.) There are no fixed prices in traditional marketplaces (*souk*) and, even in some modern shops, buying and selling requires intense communication, discussion, and negotiation. The purchasing process actually is as important as the sale itself. The market is a place without a hierarchy, where buyer and seller must come to an agreement and no one can simply impose their will – or price – on the other. Each actor has a clear objective, in the pursuit of which harsh words might be exchanged, insults hurled, and curses uttered. Yet, no matter how heated the bargaining, when a sale is concluded, seller and buyer often shake hands and part ways with a smile.

One of the most striking examples of male–female interaction in public occurs in the market. This is a place where men and women bargain fiercely with each other and women display no signs of submission or demureness. In *Gender on the Market: Moroccan Women and the Revoicing of Tradition*, Deborah Kapchan observed that the market is in fact 'a forum of transition'. She explained: 'Goods and values trade hands in the market and identities are negotiated ... . The marketplace puts rules of appropriate behaviour into question.'[17] Thus, the marketplace serves as a valuable indicator of social change. Veiled or unveiled, Islamist or secularist, male or female, the *souk* has become a great equalizer. In the past vendors and buyers were mostly men, but over the decades this has changed as women do much of the shopping nowadays and there are female food vendors in outdoor weekly markets. The marketplace is in fact a venue where changes in gender roles are tangible and occur at a grassroots level. This public sphere is no longer singularly male-dominated. To quote from Kapchan's study *Gender on the Market*:

> The rearrangement of the material economy, or its laws and rules for the physical and the social body, has influenced the transformation of the moral code. What was formerly considered private and feminine behaviour is now public behaviour in the heteroglossic marketplace. With boundaries overstepped, limits refuted, and notions of personhood and category challenged, transgression plays a major role in the hybridization process.[18]

Thus, in spite of frequent calls by conservative clerics to uphold 'tradition', new hybrid forms of social and gender identity are emerging in Morocco. Economic pressures have caused women to insert themselves into public life, and the result has been a transformation of women's sense of self. Feminist ideas manifest even when the term itself is rejected.

As the *souk* is characteristic of Moroccan life, it is a useful metaphor for the debate about women's rights that takes place there. If
the debate about women's rights in the West can be compared to an
orderly supermarket full of neatly stacked items with fixed price tags
that are taken out, observed, and shelved again if found unappealing
or not useful, in Morocco the discourse on women's rights can be compared to a *souk* where any number of ideas – from outrageous to reasonable – are entertained, vigorously discussed, and tossed around in
a seemingly chaotic manner until some useful concepts emerge. Thus,
the marketplace of ideas may follow a similar pattern to that of the
marketplace of goods, as it is an equally noisy sphere where beliefs and
concepts are put forth, discussed, rejected, and negotiated. Each side
accuses the other of unspeakable things, yet at some point a consensus
or truce will be reached.

Negotiation finesse is also part of daily routine in the privacy of
the Moroccan home. A particular sort of nonverbal communication
can be observed when gathering around the customary round table for
a meal. While most Westerners prefer to eat from individual plates,
Moroccans generally eat from one large platter placed at the centre of
the table. Eating from a communal dish requires mastering unspoken rules of sharing. Eating rituals, inculcated over generations, reveal
norms of interaction. Sharing is not equitable; a hierarchy is evident in
who gets what piece of meat. Eating habits display sophisticated skills
that carry over into aspects of life that pertain to negotiating ideas as
well. Moroccans are adept at switching back and forth between differing cultural norms for eating meals together without difficulty, a trait
much less common among Westerners. When foreigners from Europe
or North America are present, individual place settings are put on
the table to accommodate them. Such non-verbal code switching is an
integral part of Moroccan life, especially for those who interact with
foreigners on a regular basis.

Islamic discourses on women

The resistance of mostly Islamist activists to the way the women's
rights debate is sometimes framed and imposed through international

pressures or forums is to be expected, since they feel their perspectives are either ignored or not taken seriously. Those who espouse internationalist aims often fail to acknowledge that the majority of a given population is deeply vested in its own rhythms, values, and cultural norms. Westerners generally feel more secure when there are obvious rules and parameters for clearly spelled-out objectives that are adhered to by all. In Morocco, events and meetings have a way of evolving without a discernible plan and patience is an essential quality.

No person who suffers inequality needs to be reminded that he or she has been treated unfairly. How one responds to such injustice differs from person to person and culture to culture. Women in Morocco are keenly aware of their secondary status. Some accept this condition as God-given, some rebel, some employ a combination of both responses. In this age of globalization, cyber communication, and social media, information and ideas flow freely across national boundaries. Such mutual exchanges cause the West to influence the East, North, and South and the other way around. These trends cannot be stopped and change is inevitable. No matter what term is used to advance women's rights, the idea of gender equality is no longer germane to one geographic region of the world.

Though some Moroccans fear Western feminism if adopted in their country will destroy their cultures, it is actually the women's rights agenda emerging from domestic Islamic and Islamist women activists that poses a greater challenge to the patriarchal, authoritarian structures prevalent in North Africa. By Islamic women activists I mean those who use religion as an important reference point; by Islamist women activists I refer to those for whom religion is the single most important dimension in any discussion about gender. In this context, I include only non-violent activists. As discussed in the previous chapter, one of the first so-called Islamic feminists in the modern Muslim world is Morocco's own Fatima Mernissi. In basing a feminist discourse on a re-reading of sacred texts, Mernissi provided a compelling argument for improving women's status from within the existing system.

Moroccan men and women who are schooled in exegesis question prevalent gender norms. In this sense, one can compare the growth of Islamic feminism and the resistance of the conservative religious establishment to new feminist scriptural interpretations to the emergence of Liberation Theology in South America and the serious threat it posed to the Catholic Church. When Liberation Theology first appeared in Brazil in the 1950s, and later spread throughout Latin America in the 1970s, it emphasized the Christian mission of bringing justice to the poor and oppressed. The cause of poverty was attributed to the sin of exploitation of the weak. Confronted with this new gospel of social justice, the Vatican saw its authority severely challenged. It considered such teachings to be part of a socialist agenda and its exponents were disciplined or silenced. In the 1980s, Cardinal Joseph Ratzinger (now Pope Benedict XVI, suggesting that the conservative strand within the Catholic Church remains the most influential segment within its power structure) launched a vigorous attack against Liberation Theology. Today the most powerful religious institution in the Christian world continues to uphold anachronistic positions, making lamentations by the Western world about the slow progress of reform in Islam rather problematic.

Another such case in which religious authorities questioned religiously sanctioned oppression can be found in South Africa. In the 1980s, Anglican Archbishop Desmond Tutu contributed in no small measure to the struggle against the apartheid system using his church pulpit. His voice, among others, challenged the status quo in a period when most whites-only churches and their leaders supported the strict segregation of South African citizens according to skin colour. Similarly, in the United States, the civil rights movement emerged from within African-American churches; in fact, all original leaders of the civil rights movement were ordained ministers. These examples show how social transformation has emerged from the religious sphere in Christian-majority, secular countries. Nevertheless, new religious interpretations – especially when they are tied to a specific social movement – rarely go unchallenged within any organized religion. In Islam, however, there is no one central authority overseeing a worldwide organization. Thus, the Muslim world has the advantage, if one wants to call it that, of being decentralized enough to allow each country or region to develop its own discourse.

No doubt, activists and scholars who embrace a new reading of sacred texts with the goal of challenging customs and laws do undergo the risk of running afoul of local establishment authorities. Inasmuch as Islamic feminism is concerned with balancing gender relationships, it is engaged in a social endeavour that is rightfully perceived as threatening the status quo. Changing gender dynamics does not merely mean bringing about more rights for women; it means a fundamental shift in social order, in customs and traditions – in short, the way things are. Islamic feminists and Islamist women's rights activists who seek answers to gender questions in their use of the sacred scriptures are in their own right new religious authorities. In their study on 'Women in Islamist Movements', Marina Ottaway and Abdellatif Omayma made some observations about Islamist women activists in particular:

> Islamist women are concerned with the preservation of Islamist values, and as such, deny that they are embracing a Western-style feminist agenda, which they consider a rejection of women's obligations to family and community. They do, however, display increased dissatisfaction with their position in Islamist movements, and wish to be seen as potential leaders, not just foot soldiers.

> Islamist movements have depended on women to reach out to all segments of the population, leading to successful engagement in political tasks such as election campaigning, mobilizing members, and electoral monitoring. As women became active in these movements, they became increasingly aware of their importance and began petitioning for more significant roles as political actors.

> Islamist women argue that Islamic precepts originally did not aim to subjugate women, but were distorted by social and cultural norms that antedated Islam. In this view, the struggle for women's rights is a struggle to restore Islam to its original form.[19]

The authors described Islamist women as playing important roles in the movements to which they belong. Through their participation in various religiously oriented movements they are defining a new model of Islamist activism and even feminism, one that is contrary to views commonly held in the West.[20] In various Muslim-majority countries throughout the world, Islamist movements have adeptly built a broad following across social classes. According to Ottaway and Omayma, if Islamist women activists become more influential, Islamist movements could become important instruments for promoting the rights of Muslim women.

Thus far, Islamic/Islamist feminism has been studied mostly in Egypt and Iran, where it has evolved over the past several decades. In Morocco, Islamist feminist thought is still a nascent strand and various Islamist movements are at times at odds with one another. More moderate female Islamic activists reject religious rigorism; to date, no one on the religious side has formulated a specific, practical position on gender. It is, however, possible to discern a common platform that applies to Islamic feminism in general. One of the foremost experts on Islamic feminism, Margot Badran, offered this definition:

> Islamic Feminism aims to recover and implement the fundamental objectives (*maqasid*) of Islam: social justice and the equality of all Muslims, including gender equality. There can be no social justice without gender equality. Islamic feminism is attentive to the rights Islam granted to women that have withheld from them in practice, as well as the rights of any others withheld because of class, race or ethnicity. Islamic feminism is about gender, about women and men: their relations and interactions, about gender justice and the struggle to attain it, what in South Africa is called 'gender jihad.'[21]

'Islamic feminism' is among the hottest buzzwords in the contemporary study of gender issues in the Muslim world. While Islamic feminism is one of the most interesting phenomena to emerge in Morocco in the past two decades, to understand it is a little bit like shooting at a moving target. Spanish scholar Gema Martín Muñoz acknowledged in her article 'Islamists Yet Modern' (2006) that the goals of female Islamic activists are not easy to pin down. She observed that, for the most part, they do not advocate stepping back into some glorious Muslim past, nor are they manipulated, as some secular women's activists claim, to serve as puppets in the service of a male agenda to preserve patriarchal structures in the name of Islam.

Unlike self-proclaimed criminal Islamists – that is to say, terrorists – who recruit most of their adepts in the impoverished urban slums around Morocco's largest city, Casablanca, today's non-violent, religiously motivated activists are most visible on university campuses and in middle-class urban areas. This demographic marks a significant shift from previous decades, when radical leftist activists dominated at institutions of higher learning and the majority of urban women were unveiled. In Morocco today, the only really influential and well-organized campus organizations are religious ones. As Muñoz observed, contemporary female Islamic activists are less known for their adherence to Muslim traditions and customs than for their tendency to distinguish themselves through religious innovation and assertiveness in the public domain. There exists, Muñoz has argued, an 'incontestable new phenomenon of individualisation and auto-affirmation'.[22] Similarly, Gray described the occurrence of a 'personal faith' and insistence on the right to self-determination of one's own religious understanding in her study on Moroccan women and women of Moroccan origin in France.[23] Generally associated with the West, and in particular the United States, the concept of personal faith based on individual choice is becoming increasingly common among young Muslim women whether they reside in a Muslim-majority country such as Morocco or are part of an ethnic or religious Muslim minority in a country such as France.

Scholars like Ziba Mir-Hosseini and Margot Badran have described Islamic feminism as an 'original modernity', meaning it presents a genuinely new contribution that shapes modernity within a religious context. As Oumaima Abu Bakr, American-trained Egyptian scholar of Islam, wrote:

> It is true that the terms 'feminism' and 'gender' themselves are etymologically English/Western, but the ideas of egalitarianism, justice, equal rights, compassion, resistance to tyranny, activism ... etc. are not a Western invention or a monopoly by the

West. Especially the history of women in the Arab world in the 19th and 20th century shows their 'feminist activism' and discussion of 'gender' long before these terms came to the surface. Furthermore, the term 'Islamic Feminism' allows me to qualify my own indigenous brand of feminism and work out a feminist discourse stemming from within the culture and religion. There is an Islamic ethics of feminism, just as in many other things. Of course, the problem now is that I sense that the field – after it had a strong promising beginning of women scholars and experts analyzing, interpreting, and coming up with that Muslim feminist perspective/discourse – degenerated into chaos and anything goes. Any rejection, any Islam-bashing, any confrontation, any search for the shocking and the odd, and any unlearned or uninformed talk can pass now for Muslim feminist calls for reform.[24]

Though she did not explicitly say so, Abu Bakr's reference to 'anything goes' and 'chaos' is a stab at Muslim activists who advocate for gay rights in the name of Islam, as did Canadian writer Irshad Manji in her 2005 book, *The Trouble with Islam Today: A Muslim's Call for Reform in Her Faith*. The book, translated into some 30 languages, caused a stir because Manji described herself as a lesbian observant Muslim. The majority of Islamic feminists do not consider gay rights part of their struggle for women's rights. Though there are exceptions, and some do support legal protection and certain rights for minorities, including homosexuals, most Islamic feminists do not consider homosexuality as equal to heterosexuality and they would not take this stance in public in Morocco today. Manji has called for a 'project *ijtihad*', a radical re-reading of the sacred texts. *Ijtihad* encompasses the process of arriving at (mostly legal) decisions by independent interpretation of scriptures, and scholars like Abu Bakr have insisted that not everyone is equipped to engage in this process, and that some like Manji have taken the right to interpretation too far.

Another controversial author who has inserted herself into the debate about Muslim women's rights is Ayaan Hirsi Ali, a Somalia-born activist and author of three books: *The Caged Virgin* (2008), *Infidel*

(2008), and *Nomad* (2010). Hirsi Ali served as a member of parliament in the Netherlands before her Dutch citizenship was revoked on grounds that she had not been truthful on her initial application; she subsequently moved to the United States where she now works for the conservative think tank American Enterprise Institute. Her writings have reinforced Western stereotypes about Muslim women and put Islamic feminists on the defence. Hirsi Ali launched all-round attacks against the religion of Islam by portraying practices such as forced marriage, female genital cutting (FGC), domestic violence, and female illiteracy in large parts of the Muslim world as directly linked to Islam. A frequent guest on televised talk shows, Hirsi Ali's assertions have fuelled anti-Islamic sentiments. She has described her criticisms of Islam as authentic because she is a Somalia-born Muslim-turned-atheist who has been the victim of the violence she has ascribed to Islam. Although her books are directed primarily at non-Muslim Western audiences, her outspoken critique of Islam has generated a great deal of debate within Muslim communities.

Much of Hirsi Ali's critique is levelled at European countries, which, in the name of multi-culturalism, have allowed the development of parallel societies. Ali has asserted that Western societies have turned a blind eye to practices that occur in immigrant communities, such as FGC, domestic violence, forced arranged marriages, and even honour killings, in the name of cultural relativism and tolerance. She has insisted that Western norms and laws must be enforced in Western countries so as to eradicate practices that are incompatible with human rights in democratic societies. According to Hirsi Ali, multicultural tolerance can be a form of racism when minority populations are not deemed worthy to receive the same legal protection or be held to the same standards as the majority population. Her attacks on Islam have been so fierce, her 'Islam-bashing' (as Abu Bakr calls it) has been so relentless, and her popularity with television pundits in North America and Europe so widespread that other serious scholars of Islam like Tariq Ramadan have felt compelled to engage in discussions with her.[25] It is through these combative public exchanges that Hirsi Ali's positions have become known in Morocco. Provoked by assertions such as the ones made by Hirsi Ali, that women's rights abuses are intrinsic to Islam, Moroccan Islamists see a need to step up their advocacy for their religion.

The Justice and Charity movement
(Jami'at al Adl wa Ihsane)

In Morocco, one of the rising figures in Islamist feminist activist circles is Merieme Yefout, leader of the feminine section of the Justice and Charity movement (Jami'at al Adl wa Ihsane), the largest Islamist movement in Morocco. Little known even within Morocco, Yefout is active behind the scenes in developing a concept of women's rights for her country. Her research on Middle Eastern countries has left her with the sense that Morocco needs to look to itself to develop a concept of feminism and that Moroccan feminists should only take limited cues from their Egyptian or Iranian sisters. Yefout is adamant that there is no overarching Muslim identity but that identities are fluid and formed within specific cultural and geographic contexts. She fits what Turkish sociologist Nilüfer Göle called 'the avant-garde of Islamist thinkers', namely women who are developing a women's rights agenda that is in keeping with their religious beliefs; that is, who use religion as a primary source for regulating human behaviour.[26]

Yefout has argued against patriarchy as un-Islamic, and has said that monogamy should be the norm in Morocco and polygamy only the exception. Yefout believes that inheritance laws need to be changed to allow for equality between male and female heirs. She has acknowledged that Islamists disagree vehemently with each other on gender issues, and that even within the Justice and Charity movement there is no consensus on the role of women. Yefout has observed critically that women in Islamist movements are undergoing transformations that make some feel uncomfortable. An ambitious young woman, Yefout has asserted that these disagreements occur because Islamist movements are not stagnant but evolving, and there is no precedent for women in organization-wide leadership positions. Women's rights are an increasingly contentious issue among Islamists because their aspirations involve tackling larger societal issues. In my conversations with her, Yefout outlined three such major areas of concern: ignorance, poverty, and violence. Describing herself as someone who sees Islam as the source of an 'alternative socialization that affects the private as well as the public sphere', Yefout insisted on her right to be assertive, outspoken, and to assume any position for which she is qualified.

Yefout incorporates multiple minorities: she is darker skinned than the majority of Moroccans, female, from modest social class background. While the majority of lighter-skinned Moroccans rarely refer to themselves as African, Yefout does so proudly. African, for most Moroccans, means black Africans from a country south of the Sahara, and the terms black and African generally carry a pejorative meaning. As there is no such concept as political correctness in Morocco, there is little inhibition against using racial epithets.

In her doctoral dissertation, Yefout explored the insertion of Islamist women into the political arena. She herself embodies the quintessential activist one would expect to find in any progressive movement: highly educated, knowledgeable, open, interested in the world around her, non-dogmatic. Over the years, I have met Merieme Yefout at the headquarters at of the Justice and Charity movement in Salé, near Rabat, and at her university in Casablanca. Strolling with her across the main walkway of the Aïn Chok campus of Hassan II University, I saw how well known she is. Nearly every other student greeted her and many stopped to chat for a few minutes. At one of our meetings, the Political Science Department Chair handed her his office keys so that she could have a quiet place to talk with her guest. In a hierarchical culture such as Morocco it is rather unusual and a sign of trust and respect when a senior person – in this case a university department chair – offers his professional space to someone very much his junior. During our conversation several professors stopped by the office looking for the Chair but none seemed surprised that a foreign researcher would be interviewing Yefout. She is widely known on campus for her activism on behalf of an Islamist movement and, in the spring of 2011, as an active participant in mass demonstrations calling for democratic change in Morocco.

Deeply rooted in her faith, the Sufi order out of which the Justice and Charity movement has grown, Yefout used the issues surrounding the Muslim headscarf to make her point about what she considers the

Moroccan government's misguided path to modernity. Veiled herself, she insisted on a woman's right to chose if she wants to wear the headscarf or not, especially in a Muslim country. Though the Muslim headscarf is not outlawed in Morocco, there is implied government opposition to this overt show of piety. No high-ranking woman, no ambassador, mayor, or government minister (this has changed since the PJD electoral victory in October 2011) wears the *hijab*, nor does any woman interacting with the public or on publicly funded television, in the national airways Royal Air Maroc, or in any of the large national banks. The government thus sends a strong signal that this type of attire is not part of its vision of modernity, an indication of an official policy on collision course with Islamism, according to Yefout.

Even among those who are not Islamists, the *hijab* has become fashionable, and more and more young women wear a headscarf to accessorize their otherwise Western outfits, while the generation of their middle-aged mothers sport short hairdos. Women in low-paying secretarial or administrative jobs also wear the headscarf and a *djellaba*, the traditional North African floor-length, hooded robe, to work because it is less costly than having to purchase fashionable clothes and go to the hairdresser regularly. Hence, while the large number of women in headscarves is not necessarily an indication of the spread of Islamism, the popularity of Islamism helped bring the *hijab* back onto the streets and remove the stigma of its association with rural areas or backwardness. For Yefout, no matter the reason why individuals decide to wear the *hijab*, the triumphant return of public modesty is a mark of success for Islamism.

An issue of interest to Yefout and the women's section of the Islamist movement to which she belongs concerns the use of the terms gender equality versus gender justice. Yefout has said repeatedly over the years that she prefers the phrase gender justice, because this reflects more closely the language of the Qur'an wherein justice is upheld as an ideal. She emphasized that the goal of gender justice is in fact equality but that terminology matters in order to distinguish the basis of her argument from that of secular women's rights activists. Women, Yefout asserted, need to find their value as women without comparing themselves to men. Further, giving birth and taking care of children should not prevent women from pursuing career options. She blamed the patriarchal Moroccan mindset for assigning a subservient, secondary status to women and wanting to limit them to a domestic role. Yefout was adamant that it should be a woman's choice to get married or not, or to pursue a professional career or stay at home, and that all these options should be considered of equal value. (Still) unmarried and childless herself, Yefout is a strong supporter of family planning.

In contrast to some Islamists who advocate for expansion of the Muslim population worldwide by producing many children, Yefout believes in increasing the number of educated Muslims. In my interviews with her, Yefout asserted that making education more accessible to women could only be achieved by limiting the number of children a woman bears. This stance runs counter to mainstream Islamist thinking, which promotes large families and the exalted role of motherhood. Yefout explained that she despises as hypocrisy the common practice of men deifying mothers while at the same time looking down on women. Despite her support for contraceptives, Yefout expressed mixed feelings about abortion, a procedure that is illegal in Morocco. She has listened to the arguments of medical doctors who promote lifting the ban on abortion and admitted she has not yet formed a clear opinion on this issue. As an intellectual of the second generation of leaders within the Justice and Charity movement, Yefout feels she is part of an emerging trend within the movement, one that not only permits but also requires her to develop a carefully thought-out gender policy platform. She acknowledged that she represents a minority within the Justice and Charity movement but shared her hope that one day her ideas will become mainstream thought.

The Justice and Charity movement is the most controversial yet most influential Islamist movement in Morocco. Due to its outspoken stance against the hereditary and sacred monarchy, the movement is a constant thorn in the side of the palace, and its members are occasionally rounded up or apprehended. The movement's opposition to the monarchy stems from the belief of its founder, Sheikh Abdessalam Yassine, that past and present Moroccan monarchs have neither automatically embodied nor adequately implemented Islamic teachings. Yefout joined the movement in part because she felt inspired by its religious teachings, and in part because she viewed it as the best outlet for her ambition to effect lasting changes in Moroccan society. Further, because she saw the government as corrupt and nothing more than an instrument for carrying out the monarch's decisions, she has not considered joining a political party. In the spring of 2011 Yefout came out as a political activist by supporting the so-called February 20 Movement (Conseil National d'Appui au Mouvement du 20 Février, CNAM20), a loose organization of individuals calling for democratic reform in Morocco that was created in the wake of the mass uprisings that led to the overthrow of North African dictators Zine El Abidine Ben Ali of Tunisia and Hosni Mubarak of Egypt. She and others of the Justice and Charity movement joined ranks with secularly minded protestors. Yefout feels that the demand for democracy is not limited to the young or to Islamists of her ilk but that Moroccans of various persuasions and ages are united in this quest.

Yefout expressed her admiration and support for Nadia Yassine, the daughter of Sheikh Yassine, who may succeed her father as the next leader of the Justice and Charity movement. Nadia has taken Merieme Yefout under her wings and encouraged her to take on a more prominent role within the feminine section. At the same time, like all Adlists (as members of the Justice and Charity movement are called), Yefout reveres Sheikh Yassine as a saint-like, larger-than-life figure.

Sheikh Abdessalam Yassine and his daughter

Sheikh Abdessalam Yassine separated from the large Moroccan Bouthchichia Sufi order in 1973 and began to engage in political activities in his home country. Around 1985, he founded the Justice and Charity movement, a pacifist group with political aspirations. According to Mohammed Tozy, who studied Islamist movements in Morocco, Yassine gradually evolved as the chief ideologue of Moroccan Islamism.[27] Since its early days, Islamism in Morocco has undergone several transformations, from spiritual Sufi movement to social organization, and now to extra-parliamentary opposition. Of the various Islamist organizations in Morocco, the Justice and Charity movement is the only one openly opposing the monarchy in Morocco.

Yet today, because the charismatic Sheikh Yassine is ageing and in failing health, the future of the movement, as with all movements led by messianic figures, is in question. There is no apparent successor; neither is there a process in place to elect or appoint one, despite assertions to the contrary by the movement's official spokesperson, Fatallah Arsalane. Nadia Yassine, the Sheikh's daughter, is believed to be her father's choice as future leader, but senior members have said that a woman cannot hold a position of such power and influence. Men close to the Sheikh draw on their religious understandings to argue that women cannot occupy such positions of authority. Thus, despite Yassine's alleged belief that his daughter is entitled to a special providence due to their blood relation, leading figures in the movement do not share this sentiment. A shroud of secrecy surrounds the inner workings of the movement; therefore much of the information concerning succession is based on hearsay or second-hand information.

As stated above, a major *raison d'être* of the Justice and Charity movement is its opposition to the monarchy and the monarchy's apparatus, *makhzen*, a Moroccan Arabic term for the governing elite in Morocco. The *makhzen* in Morocco centres on the king and the royal notables, businessmen, wealthy landowners, regional leaders, top-ranking military and security service personnel, and other well-connected members of the establishment. Due to its inscrutable nature and its far reaches of power (it is considered more powerful than the government itself) *makhzen* has a mostly negative connotation. Nevertheless, it is interesting to observe the similarities between *makhzen* and the structure of the Justice and Charity movement, though its members are insulted when their organization is said to replicate that of the *makhzen*.

Within the Justice and Charity movement, Sheikh Yassine is the supreme leader. He is revered, adored, obeyed; his texts are read alongside the Qur'an. Erudite and well read in both Eastern and Western thought, Yassine has authored over 20 books. His daughter enjoys all the privileges accorded to royal offspring. She is a gifted orator, spirited preacher, and acute public debater in her own right. Yet all is not well within the Sheikh's own family. His sons left the movement long ago and consequently fell from grace; their existence is rarely acknowledged today. As with the royal *makhzen*, secrecy is an integral part of the power structure of the Justice and Charity movement; it is unclear exactly who belongs to the inner circle of the Sheikh and who wields what kind of power. Within this Islamist association, as in the royal palace, transparency is not considered a valued asset.

The conflict between the Justice and Charity movement and the Moroccan royalty dates back more than 30 years and offers insights into the power struggles between various forces aiming to take the lead in Morocco. Abdessalam Yassine rose to prominence in the 1970s when he published an open letter titled, *Islam or the Deluge*, in which he called on the late King Hassan II to content himself with his role as head of state and step down as a religious leader. As with most Islamist scholars elsewhere in the world, Yassine holds that the most perfect human society, the one closest to realizing God's message, was the one created and directed by the Prophet Mohammed in the last ten years of his life, and perpetuated by his four 'rightly guided' successors. Yet, like other Islamist leaders in the world, Yassine has contended that from that point until today, absolutist rule and bad governance have dominated Muslim-majority countries.

For decades now, Yassine has advocated for separating the dual powers vested in the king of Morocco. When he first demanded that religious leadership be ceded to a religious figure, he implicitly offered himself as supreme spiritual guide. In this way, he envisioned himself complementing the monarch in his role as head of State. As expected, King Hassan II would have none of this and put the Sheikh first in a psychiatric ward and then under house arrest. The fact that Hassan II survived two attempted *coups d'état* was presented by the palace as proof that he enjoyed special divine blessings, *baraka*, and could very well serve as spiritual leader himself. To this day, Moroccans marvel at how, in the early 1970s, the king almost miraculously remained unharmed in two carefully planned assassination attempts by the military. In keeping with the old Sufi saying 'Trust in God but tie your camel's legs', the king did not count solely on divine protection but responded to the attempts on his life with crude force, ushering in the 'leaden years'. Mass incarcerations followed, even of those suspected of having even the remotest connections to the plotters, including wives and children of real or imagined foes. Hassan II had special prisons built in the desert in which more than half of the inmates perished. Leaders of the attempted *coup d'état* are said to have committed 'suicide' upon discovering that their plots to overthrow the monarchy had failed. The swift action taken by the king to eliminate once and for all opponents to his regime, as well as the iron hand with which he ruled until 1999, made Hassan II one of the longest reigning monarchs in modern times. Whether his subjects loved or loathed him, under his rule the country remained united and peaceful – as well as poor and illiterate – and never again did a serious threat to the monarchy occur. It was in this climate of heightened sensitivity for criticism of the monarchy that the Sheikh was banished.

Sheikh Yassine's punishment conferred on him something of a martyr status, and his movement began to flourish in the years that followed. Yassine drew inspiration for his vision of a state guided by a religious authority from the Iranian revolution of 1979, in which the spiritual leader, the late Ayatollah Khomeini, wielded more power than political authorities, a situation that continues to this day despite challenges to the system that have recently erupted. Over time, the Iranian model became more and more engrained in the Justice and Charity movement's own idea of a national hierarchy. In this, the Sheikh's views go against the core of the Moroccan monarchy, whereby both the religious and political leadership are unified in the person of the king, who is additionally held to be sacred according to the Moroccan constitution.

King Hassan II died in 1999, and within a year of his son King Mohammed VI's ascension to the throne the young monarch lifted the house arrest of Sheikh Yassine that had been imposed by his father. The Sheikh's release was a major event in Morocco and proved to be an astute move by the new king. No longer locked away, Yassine lost his martyr status, and Mohammed VI was hailed as ushering in a new era of openness and reconciliation.

In March 2000, soon after Sheikh Yassine was released, the Justice and Charity movement experienced its highpoint when Adlists, in collaboration with members of other Islamist organizations, mobilized over a million people in Casablanca to demonstrate against the impending introduction of the Personal Status Code reform, described by the then-government of Prime Minister Abderrahmane Yousoufi[28] as, 'a plan for integrating women into the development of the country'. Testing its new clout, the Justice and Charity movement again mobilized thousands of people in July 2000 in a campaign to 'clean up the beaches' – a reference to their demand that women remain fully clothed on public beaches and not expose themselves in swimsuits. Obviously, no such demands for 'modest' attire were made of men, who enjoyed jumping into the waves of the Atlantic Ocean or the Mediterranean in nothing but swimming trunks. Looking at beaches in Morocco today, the impact of these Islamist campaigns is evident. Each year, urban beaches are packed in the summertime, yet women in bathing suits are now conspicuously absent. While men and children frolic in the waves, women lift their floor-length robes and tip their toes in the water or sit under large beach umbrellas. Many women don't go to public urban beaches at all anymore. Those who do want to swim in a bathing suit visit private beachfront clubs further afield. Thus, the Islamist campaign succeeded in striking a sensitive chord by appealing to Moroccans' widely shared sense of piety and modesty in public.

Soon thereafter, the Justice and Charity movement once again decided to stage a demonstration commemorating the inauguration of the Universal Declaration of Human Rights in 1948. Government forces intervened, preventing the movement and other Islamists from appropriating the human rights agenda. Demonstrating its ability to mobilize tens of thousands of people on three separate occasions allowed the Justice and Charity movement to establish itself as the most important extra-government opposition group in Morocco without ever forming a political party. In fact, some observers have argued that the movement represents the only real organized opposition group in Morocco today, as political parties – even those in the opposition – are seen as having been co-opted by the palace and the *makhzen* and thus are part of the power structure. In organizing mass demonstrations, this Islamist movement proved that it is indeed possible to stand up to the palace and the government.

Al Adl has effectively asserted itself in other areas where the state has let its people down. The movement offers social and community services that government-run mosques fail to provide. Nevertheless, following its high point in 2000, the movement experienced a deep low when the much-heralded 2006 apocalypse prophesized by Sheikh Yassine did not take place. At the time, the Sheikh was said to have had dreams and visions that the Moroccan monarchy would come to an end, ushering in a new era of true Islamic rule. Yet 2006 and subsequent years passed with the monarchy intact, once again confirming the belief that the monarchy enjoys more *baraka* (blessing) than any other institution in the country.

More recently, the Justice and Charity movement has taken on the Palestinian cause and is fashioning itself as the most vocal defender of Palestinian rights in Morocco. Maddy-Weitzman examined the writings of Sheikh Yassine and found that his support of Palestine is based in no small measure on anti-Semitic notions.[29] To be sure, his daughter is emphatic that she does not share the same sentiments and is keen to distinguish between Jews and those who support official Israeli policies. In fact, Adlists compete with the government in organizing demonstrations in support of Palestinians. While Adlists count on Arab/Muslim solidarity for a large turnout, the government offers free train rides to those who wish to participate in such demonstrations. Channelling anger towards a cause in a faraway place is a facile way of diverting resentment against local incongruities. And yet these protestations against injustices far afield do not eclipse the growing dissent within the Islamist organization.

Though the internal goings-on of the Justice and Charity movement are well guarded, with outsiders gaining only occasional glimpses, the battle over leadership succession has not remained a secret. Interestingly, this conflict revolves around the question of the role of women. Nadia Yassine, Sheikh Yassine's daughter, feels entirely qualified, if not entitled, to assume leadership of the movement her father founded. In fact, as the unofficial spokesperson and national and international public face of the Justice and Charity movement, Nadia Yassine is more often in the public spotlight than the movement's official spokesperson, Fatallah Arsalane. Without a doubt, Nadia's popularity and media-savviness contribute substantially to the internal conflict.

From information that can be obtained, the inner circle around Sheikh Yassine is firmly opposed to a female leader. It is unclear if

Yassine's own presumed preference of his daughter over other leaders is based on her blood lineage or on her qualifications, or possibly a combination of both. Thus far, the Sheikh has refrained from officially installing his daughter as his successor, most likely because such an action would risk the break-up of the movement. Nonetheless, if the various factions within the Justice and Charity movement fail to reconcile, such fragmentation may happen anyway once the Sheikh passes away.

Over the years, Sheikh Yassine has addressed the issue of women in some of his writings. In one of his most notable books, *Islamizing Modernity*, he wrote:

> A model homemaker actually is the opposite of the insignificant and oppressed creature that we see today in our society. Widespread illiteracy is one of the results of unjust patriarchal traditions. At the time of the prophet, when women suffered the worst infamy, Islam introduced new laws and a new model for women. Today's Muslim women suffer doubly. Torn between the unfortunate situation resulting from male injustice and the attractive occidental model of freedom, they transform into a European imitation as soon as they find the means to do so.[30]

In an earlier book, *The Illumination of the Faithful*, Sheikh Yassine wrote approvingly about certain historic women who had assumed important positions within the Muslim community. Some say he emphasized the contributions of these women as a part of an historical analysis that would establish a precedent for leadership roles for women in Islam in order to pave the way for his daughter's future leadership.

Born in Casablanca in 1958, Nadia Yassine embodies what the Sheikh envisions for women; she is highly educated, forging her own path as a faithful Muslim woman without modelling herself after emancipated European women. Since the early 1980s, she has sought to take a more prominent role within the Justice and Charity movement by founding a 'feminine section'. This quest was initially met with fierce opposition by then second-in-command Mohammed

Bashiri. Internal wrangling ensued over her initiative and other matters of disagreement between the Sheikh and Bashiri, who until then had been his most loyal follower. A superb organizer and strategist, Bashiri nevertheless was eventually relieved of his position following these internal disputes. It is unclear if he left the movement of his own volition or because he was expelled. Soon after his departure, Bashiri died suddenly. According to Justice and Charity members, his fate serves as a lesson of what can happen to those who part ways with the Sheikh and no longer behave in accord with what the movement sees as divine providence.

The departure of Bashiri, however, did open the way for Nadia Yassine to finally establish a feminine branch. Though the semi-clandestine status of the Justice and Charity movement makes statistics on the group unavailable, it is widely known that women make up at least half the movement and form the most active section. The popularity of the group among women attests to Nadia's talent for mobilizing supporters. Despite Merieme Yefout's official position as leader of the feminine branch, Nadia Yassine undoubtedly is the power behind it. In addition, since she has no official position as spokesperson or as the person in charge of a section, Yassine can focus on establishing herself as an overall spiritual leader. Female members already treat Nadia Yassine with great reverence, a veneration many male members argue is due only to the Sheikh himself. In their respect for Nadia Yassine, female members replicate to a certain degree the admiration they have for her father. The saint-like status of Abdessalam Yassine and the cult surrounding his personality make the Justice and Charity movement unique in Morocco. Nevertheless, such reverence for an individual is not inconsistent with the country's long and enduring tradition of saint-worship – a practice not condoned by conservative Islamists in the Middle East, who consider veneration of saints as un-Islamic.

Just like her father, Nadia Yassine is at once an outspoken yet enigmatic figure. She combines what Mohammed Tozy has called 'the charismatic with politico-religious activism'.[31] Nadia Yassine emphasizes that her activities follow two main trajectories, the spiritual and the practical, both expressed in volunteer activities. At one of our meetings she said, 'If you solve social problems, you help women.'

Still, she has publicly rejected the term feminism because it is derived from a Western historical context that she feels is not applicable to the Muslim world. 'I don't want to be identified by a Western label,' she has stated categorically. In an article published on the website oumma. com in December 2008, Nadia Yassine explained that she considers the term Islamic feminism an oxymoron because it misses the point of what female Muslim activists are all about. Later in the article, however, she mentioned 'points of convergence between feminism and Islamism' and described women's liberation as a 'sacred duty'.

Nadia Yassine is fiercely independent, and by now much more powerful than her husband, Abdallah Chibani, whom the Sheikh had at one point – in vain – tried to nurture as a possible successor. She is not afraid to take on the male leadership of the movement, and frequently speaks out on issues of injustice and corruption within her own circle and in society in general. Because she has become one of Morocco's most famous opposition figures and also has been successful in presenting Morocco's moderate Islamist positions in the international arena, the male leaders within her circle cannot ignore Yassine. She has authored the book *Full Sails Ahead* (2006), raised four accomplished daughters, and cherishes her role as a young grandmother. Over the years, her positions have changed and evolved as she carves out a role for herself in the movement – and possibly on a larger scale in Morocco. In private, when I met her in her apartment, she has admitted that for all intents and purposes she is a feminist. Her public rejection of the term feminist, however, speaks to her desire to remain independent of any kind of label and her insistence on being viewed on her own terms.

Nadia Yassine holds that women's liberation is not primarily a matter of changing laws, but, first and foremost, a matter of changing mentalities. According to Yassine, such liberation happens by way of re-reading the scriptures at the grassroots level. She believes strongly that exegesis should not be limited to scholars but extended to ordinary believers, who need to engage critically with sacred texts. In an interview at the Movement's headquarters, she asserted that women need to reclaim the liberating message of the Qur'an: 'our sacred texts give us many rights. But men, these machos, have robbed us of that.

It's their fault that the whole world believes the opposite.' Like almost everyone in Morocco, she invoked Sufism when referring to religion:

> Our movement is grounded in Sufism; we are concerned with eternal life and to make sure our life here on earth is lived in such a way that we can meet our maker on the Last Days. Life on earth is not a 'Club Med;[32] it is rather, as the Bible says, 'a valley of tears'.[33] Life is difficult for most people, men and women. It requires endurance and finding value within oneself.

Nadia Yassine has pointed out that her values are in stark contrast to those of a consumerist society, which places value on 'having' rather than 'being'. To this end, she emphasized the importance of the education of women:

> It is by meeting the challenges here on earth with a serene mind that we ultimately effect change. We are striving for women to become experts not just in the domain of religion but also in areas such as psychology, political science, law, medicine, etc. By doing this we revive the prophetic tradition which elevates the value of human beings. We have to remember the history of Islam and reject the paternalistic (machist) readings and interpretations that have marginalized women. It is necessary for women to have their own interpretations.

On some level, Yassine's assertions are strikingly reminiscent of those of Fatima Mernissi, for whom she expresses high regard. The mutual respect of an Islamist leader and a secular academic is again indicative of Morocco's history of peaceful resolution of conflicts.

Sisters of Eternity

Organized religious congregations solely constituted of women are unusual in Morocco. Though women are not formally forbidden from entering mosques there, the reality is that the women's sections in most mosques have been taken over by men. With few exceptions, the partitions separating the men's space from the one reserved for women have been taken down, depriving women of a required designated women's section in mosques. This leaves women with no official place of worship because men and women do not mingle in a mosque. If the mosque is a religious space that expresses ideas about authority, participation, and roles, the practical exclusion of women from such places sends several important messages: women do not belong there, the official practice of religion is a male domain, a woman's place is in the home.

The all-female religious gatherings of the Justice and Charity movement, therefore, meet a specific need of Muslim women in Morocco. They elevate their status and offer a structured approach to their spiritual observance. Members of the Justice and Charity movement, or Adlists, male or female, are not permitted to address congregations in state-run mosques and therefore organize their own gatherings. The services of the Sisters of Eternity, on the other hand, are led by women, sending an empowering signal. Because of their potentially subversive character *vis-à-vis* the religious establishment (official state mosques and their *imams*), such services are not advertised and participation is by invitation only. In fact, it is rare for a non-member to be allowed to sit in on meetings of the Sisters of Eternity. I was invited to attend some sessions. Their reunions are held at the Movement's headquarters in Salé, Rabat's comparatively poor twin city on the other side of the Bou Regreg River. The headquarters are housed in a whitewashed villa in a residential neighbourhood on one of the unusually clean back lanes.

At any given meeting, hundreds of veiled women sit on a carpeted stone floor, crammed into several large adjoining living rooms that have been converted into a hall. Women of all ages and backgrounds attend. Most are professionals; some are homemakers, some students. Given that the meetings take place in a city, the majority of women in attendance are urban. The absence of rural, illiterate women – who make up the majority of women in Morocco – is apparent. This has been pointed out by secular women's rights organizations, most notably ADFM, the Democratic Association of Moroccan Women. Ironically, the members of ADFM also have been accused of representing only the urban middle and upper classes. Among those attending the gatherings of the Sisters of Eternity is a small group of atypical students: mature women who, after raising their children, returned to universities (mostly in Europe), to pursue graduate studies. In Morocco it is rare for adults, and especially women, to return to higher education, so these women embody the Justice and Charity movement's sincerity and commitment to supporting women's professional advancement.

At one such assembly of the Sisters of Eternity, Nadia Yassine sat on a plush chair in the front of the hall and guided the proceedings. She proudly introduced some of the middle-aged pioneers as role models to the congregation and asked them to offer testimony about how they transitioned back into student life after having been out of school for decades. Yassine encouraged her listeners to pursue a path of life-long learning. Obtaining an education, she noted, is the first calling of a Muslim woman. She then moved to the centrepiece of the gathering, her sermon. Speaking without notes, Nadia Yassine captivated her audience for several hours at a time. Yet, there is no shuffling, no exiting to stretch legs, no yawning; everyone remains attentive throughout the service in their crouched position on the floor.

The following is a very brief summary of the sermon delivered at the service I attended. This abbreviated version does not do justice to the lengthy and detailed elaborations that were included in the actual sermon, but conveys the fundamental essence. It focused on certain themes that Nadia Yassine emphasizes in most of her addresses. As is the case in cultures with a strong oral tradition, there is much spoken reiteration and loud affirmation by the congregation, a practice that keeps listeners engaged and active. The way Nadia Yassine delivered her sermon is best compared to the interactive way preachers conduct services in African-American churches. There too, the congregation does not silently receive the word from the pulpit but punctuates the delivery with affirmative exclamations. In a similar manner, Yassine repeated important points, raised and lowered her voice for effect, and encouraged her congregation to vociferously express their support and understanding.

Our objective is to prepare us so as to be ready to meet God one day. This objective cannot be met without concrete projects with people while here on

Earth. It is by being active with people and in this world that we transmit our message. Interaction with people occurs on various levels: primarily in the family and also the larger society. In both settings, dialogue is necessary. Apart from dialogue, we need something concrete to do, we cannot just mediate and pray and feel good about ourselves and our relationship with God. We cannot just associate with like-minded people simply because this is easier and feels better. We need to participate in all levels of society. We need to reach out and challenge ourselves. We cannot be content with silent contemplation.

Members of our movement are critical of the sermons given by government-appointed imams *in mosques throughout the country. The* imam *stands there above the congregation and gives his sermon, literally talking down to the congregation. We must not do the same thing. Real learning is participatory. We have to feed the heart as well as the rational mind. We need to allow questions to be asked. Believers have questions; they don't need to be told what to believe. You cannot understand without asking questions. The same goes for doubt. Doubt is an integral part of a life of faith. We should never feel too sure of ourselves. You should not sit here just agreeing with what I say. If you don't understand something, you need to ask.*

The tyrants of the Muslim world want us to be estranged from the memory of the initial Muslim community. People don't remember the beginning of Islam, the beginning of our religion. In this we are unfortunately very different from Jews. Jews place great value on memory, something that has given strength to their community throughout the ages. Without memory of the past, we don't have a future. If we want to strengthen our community, we need to learn to remember:

1. *The creation of human beings*
2. *The Muslim history*
3. *The history of Al Adl wa Ihsan*

It is important for people to be accountable for their actions. It is important to monitor oneself rather than to wait for the reprimand of others. You should keep track of your deeds before God does. God can forgive anything but to obtain forgiveness between people is more difficult. Self-monitoring also includes repentance. Every true believer has to question him- or herself daily. The one who transgresses does not question his own behaviour and actions.

In the West, there is great emphasis on civic consciousness, doing things for the good of the whole, for the good of humanity. This is one way of overcoming selfishness and building a common bond. We need to learn from that and not only take care of our own community. This is something we should learn from the West. When there is a humanitarian crisis, they don't ask if the people affected are Christian, or Jews, or Muslims, they offer assistance to suffering people regardless of their religion or which country or community they belong to. Here we are too much concerned with our own community. We need to go beyond, get out, and get involved. Don't be afraid to learn from others.

You should treat your soul like a good business partner. We Moroccans understand parables that relate to business. We know money matters. So let me apply this to our spiritual life. Do not cheat your soul! You may gain something in the short run, but you cannot afford to lose your soul. You can call this public-mindedness or a spiritual practice; the result is the same, namely to overcome self-centredness. It is thus that we purify our soul ...

Once Yassine concluded her sermon, she invited congregants to ask questions or make comments. As it is not a Moroccan custom to pose questions to someone in a position of authority, most of the women expressed their gratitude for her words or reiterated the points they considered most relevant. Some asked for clarification or asked which passages of the Qur'an relate to what they had just heard. There were no probing questions that would lead to further discussion, however. As much as Yassine encouraged her listeners to engage critically with the ideas she presented, the congregation remained mostly in awe and in agreement.

Moving the meeting along without a break, Nadia Yassine next read from Sheikh Yassine's texts, pausing to explain and elaborate. About five hours passed before there was a break. Throughout this period, congregants exhibited no signs of fatigue or boredom. Despite some recent serious health problems, Yassine remained alert and in charge, and graciously accepted displays of reverence. Once congregants rose and prepared for the ritual prayer, there was some shuffling and movement. A number of women left the room and stood in the cold, rainy courtyard, patiently waiting until the prayers were concluded. Those who did not bring an umbrella huddled close together. Eventually they re-entered and continued their participation. This procedure was repeated each time another prayer was offered.

Women's special dispensation

The women who left the hall while others prepared for ritual prayer were menstruating. The scriptural directives for menstruating women can be interpreted in various ways. Some say the Prophet understood that women often are in pain during this time of the month and he sought to offer them some relief. Other interpretations hold that the monthly cycle is unclean; therefore entering the house of prayer is forbidden. Neither Nadia Yassine nor Merieme Yefout could explain why their feminine reading of the scriptures does not contradict an interpretation that considers menstruating women unclean. Though the Qur'an refers to menstruation and admonishes men not to approach their wives for sexual intercourse during that time (2:222), there is no verse that explicitly requires that women be barred from houses of worship during this period of the month. Clearly it is more uncomfortable to stand outside in the rain than to remain indoors for prayers, so maintaining the custom of having menstruating women go outside while others pray does not appear congruent with the feminine reading of the scriptures the two leaders advocate. Several possible reasons might account for their disposition toward this issue. One is that a new feminine interpretation of the scriptures has not been completed yet, and adjustments may be made along the way that will remove barriers to participation based on biological factors. Alternatively, it is possible that even women who reject patriarchy have interiorized their subordinate status and accept that there are no routine biological circumstances that preclude men from entering a house of prayer.

Female Islamist activists still accept certain tenets without considering their larger implications. Those who support the specific exclusion of women from religious practices based on biological factors do, in fact, support basic gender inequality. They affirm determinism over choice. Every menstruating woman is limited in her religious observance and reminded on a regular basis that biology is the basis for public exclusion from participation in a religiously required ritual. In addition, the prohibition on participation in prayer during menstruation brings up privacy issues. Not every woman is comfortable announcing to the world when she is menstruating and may consider this a personal matter. In gatherings where people know each other, pregnancy, miscarriage, and menopause are not private affairs, as fellow congregants will notice when a woman does or does not leave the room for prayer for several months in a row. However, given the large number of Islamist women who obtain higher education – frequently in Europe – and strive for careers and professional fulfilment, it may only be a matter of time before they insist on being able to choose for themselves if they want to remain in the room for prayer while menstruating. One probably should not assign disproportionate importance to this issue, yet it does underscore the limitations of self-proclaimed anti-patriarchal interpretations of Adlist women's activists.

On several occasions, I have visited Nadia Yassine in her home. Away from the public meeting hall and in private, she acknowledged some inconsistencies in her feminine interpretation of the Qur'anic scriptures and explained that *ijtihad*, the process of interpretation, is an ongoing one. Whereas her public persona was disciplined and controlled – and often provocative – she was relaxed and gregarious in private. Nadia and her husband live in a modest apartment not far from the prison where her father, husband, and other members of the Justice and Charity movement have been incarcerated at one time or another. She admitted that these arrests – without trial – were traumatic events in her life. They have infused her with a sense of mission to fight government corruption and injustice and steeled her resolve to audaciously pursue her own goals. At home, she was a gracious and generous host who insisted on serving her guests, even those who earlier had expressed great deference to her.

An expert debater, Nadia Yassine was hard to pin down when it came to specific questions about her vision for a future Morocco and the role of women therein. In public she rejects being called a feminist, though in smaller settings she acknowledges being one. She is, in fact, one of the very few women, or possibly the only woman, to hold a position of considerable authority in an Islamist movement – not only in Morocco but also throughout North Africa and the Middle East. At times, she has advocated for an Islamic state following the Iranian model of Ayatollah Khomeini, an ideal her father has long espoused.

More recently, she has joined public rallies and called for Morocco to become a republic. At other occasions, to smaller groups more familiar with her work, Yassine has said that she favours the idea of a secular state that guarantees religious freedom to its citizens. One could say that she is performing something of a high-wire act, trying to prove herself loyal to her father's vision (the prime source of her legitimacy) while at the same time developing her own positions, more in line with contemporary reality. Thus, she seeks to sidestep the utopian model upheld by her father and take the movement from the margins to the centre of public life in Morocco. She frequently laments that her movement has been 'demonized'. Yet for a shift toward official legitimacy to occur, the Justice and Charity movement needs to shed its cult-like image, become more transparent, and distinguish itself through a tangible plan for development rather than primarily through venomous – if justified – attacks against an often corrupt government. Though faith is believed to move mountains, practical problems such as illiteracy, unemployment, and women's unequal status call for practical propositions. Yassine's constant appeal for a 'change of mentality' ultimately will not be sufficient to address the country's manifold challenges.

The divergence between Nadia Yassine's public and private personas is reminiscent of those representing minorities who must straddle vastly differing constituencies. The work of civil rights leader Dr. Martin Luther King Jr. exemplifies such a balancing act, and his seemingly contradictory speeches to different audiences reflected this effort. King's sermons to predominantly black church congregations differed significantly from speeches he made to predominantly white audiences. Rieder analyzed King's oratory and pointed out that he used 'black and ethnic' idioms when speaking to African-American audiences and 'universal and civic discourse' when addressing white audiences.[34] Rieder described the difference between a 'triumphalist and particularistic backstage persona' and a more accommodating 'front stage persona', interpreting the inconsistency as strategy rather than doublespeak. The same may apply to Nadia Yassine, who has to maintain integrity within her own circles while at the same time trying to connect with a larger public.

There is one message Yassine communicates consistently no matter the setting, however. Every chance she gets, she reiterates that women's secondary status is the result of centuries of patriarchal reading of scriptures and goes hand in hand with other forms of discrimination based on race, religion, and social class. Thus, she considers the 'liberation of the mind' as one of the most urgent tasks of our time, both for men and women. This liberation requires education and has to be conducted according to specific regional and cultural settings. In a country where public education has not reached rural areas, such liberation comes slowly. Rural life in Morocco is in stark contrast to the rapid economic development and modernization of the urban centres. In the hustle and bustle of modern cities like Rabat, Casablanca, or Tangier, a casual visitor can easily overlook the fact that Morocco is still a global South country that suffers from illiteracy and severe poverty, and has regions where donkeys are still the main mode of transportation. In fact, even urban middle-class Moroccans often are not aware of the extent of poverty and deprivation in their country. When Nadia speaks of liberation of the mind, she refers not only to Moroccans generally but also to the men in her own movement, whom she says are intent on limiting her range of activities. In addition, despite her efforts to make the Justice and Charity movement known throughout the world as an exceptional Islamist movement committed to non-violence, her ardent promotion of women's rights rubs many of her male peers in the movement the wrong way.

Yassine's brand of Islamism is at odds not only with the higher ranking members of her own organization but also with other fundamentalist religious interpretations, such as Wahabism, a conservative brand of Islam from Saudi Arabia. The influence of Wahabism is increasingly evident in Morocco, where more and more women cover themselves in attire common to Wahabism's adherents: tent-like black cloaks, a face veil (*niqab*) that leaves uncovered only a slit for the eyes, long black gloves, and socks, even in the heat of summer. In the past, even conservative Moroccan women did not cover themselves in this manner, although some older women covered their mouth with a little piece of cloth. While a male guardian, husband, brother, or son routinely accompanies Moroccan women influenced by Wahabism who are fully covered, women who wear just the Muslim headscarf go about their business alone, in pairs, or in groups, just as unveiled women do.

Nadia Yassine is adamantly opposed to Wahabism. She described it as a 'misguided sect of Islam' that requires women to wear clothing that is without justification in the religion. She feels people should be honest and call this a personal preference or fashion instead of a religious duty. Further, she argued that such full-body covering is misguided because women who dress this way are excluded from participating in public life, since they can barely write due to their woollen gloves or drive a car because of their limited range of vision. Even walking is difficult for women fully covered in this way, as they cannot easily detect potholes or other obstacles before them. In fact, their mobility is so restricted that independent movement or activity in public, including a professional career, is all but impossible. Nadia Yassine also bases her opposition to this attire on the rule which prohibits face covering during the pilgrimage, *hajj*, to Mecca, one of the five pillars of Islam. According to Yassine, if the *niqab* is not allowed when visiting Islam's most holy sites during the *hajj*, it cannot be a recommended practice, let alone a requirement. Nevertheless, Wahabism in Morocco poses a challenge to Yassine's Islamist Justice and Charity movement because it attracts pious women away from her circle. Certainly, Moroccan Muslims understand the subtle distinctions and messages sent by religiously inspired attire better than the majority of populations in Europe or the United States; that is, they know the difference in meaning between the Muslim headscarf and the full-face veil. Despite her opposition to the full-face veil, Yassine decried the 2011 legal ban in France on what the French call the *burqa* because it singles out a very small minority and fails to address larger issues of discrimination and disenfranchisement of North African immigrant communities in France.

All female members of the Justice and Charity movement wear the *hijab*, the Muslim headscarf that covers only the hair, so the debate about the various veil types among women who themselves are covered to different extents points to the complexity of the 'veil issue' in Morocco and elsewhere. The divergent opinions among Islamists make for unlikely alliances among those who are against the full-face veil.

In his opposition to ultra-conservative forms of Islam, Yassine agreed with French President Nicolas Sarkozy, who stated in 2009:

> The problem with the *burqa* (which is a Muslim attire common in Afghanistan, similar to the face veil, except it covers the entire face and leaves the eyes behind a mesh) is not a religious problem. It is a problem of liberty and a woman's dignity. It is a sign of servitude and it is demeaning. I want to state clearly: the *burqa* is not welcome on the soil of the French republic. In our country, we cannot accept that women be imprisoned behind a mesh, cut off from all social life, deprived of their own identity. This is not our understanding of women's dignity.[35]

Islamists like Nadia Yassine could not agree more with Sarkozy's characterization of the *burqa*, even when they oppose legal sanctions against women who dress in this manner. It should be noted that European countries are not the only ones that have outlawed full-face coverings. Muslim-majority countries such as Syria, Egypt, and Turkey have imposed their own limits on the extent to which women can cover in public. Moroccans recall how the first king after independence, the revered Mohammed V, publicly unveiled his daughters. Nadia Yassine has frequently said that her goal is to engage with a changing world and that she does not want a return to the archaic system in place at the founding of Islam.

Abortion

The veil is not the only issue on which there is agreement among unlikely allies in Morocco. In contrast with the United States, where abortion is a subject that incites much emotion, abortion is not a major issue of contention in Morocco. In the United States it divides conservatives from liberals, and certain segments of the Christian community from people with more liberal Biblical interpretations. Some there have such strong feelings that they do not shy away from harming, even killing, physicians who perform such procedures. In Morocco abortion is illegal, but l'Association Marocaine pour le Planning

Familial, or the Moroccan Association of Family Planning, is working toward legalizing the procedure. In 2009, it launched a five-year campaign against clandestine abortions and began advocating for a public national debate on this issue. According to Mohamed Graigaa, the family planning association's director, his organization is not a supporter of choice in the Western sense; rather, he wants a lifting of the ban on abortion in cases of rape, incest, or for mentally ill women. According to a report by the association, the majority of women who request abortions in Morocco have become pregnant due to one of these situations or as a result of pre-martial sex, which is taboo.

Not permitting legal abortions, Graigaa says, has disastrous social consequences for Morocco. Orphanages are full of unwanted, abandoned children, and the sight of single mothers begging in the streets with their infants by their side is common in cities throughout the country. Women who bear children out of wedlock are considered outcasts and often are shunned even by their own families. Medical associations in Morocco other than the Moroccan Association of Family Planning take a more aggressive stance and promote lifting the ban on abortion altogether. They view it as a public health issue and support their contentions with staggering statistics on botched abortions, determined by the number of women who come to hospitals or emergency rooms with life-threatening health issues as a result of illegal, back-room procedures. Single motherhood is not an option in Morocco; not only do the mothers face grave consequences such as often being cast out by their own families, but their children experience life-long difficulties as well. In order to obtain official Moroccan documents, such as a birth certificate, national identity card, or passport, state agencies require that the name of the father be provided. When no father is named, which would be the case in a number of instances, as when the father is married to another woman, is a relative, or the mother was underage at the time of birth, a document can be considered invalid. In addition, fatherless children do not obtain full citizenship rights, since official documents are needed when registering a child for school or to receive public health care and other services. Often single mothers are too ashamed to present a document that attests to their having had a child out of wedlock. As a result, children of single mothers frequently do not attend school and do not receive proper health care. The increasing number of child prostitutes in Morocco is another consequence of the stigma of single motherhood.

Chafik Chraïbi, president of l'Association Marocaine de Lutte contre l'Avortement Clandestin, or the Moroccan Association against Secret Abortion (AMLAC), estimates that about 600 clandestine abortions are conducted every day in Morocco. This high frequency is due in part to an increase in sex tourism in the beach city Agadir, the port city Tangier, and the prime tourist destination Marrakesh. Chraïbi laments the silence of the king concerning this issue. The Islamist Parti de la Justice et du Développement (PJD), or the Justice and Development Party, formerly in opposition and since November 2011 the ruling party, has thus far been the most vocal supporter of legalized abortion. Their members argue that the Qur'an contains no explicit reference to the beginnings of human life and that the Malekite position (on which Moroccan religious law is based) holds that a foetus does not possess a *nafs* (soul) in the first trimester of a pregnancy. The Qur'an clearly condemns the killing of children, born and unborn, for selfish reasons: 'Do not abandon your children out of fear of poverty. We will provide for them and for you. Killing them is certainly a great wrong' (17:13). Nevertheless, no widespread agreement exists about how to interpret this verse with regard to ending a pregnancy. Most Islamic scholars concur that abortion is always a painful choice of last resort and certainly offers no pleasure. PJD leaders argue that the complete ban on abortion in Morocco is part of a colonial legacy, and is based on old French law and not the religion of Islam. Interestingly, in Morocco it is the conservative religious political party that supports revisiting abortion laws, whereas the modern monarchy so far has not taken a stance on the matter. However, leading members of the Justice and Charity movement have not formulated an official position on the issue of abortion, although they have said that such laws need to be reconsidered carefully in light of the misery suffered by large numbers of women and children.

The founding figures of Christianity and Islam provide two very different life examples: Jesus died young and unmarried, while Mohammed lived to a ripe old age, married multiple wives, and left numerous daughters behind. In Islam, sexual relations are considered an integral part of life and marriage is akin to a religious obligation. There is no virtue associated with celibacy and no religious order requires it of its members. However, birth control and abortion touch on issues such as single motherhood and sexual morals, which are of concern to Islamists. While they hold firm to the view that sex belongs in marriage, they acknowledge the reality of street children, rape, and incest, and see the need to develop a response to those problems. Complicating the issue of abortion in Morocco is the fact that adoption does not exist in legal terms because it is tied to inheritance laws. What is legally possible instead is *kafala* (the gift of care), a contractual relationship allowing a family to take in a child and treat him or her as a family member, even if this relationship is not a parent – child relationship in the eyes of the law. Though the laws pertaining to abortion, paternity, and citizenship present serious dilemmas for single mothers and their children, the discourse on the legality of abortion in Morocco has thus far been reasoned and conducted with few religious overtones.

Gender equality versus gender justice

There are, to be sure, many issues that generate heated debate in Morocco. One is the distinction between the concepts of gender justice and gender equality or equity. The West aspires to achieve gender equality, which includes legal equality and the elimination of all aspects of discrimination and inequality based on gender. In the West, gender equality also is seen as an important building block of economic prosperity. The United Nations Millennium Project has declared gender equity one of its main goals in the fight against world poverty: 'Every single goal is directly related to women's rights, and societies where women are not afforded equal rights as men can never achieve development in a sustainable manner.'[36] The United Nations Population Council defined gender equality as 'first and foremost, a human right. Women are entitled to live in dignity and in freedom from want and from fear. Empowering women is also an indispensable tool for advancing development and reducing poverty.'[37] Thus, gender equality is defined in terms of human values and seen as essential to the achievement of tangible goals, such as the eradication of poverty.

Gender justice, by contrast, is a religious concept used by Christians and Muslims alike in an effort to define women's rights within the context of scripture and in keeping with the divine order. Both the Bible and the Qur'an contain numerous references to justice, but the term equality is not found in either text. Arguing from a religious perspective, neither men nor women can claim rights that God did not endow them with. Conversely, humans have no right to restrict God-given privileges. Male and female Islamist activists fear a blurring of gender roles if women seeking equality take men as the standard and demand the same rights men have. Islamist activist Merieme Yefout, for example, has said that she fears women will 'lose their souls' when aspiring for gender equality because they will focus on acquiring 'sameness with men'. Furthermore, gender equality evokes the spectre of gay rights, queerness, and androgyny, topics that find no resonance in contemporary Morocco. In North Africa, the pervasive perception that gender equality means sameness can put an unnecessary strain on discussions about women's rights. Feminist scholar Toril Moi has pointed to an essential flaw in the thinking about 'difference and equality', however. Moi has argued,

> This is both a logical and historical mistake. In the context we are talking about, the opposite of equality is not difference, but inequality. To speak of women wanting to be like men is beside the point here, for we are not talking about what human beings are like, but about social and political rights.[38]

According to Moi, references to biology and differences between men and women miss the point in discussions about rights. She has also pointed to a problematic use of terminology: the French term for human rights, *droits de l'homme*, has a distinct gender reference that to many Moroccans means that if women are given equal rights, they are like men (*l'homme* in French). Though the term *droits de l'homme* originated in France, some human rights advocates propose the adoption of the gender-neutral English term 'human rights' so as to avoid possible confusion over the gendered French usage.

The concept of gender justice to which Islamists subscribe is based on the notion of biologically determined complementarities, meaning the dependence of men and women on each other in order to generate a family. Since God is the ultimate creator, biological distinctions are considered part of an immutable divine design, and men and women are seen as having distinct roles that need to be reflected in legislation. Islamists across the board demand job protection after childbirth, a reflection of their belief that mothers require special provisions in the law. They also insist that employers, both public and private, should be required to provide affordable childcare for preschool children and summer camps for all children regardless of the parent's ability to pay. Modern Moroccan men are not accustomed to playing a major role in raising their young children, thus women need to be allowed certain types of leave for their children's school or medical appointments without repercussions from their employers. The concept of gender justice, then, implies that equality in and of itself cannot be a goal, and that instead women need to advocate for a set of rights and provisions that take their particular needs and familial obligations into consideration.

Most Islamist women's rights activists agree that biology has been used as an argument to justify women's subordination to men. They also agree that men have used the absence of certain topics in the Qur'an as an opportunity to fill in the blanks and draw conclusions that serve their self-interest. The Qur'an makes no link between physical strength and intellectual superiority, for example, nor connects the ability to bear children to the inferiority of women. Nevertheless, male exegesis has focused on verses that emphasize men's superior status: 'Women also have recognized rights as men have, though men have an edge over them' (2:228) and 'Men are the support of women as God gives some more means than others, and because they spend of their wealth to provide for them' (4:34).

Though most Islamists use the terms gender justice and gender complementarity interchangeably, some emphasize one term over the other. Generally speaking, gender justice can be seen as more compatible with gender equality because, despite the difference in terminology, the goals are largely the same. Gender complementarity, on the other hand, emphasizes women's role as wives and mothers. To date, there has been no clear articulation by proponents of gender complementarity as to how this notion translates into laws that lead to more rights for women that are unrelated to motherhood. Complementarity implies relationship; hence, if women's rights derive from their relation to men, it is their role *vis-à-vis* men that forms the basis for women's rights legislation. The idea of complementarity affirms the primary role of woman as wife and mother and of man as father, provider, and decision-maker. Islamists like Merieme Yefout or Nadia Yassine, by contrast, emphasize the importance of education for women and their right to pursue a professional career. Such choices do not flow directly from a belief in complementarity but from an affirmation of women as individual agents. At this point in time it seems that the concept of gender complementarity is either not fully thought out or that those who embrace this idea do, in fact, believe that collective cohesion trumps individual agency. Again, those who insist on using vague concepts such as gender complementarity are mostly Islamists who prefer to focus on cultural renewal or a change of mentality rather than working to achieve concrete goals with regard to women's rights. The idea of gender complementarity is neither novel nor Muslim in origin; it has been advanced in other religious contexts as well, most notably Catholicism, which has its own version of gender complementarity and is based on the understanding that men and women are so distinctly different that they cannot be treated the same even in the eyes of the law.

A renewal of feminine consciousness

One prominent Islamist women's activist who stresses gender complementarity is a high-ranking member of the Islamist Justice and Development Party (PJD). Bassima Hakkaoui, PJD member and since the election in November 2011 the only woman in the newly formed government, holding the post of Minister for Solidarity, Women, Family, and Social Development, is also a leader in l'Organisation de Renouveau de la Conscience Féminine (ORCF), the Organization for Renewal of Feminine Consciousness.[39] The PJD itself grew out of an Islamist religious movement, namely Harakat al-Tawhid wa- al-Islam, or in French Mouvement de l'Unité et de la Réforme (MUR), the Unity and Reform Movement, in the 1990s. The MUR is a group that periodically has inserted itself in the public domain but, in contrast to the Justice and Charity movement, it has never questioned the role of the king. MUR members eventually formed the Islamist political party PJD, which is unequivocal in its support of the monarchy. Adlists deride such loyalty to the monarchy; they have described PJD members as the 'King's Islamists' who cannot claim to offer a credible Islamist plan for reform which by Adlists' standards must include a questioning of the absolute power of the king. It is thus not primarily on the issue of women's rights that Islamists differ but on their understanding of the role of the monarchy in a future Morocco.

One of the leading members of the PJD, Mustapha Ramid, has asserted that the PJD supports the rights of women to participate fully in the public sphere. To underscore his claim he pointed out that more women hold office within the PJD than in any other political party. However, Ramid is adamant that his party will not support any changes to *shari'a*-based laws, including inheritance laws that blatantly privilege male over female heirs. Ramid has repeatedly and categorically stated that the laws of inheritance are sacred, as they are based on the Qur'an. When I questioned Hakkaoui about Ramid's position, she responded with a sardonic smile and observed that such pronouncements are to be expected from her male party colleagues, though she refrained from offering her own opinion on inheritance laws. Hakkaoui emphasized instead the importance of becoming part of the political process, of inserting herself into public life, rising within the party hierarchy, and then making changes from within.

Hakkaoui was careful not to divulge the details of the changes she envisions, but she was forthcoming about the religious convictions that undergird her activities. I met Hakkaoui in the elegant Parliament Building in Rabat. Given that this is the seat of government in Morocco, security is tight and the clearance procedures long. But Hakkaoui wanted to make a point that parliament is as good a place to talk about her faith as any other. In fact, she preferred to talk about her religious views rather than comment on specific political and legal matters:

> We look for God's grace in our life. When I get up in the morning, I pray. God is my inspiration; it is this kind of divine

inspiration that sets us apart from animals. God is my point of reference. Of course I am also a product of my culture. Basically, I believe that humans are meant to be free. The Qur'an provides spiritual guidelines and a basis from which to develop certain positions but it is not a day-to-day guide on every single issue.

Hakkaoui wore a headscarf, a simple grey pantsuit, and little make-up. Sitting in the heavy leather chairs of the official government lounge, she likened the teachings of the Qur'an to traffic rules. Although each driver has his or her own driving style, this style has to fit within the general traffic guidelines. Rules provide the structure; yet within that general structure everyone is free to drive as fast or slowly as they want. She compared the enactment of individual preferences within a larger set of rules to the practice of *ijtihad*, the interpretation of sacred scriptures. Hakkaoui, a social psychologist by training, insisted that the gate to *ijtihad* is always open, as it has been throughout history. Unlike those who assert that the practice of *ijtihad* ended centuries ago, Hakkaoui was resolute about her right and the right of individual believers to interpretation. Referring to Muslim sources for guidance on women's rights is more germane to Morocco than looking to the model of Western feminism, she maintained.

Hakkaoui has proposed to work across ideological and transnational lines on issues such as gender-based violence, however. According to Hakkaoui, domestic violence is the single biggest issue that neither Western feminism, nor Islamism, nor socialism has been able to resolve. Since gender-based violence in the home and in society is a recurring, serious problem the world over, she believes women of all nationalities, religions, and cultures need to collaborate in order to combat such crimes. On most other issues, however, she feels her approach is different from feminists in the West:

For me, being a woman's rights activist and a religious person go hand in hand; there is no contradiction here. Even if in reality this is the case, there is philosophically speaking no contradiction between freedom and religion.

Hakkaoui explained that her organization, the ORCF, supports the elimination of discrimination against women, but not as it is laid out in the Convention on the Elimination of All Forms of Discrimination against Women (CEDAW), an international convention adopted in 1979 by the United Nations General Assembly. For example, Hakkaoui stated that she supports paid maternity leave for women but would not support paternity leave for men, as in her view children need a mother more than a father in their first months of life and paternity leave would not be in the best interests of the child. Plus, she added only half-jokingly, 'Our men would jump at the opportunity to take parental leave but they would not spend a minute actually taking care of the baby.' Hakkaoui supports an extension of maternity leave from three to six months, possibly even a year. She advocates for adjusting vacations for working mothers to coincide with the school calendar, as well as for day-care centres in workplaces. For this quietly resolute politician, women's rights need to be first and foremost grounded in safeguarding not just the rights of individuals but also those of children and the family.

In choosing to enter politics, Hakkaoui has had to insert herself into public life in a way that sometimes contradicts her own beliefs. Married to a professionally successful husband, she decided to embark on a career of her own. Yet her organization, the ORFC, has been known to support the idea that women should not work outside of the home if the husband has the financial means to maintain the family. Hakkaoui defended such claims by saying that the work of a homemaker needs to be recognized as an economically valid activity that serves the goals of national development. She even wants homemaking to be a recognized profession, and to be included on Moroccan identity cards and passports, which contain a line specifying the profession of the holder. Hence, she contended that the concept of gender complementarity is more inclusive of women's multiple roles than gender equality, which, according to Hakkaoui, leads to confusion and depreciation of a woman's role as wife and mother. In an interview with the *Arab Reform Initiative*, however, she is quoted as saying:

> Equality is an extremely important matter, which should be conceptually subject to a philosophical argument, because the

question is what it is that we want from equality, and the answer
is to abolish injustice and disadvantage. Can mechanical equality
achieve that? Or do we want equality with the logic of justice?
Justice recognizes that every person has needs, and the fulfill-
ment of these needs is what equality achieves. I am in favor of
equality as a goal and a principle that we start from and end
with. But between the outset and our arrival at the goal we must
use the tools that enable us to achieve justice. And when we
strive for equality with the logic of justice, we will achieve it.[40]

The ORCF, founded in 1995, has two main objectives: resolving family disputes and training political leaders. The association primarily
takes up the cases of women that it finds of particular interest, such as
women discriminated against in the workplace because they wear the
veil. The ORCF also offers limited legal advice to victims of domestic
violence. From its headquarters in Casablanca, it encourages members
to become politically active on the local level. The ORCF receives funding from the Moroccan government, but unlike secular women's advocacy groups it does not receive any international financial support.

Though the political party she belongs to calls itself Islamist, she
preferred to describe the organization she leads as a 'women's rights
association that attracts observant women'. She stated that she feels
that the ORCF contributes to 'careful policy planning based on exact
study of the country's actual conditions'. A slight woman in her early
fifties, Hakkaoui lives in Casablanca but commutes daily to the parliament building in the capital city of Rabat, a two-hour drive depending
on traffic. She both runs her women's advocacy organization and raises
her children. Though Hakkaoui often feels stretched to the point of
exhaustion, she said it was important to her to have her own association as it gives her an outlet to implement her ideas without always
having to conform to the party line despite the fact that she is a member of the policymaking general secretariat of the PJD. Further, her
position as an elected representative of a district in Casablanca allows
her to develop her own outreach activities without having to rely on
the Justice and Development Party apparatus at all times. Of course,
she is aware that her standing within the party is tenuous, as some of

her male peers do not look kindly on women holding public office – despite official declarations to the contrary. Some observers have raised the suspicion that Islamist parties such as the PJD promote women in order to gain widespread recognition, but once these women become more established and powerful, the PJD relegates them to more traditional roles.

Though the PJD is officially an Islamist party, Hakkaoui pointed out that her party's electoral programme does not contain religious slogans. Rather, it advocates for national development that is in keeping with Morocco's own cultural and religious traditions. She was eager to point out that this is unlike such religiously based political movements as the Muslim Brotherhood in Egypt, for whom Islam is at the same time a religious and political programme. The more pragmatic approach of the PJD is indicative of the approach to Islam in Morocco, where neither the designation 'Islamist' nor 'secular' fully captures anyone's aspiration and goals.

Common to those who argue for women's rights from a religious standpoint, when interviewed Hakkaoui offered a somewhat vague or overly general perspective on emancipation, though she is proud to say that she was part of the committee that proposed the Personal Status Code reform. Like Nadia Yassine, Bassima Hakkaoui faces opposition within her own political party, where her role is heralded publicly but, she admitted, questioned in internal meetings. Both Yassine and Hakkaoui shared that they feel the need to tread carefully so as not to alienate the people within their own camp by taking a strong stance on women's rights. This concern might explain their apprehension about outlining specific goals, since explicit objectives may put them in a defensive position and cause conflict with the men who currently hold power within their larger organizations.

The seeming absence of a specific catalogue of demands or proposals by the feminine branch of the Justice and Charity movement and ORFC also allows women leaders room to navigate and reformulate their positions, not only on women's rights but on larger societal issues. Even the name Organization for the Renewal of Feminine Consciousness is vague enough that it can refer to an association engaged in anything from religious instruction to legal advice to community organizing.

Hakkaoui's group is not unlike Nadia Yassine's Sisters of Eternity – even Yassine's plea for a 'liberation of the mind' resembles Hakkaoui's call for consciousness-raising among women. Nevertheless, the ORCF can be mobilized as a political machine during election times. Hakkaoui made it clear that she feels she can be most effective by being part of an established party, while Yassine, for her part, was unambiguous about wanting to work within the movement her father founded. Both believe that setting out on their own would leave them isolated and, consequently, less successful. One of the main differences between Hakkaoui and Yassine, however, is that the former has adopted a more realist approach using her strategic advantage as a high-ranking member in an important political party to pursue her goals of women's rights, whereas the latter remains part of a utopian movement that rejects the limits of mainstream political organizations. While these two women have chosen to work within their respective systems, there are others who have ventured out on their own.

Going it alone

Being a devout Muslim, or even an Islamist, as we have shown, does not mean one must be meek or docile. Meet Khadija Moufid, erstwhile Justice and Development Party (PJD) member who eschewed the confines of that organization and launched her own small non-governmental organization (NGO) after finding the internal wrangling within the Islamist PJD unbearable. A co-founder with Hakkaoui of the ORCF, she had risen quickly through the ranks of the Justice and Development Party before quitting because, as she told me, 'independent thinkers are not welcome there'. Moufid rejected the idea that she should be relegated to those commissions within the political party that dealt with women's issues. After leaving the PJD, Moufid proceeded to found her own social service association, Al Hidn (roughly translated: a place of nourishing) in 2002. Al Hidn's goal is to serve families by tending to the needs of mothers, fathers, and children. Its services also extend to orphans and widows, and include literacy classes and study courses that educate men and women in the Qur'an.

In my interview with her, Moufid referred to a 'psychological block' in Morocco that prevents women from assuming decision-making roles. This tendency, she has argued, applies not just to Islamist movements or political parties but also across the board to all groups and associations in her country. Moroccan women who serve in high offices like ambassador, government minister, or mayor generally hail from well-connected, prestigious families or are in some way linked to the *makhzen*. Such women, Moufid asserted, are promoted because they belong to a particular social class or family rather than because of their own merit. Moufid asserted that, at the present time, there are not enough female role models whose achievements are based on their own merit. Islamist organizations further disadvantage women by limiting their involvement in decision-making processes based on what she has called 'religious misconceptions' about the subordinate role of women.

I met Moufid in the modest, almost austere office of her association in Casablanca. Though it took more than an hour for Moufid to arrive, I was made to sit by myself in her office behind closed doors and was given pamphlets of the association to read. Her staff milled around but none felt comfortable talking to a foreign guest. When Moufid finally arrived, her staff sprang into action, quickly sitting at their desks and working on their computers. Moufid asked her staff for a brief report on what had been happing throughout the day and then joined me. Tall, strong-boned, and with an air of authority, Moufid arranged her headscarf before sitting down at her large, orderly desk, ready for our conversation. According to Moufid, in her understanding of Islam the most competent people should lead, whether male or female. Though the government has a quota for the minimum number of women on the ballot, Moufid's own experience is testimony to the continued resistance of political parties against women in public life. In her assessment, women 'who know how to toe the line and will not overstep their boundaries' are those who eventually are promoted, largely to satisfy government quota requirements. Moufid asserted that this propensity exists not only in Islamist circles but in palace circles as well, such that women who serve at the king's discretion are bound not to challenge the monarch's course of action. Moufid told me, 'after all, we live in an autocratic society, and so autonomous thinking is not encouraged'. At the same time, she acknowledged that changes are appearing in some areas of Moroccan society, most notably business and commerce:

> In today's global environment, Moroccans are getting more and more creative and successful in business ventures. Women are now in upper management positions of some large companies. It will take time before this is translated into the political realm.

Moufid said that no one openly would admit to blocking women from running for office or assuming positions of authority in Morocco, but contended that daily practices make it clear that women are not welcome at the top echelons within the political establishment. As a case in point she explained that official party meetings frequently take place in the late afternoon or early evening and run until late at night, a time when most women feel compelled to be at home with their children. She recounted the hypocrisy of men who chide women for wanting equality but at the same time do nothing to enable them to attend meetings. As Moufid noted:

> They organize important meetings always at times when they know women cannot attend. I am not sure they do this intentionally or if they are oblivious. But my demands for holding meetings during regular working hours have always been ignored.

For Moufid, one of the major obstacles to women's participation in political life is that women's multiple roles are not considered, much less valued. She raised the same issue as her former party colleague Hakkaoui when she observed that the state is complicit in preserving male dominance by making no provisions to take into account the multiple responsibilities of women, which they could do by providing subsidized childcare, for example. Not only does such a system preserve male dominance, it also makes less likely opportunities for promotion based on merit and not social class. Upper-class women have access to private childcare, around-the-clock nannies, housekeepers, and/or cooks, something most lower-middle-class or even middle-class women cannot afford unless they resort to employing *petites bonnes*, ill-qualified domestics. Sharing childcare responsibilities between both parents is not a widespread practice in Morocco. For Moufid, such encrusted views of class and gender roles can best be battled from within the Muslim religion, since justifications for the order of things always rely on Islam. As Moufid shared, 'It makes me sick to hear the argument that this or this or this is "un-Islamic." It has become such a catchphrase and is used to condemn or support just about anything.' Thus, like other Islamists, Moufid is intent on using the sacred scriptures of Islam as a basis for her argument in support of full emancipation for women.

As a well-trained Islamic scholar, Moufid has spoken repeatedly and publicly about the problems political parties pose for women. In a 2007 speech delivered to women voters, she said:

> There seems unanimous agreement on the role of women in political parties across the spectrum. Women are used for the purposes of mass mobilization. In all political parties, women are either absent from executive positions or have subservient positions. Their influence in the decision-making process is exceedingly limited. Women are rarely present when it comes to formulating political platforms or occupying specific functions of influence, other than on so-called 'women's issues' or women's committees, or committees that pertain to family or children's issues. ... In fact women appear more as an ornamental object in political parties; they are neither selected for their opinions nor their original contributions.

Moufid has studied Western feminism with the goal of understanding successful change strategies. She feels that Western feminist thought offers legitimate resistance against male oppression and discrimination. At the same time, she contends that the Muslim world now needs to find its own path of resistance against patriarchal forms of domination. Like other Islamist feminists, she sees a need to point out that the promotion of gay rights is 'an aberrant goal and not an integral part of women's struggle for emancipation'. She is equally opposed, however, to literalists who stick to outmoded interpretations without looking at the deeper meaning of the text, especially when it comes to laws pertaining to women. As Moufid observed:

> Everybody gets all religious when it comes to women's rights. Even people who rarely talk about religion, much less practise it, when it comes to women's emancipation, they all of a sudden draw the religious register as if they spend most of their time pondering the Qur'an. They pronounce that things cannot be changed because this would be un-Islamic when these very same people do 'un-Islamic' things all the time.

Moufid advocates for a systematic approach to studying scriptural verses that pertain to women and creating modern laws derived from this analysis. She feels that the crisis over the status and role of women in Morocco has been aggravated by a mixture of laws, some Western, some based in Islam, which have left Morocco in an ambiguous state between tradition and modernity. In order to move forward with a women's rights agenda, Moufid argued, women first need to understand the rights granted to them by their own religion. Then the entire legal code should be aligned with this understanding, rather than singling out certain laws. When pressed to reveal if by this she means she supports changing Morocco's entire legal code to one based on *shari'a*, Moufid did not answer.

Moufid has found a way of using time-honoured Muslim traditions to suit her own goals. This forceful and self-assured woman is in a polygamous marriage, the second wife to a husband who was already married at the time they met and had several children with his first wife. In keeping with Islamic law, her husband maintains separate households for his two wives and provides for all of his children, including his three with Moufid. Due to his obligations to both wives, Moufid only sees her husband every other week, an arrangement that suits Moufid just fine because it leaves her free to pursue her own interests in the week that she does not have to attend to her husband. She explained that even in today's Morocco, a woman is still expected to serve her husband and be there for him when he is at home. As a college professor, the leader of a social service organization, an international women's rights activist, and mother, to be at the beck and call of a husband is not something Moufid said she was willing to submit to on a daily basis. Likewise, she never entertained the option of remaining single. For this independent woman who cherishes her career, polygamy is the model of family that suits her best. When asked about jealousy between the two co-wives, Moufid responded matter-of-factly that jealousy is part of every marriage. 'In my case, at least I know the other woman,' she quipped. As for her husband, she feels he is in two committed, legal relationships, both permitted by her religion. Moufid believes that as long as the division of labour in the house remains clearly divided between men and women, not having a man around every day allows her the freedom and independence she desires. She skilfully skirted a question about how she would feel about polygamy had she been the first wife and found herself suddenly confronted with a co-spouse. She did admit, however, that she could not envision her husband taking a third wife. To make her point about her independence, she spontaneously invited me to have lunch with her at her apartment, which is only a short drive away from the offices of her association. She became very animated as we ate in a corner of her spacious living room, which contained wall-to-wall bookcases filled with volumes about Islam, Islamic jurisprudence, and philosophy.

No longer affiliated with a major political party or movement, Moufid is at a comparative disadvantage in creating a platform, and she is struggling to maintain her public profile by organizing national and international conferences. In the process of doing so, she has come to realize that the best way to insert herself in public discourse in Morocco is by focusing on the very topic she did not want to be limited to while still a member of the PJD: women's issues. She also has aligned herself to one of the Islamists' pet projects, namely the covering of women at public beaches. Moufid agrees with the views of Hakkaoui and Yassine on this matter. In a country that stretches along the Atlantic and Mediterranean coastline, where most major cities are situated along the seaside, beaches are popular public spaces in the long, hot summers. Yassine, Hakkaoui, and Moufid strongly support the convention that women remain fully clothed at public beaches. They also support the idea of gender-segregated beaches because women should be entitled to a space where they can swim or play in the water in peace without being subjected to male gawkers or, worse, sexual harassment. For these women activists, women's rights does not mean being allowed to swim in bathing suits or bikinis alongside men, but being allowed to choose a segregated, women-only beach.

The debate about beaches comes up each year and is one that never ceases to inflame public opinion. Yassine, Hakkaoui, and Moufid all agreed that women at co-ed public beaches should dress 'modestly'. Although they did not explicitly say that women should swim fully dressed instead of wearing bathing suits, for all intents and purposes 'modest' in Morocco means no naked arms or legs. Islamists of all stripes have been successful in their campaigns to 'clean up the beaches', so today there are virtually no public beaches – except in the tourist centre of Agadir – where local women can be seen in swimsuits or bikinis alongside foreign tourists. However, there are Moroccan women who would like to be allowed to swim at any public beach in any outfit they choose, rather than having to drive out to an expensive private club that permits women to wear Western swimming attire. Yet, the voices of these women largely have been marginalized, as few women in Morocco would go out into the streets and demonstrate for their right to wear skimpy clothing in public.

Islamist women leaders

Though all Islamist women's rights advocates bemoan authoritarian, patriarchal systems, to a large extent the organizations to which they belong or which they lead mirror the norms of the society in which they live. Those women who hold leadership roles in Islamist associations are strong and forceful and dominate their respective associations. Ordinary members do not feel empowered to make their own decisions but defer to those in positions of authority even in these women-led groups. Members frequently declined to answer my questions and insisted that only their leaders could respond to inquiries.

An authoritarian approach is ingrained in both leaders and followers. In recent years Nadia Yassine has encouraged women to step forward and speak their minds, but often Justice and Charity movement members – with the exception of Yefout – continue to defer to her and decline the opportunity to develop their own ideas.

Though they might echo each other's opinions, Islamist women's activists do not collaborate overtly. Instead, each leader insists that her particular group represents the newest, most authentic Islamist platform. Although there may be some philosophical differences among the various Islamist women's groups, with regards to gender rights, they are, in fact, quite similar in outlook. The differences that do exist actually are more personal than ideological. Personal ambition leads Islamist women's rights activists to view each other as competitors rather than to capitalize on the rising popularity of Islamist positions and join ranks to formulate a clear, uniform agenda and set of demands. In fact, the fractured approach of Islamist women's organizations weakens their momentum. If multiple organizations, associations, and movements with similar aims would pursue their goals cooperatively, they could demonstrate the heterogeneous character of Islamism by allowing the various discourses to be heard and offering more choices to potential supporters.

In rejecting the label 'feminist' and the gender equality agenda of the West, Islamist women's rights activists are seeking to chart their own paths to gender equity in the twenty-first century. While they express their visions in general philosophical terms rather than as clear and tangible goals, there is no sense of complacency. Clearly, these religiously motivated women are not reluctant to take on the patriarchal establishment and work towards claiming the rights they believe their Creator intended them to have.

CHAPTER 3

A THIRD WAY

Several scholars – not only religious ones – have put forth the idea of a 'third way', an alternative paradigm of gender equality that de-secularizes the project of women's emancipation while at the same time employing a non-confrontational attitude toward the West. Third way proponents presuppose the existence of a basic set of human values that reaches across borders and cultures. In Morocco, their focus is on finding a valid way of advocating for women's rights within the modern Moroccan religious and cultural context, thus avoiding the cleavage that currently exits between secular women's rights activists and certain Islamists.

The third way approach is based on premises expounded by theologian Annemarie Schimmel in her seminal book, *My Soul is a Woman*: 'For a theologian the rule applies that ideals have to be compared to ideals and reality to reality ... Hence, in the realm of spiritual life, there should not be a difference between man and woman'.[1] Schimmel argued that a look at the daily reality of Muslim women clearly indicates that their circumstances are not equal to those of men. Further, she cautioned against inferring from this reality that such unequal treatment is divinely sanctioned, and pointed to the contradiction between what people actually do and the ideal laid out in the Qur'an. A discrepancy between ideal and reality with regard to gender parity is, of course, not limited to Muslim-majority countries; it is prevalent in the West just as anywhere else in the world. Yet, in a country with an official state religion, it is easy to infer that unequal practices are rooted in religion and therefore divinely sanctioned. The approach of Islamists seeking gender justice is to work largely within a spiritual framework and promote a change in mentality or consciousness rather than offer concrete proposals for change. Yet, while important, modifying attitudes is a somewhat elusive undertaking, since goals and results are hard to measure.

Third way ideas are not limited to gender issues, though these are the focus of this book.[2] In Morocco, the idea of a third way grew, in part, from an informal survey of Moroccan women conducted by a group of scholars from the social sciences and religion. One of the questions asked respondents about their concerns about their religion. The overwhelming majority of women described a chief concern as 'fear of posing questions'. They said that there were many aspects of the practice of Islam that troubled them, but that they did not want to risk being considered unfaithful and so preferred not to ask questions about these practices. Fear of being regarded a 'disbeliever' was of paramount concern among the women surveyed; they did not want to risk being ostracized by their community for overstepping real or imagined boundaries. Many respondents said it was more important to be viewed as a faithful person by their co-religionists than to pose questions that could potentially create trouble for them.

The concept of submission, or to use a less inflammatory term, obedience, is deeply woven into the cultural fabric of Morocco and does not apply only to religion. In Morocco as throughout North Africa, obedience is an inseparable part of an educational system that does not encourage critical thinking. Further, the expectation of obedience, by definition, creates fear, a recurring theme in Moroccan society. The patriarchal society and authoritarian government of Morocco is built on obedience and subservience. Submission to God has become synonymous with women's obedience to men, students' compliance with their teachers, and subjects' deference to their monarch. Submission, then, is rooted in the patriarchal culture and sustained by the instrument of religion. In authoritarian societies such as Morocco, deference to a higher authority (in Morocco the highest authority among humans is the king) is expected on many levels by men and women alike.

Compounding the difficulty for women who reject gender inequities is the infusion of religious meaning in the act of submission. Hence, in the name of religion, women choose to be silent. However, proponents of a third way argue that they want to live their religion in serenity and peace rather than in a spirit of resignation, resentful compliance, or, most importantly, fear.

Conventional conservative Islamist discourse has identified women primarily as relational beings; that is, in terms of their function as a mother, wife, sister, or daughter rather than as an individual. Rarely does such a view present a woman as an independent, autonomous agent. And yet the Qur'an portrays women not as sub-species but as human beings who, like men, are endowed with the right to freedom of individual agency or autonomy. Proponents of a third way call on this portrayal in the Qur'an and insist that women are to be considered as individuals and not defined primarily through their relationships with men: their father, husband, brother, son.

The third way approach to gender equality attempts to avoid the trap of what Mehrzad Boroujerdi has called 'Orientalism in reverse', meaning a discourse that is primarily conceived in terms of opposition to the West.[3] Orientalism, we recall, is a theory advanced by Edward Said that described a reductionist – and often false – depiction of Eastern cultures through a Western lens. Though Boroujerdi's research pertained mostly to Iran, his analyses apply to Morocco as well, since he proposes that it is indeed possible to devise a culturally authentic approach to questions of modernity in Muslim-majority countries. Thus, third way proponents are careful not to take the West as the sole yardstick against which to develop 'nativist' concepts. Further, those who are obsessed with an essentialist reading of the West, Boroujerdi argued, fall into the same trap as Orientalists.

Third way proponents are not opposed to some forms of secularism, such as the separation of religion and state in matters of religious practice and individual freedom of religion. Legal scholar Abdullahi Ahmed An-Na'im, who has written extensively on Islam and the secular state, asserted that secularism should not be feared by Muslim societies but should be examined as a 'state-form' that developed differently in different countries and for different reasons. An-Na'im favours the institutional separation between religious and political authority; however, he does not advocate the complete privatization of religion. While Islam should be separated from the state, An-Na'im has argued, it need not be left out of politics. His proposal is more in line with the American concept of separation of church and state as spelled out by Thomas Jefferson than the French idea of *laïcité*, developed to curtail the influence of the Catholic Church in state matters, with which Moroccans are more familiar due to their historical connection with France.

The French notion of *laïcité* grew out of the struggle to find a balance between secular and religious powers following the 1789 French Revolution that ended the Roman Catholic Church's domination over government affairs. About a decade later, in 1801, Napoleon reached an agreement with the Catholic Church in a concordat that brought the Church under state auspices and confined it to making decisions only on religious matters. A landmark law was passed a century later in 1905, formally instituting the separation of church and state and marking the beginning of *laïcité*, a term that stems from the Catholic lexicon, in which 'lay' refers to people not ordained or belonging to the clergy. While the French law grew out of an adversarial relationship between the Roman Catholic Church and the French government, and led to a decidedly anti-clerical stance, the American notion of separation of church and state was part of the foundational design of the country. In the newly formed United States of America, the separation of church and state was intended to offer freedom of religious expression and to shield citizens from government interference in religious matters. Nevertheless, neither French Republican *laïcité* nor US secularism means that religious belief is to be banished from public spaces. As Olivier Roy argued, 'secularization does not mean the end of transcendence but the establishment of a non-theological transcendence, in a sense of a secularized religion'.[4]

Though there is no separation of the religious from the political sphere in Morocco, the issues surrounding a shift to a more secular society are discussed frequently and are anything but a taboo topic. In fact, a front-page article in Morocco's weekly news magazine *Tel Quel* asked, 'Islam and secularism. Is it possible?'[5] – and answered in the affirmative. The article referred to two organizations that have openly campaigned for a secular society, the Mouvement Alternatif pour les Libertés des Individuelles (MALI), or Alternative Movement for Individual Liberties, and the Association Marocaine pour les Droits Humains (AMDH), or the Moroccan Association for Human Rights. MALI members incurred public ire – and brief arrest – when they defied fasting during the month of Ramadan and congregated to eat in public. They claimed it was their right to observe the fast or not and that religious observance should not be state-imposed. The mostly young members of MALI argued that that it is easier to practise religion freely in a secular society than in a country with a state religion.

Sacred or secular

The difference between the separation of religion from politics in France and most of Western Europe as opposed to that in the United States is also reflected in the standards applied to public officials. More than their European counterparts, elected officials in the United States are routinely put under a magnifying glass to see how well they conform to religiously based personal morals, sexual in particular. From Finland to France, Germany to Spain, the personal morality of public persons – albeit of voyeuristic interest – is ultimately of little consequence. When the mistress of French President François Mitterrand attended his funeral in 1996 alongside his wife, no eyebrows were raised in France. The fact that former German Chancellor Gerhard Schröder (1998–2005) was in the process of entering his fourth marriage when he ran for office did not prevent him from winning the election, a phenomenon unthinkable for a contender to highest political office in the United States. The personal sexual morals – or lack thereof – of President Bill Clinton caused an enormous outcry, led to his impeachment, and very nearly cost him the presidency in 1998.

Though secularism in the United States keeps religious instruction out of public schools, religion infuses public and political life. Sexual infidelities are of great public concern and consequence. In recent years, numerous elected public officials resigned or saw their political careers unravel as a result of extra-marital affairs, an outcome unthinkable in most European countries. In Morocco, public officials face no such scrutiny; personal morals are of little significance for their public office. For public officials, religious matters are chiefly of concern with regard to their observance of the five pillars of Islam. Public officials are not expected to serve as role models and are therefore exempt from examination of their personal life choices; they are actually given much greater licence than in the secular United States. In fact, because the king is above all public scrutiny (it is against the law to criticize the monarch) public officials see themselves as miniature kings who expect to be equally free from having their private lives and their business practices examined. Instead, in Morocco, scrutiny is applied to ordinary citizens who find themselves under the watchful eye of family, neighbours, and other members of the community.

The term secularism is often invoked in a polemical sense to connote a diminished role of religion in public life. To most Moroccans this is unacceptable. However, as the US example demonstrates, religion can be alive and well in a secular state even when the state is not imposing any particular religious belief, practice, or oversight on its citizens. In fact, one could argue that personal faith can be practised best in a secular state where there is little interference in personal religious matters and where everyone is free to worship and be religiously observant according to their own understandings. Research supports this contention. A Pew Research Centre poll conducted in 2007 has shown that Muslims who migrate to the United States find themselves at greater liberty to practise Islam according to their own beliefs than in their respective home countries, where Islam is the state religion. The study also found that Muslims in the United States saw no conflict between being a devout Muslim and living in a modern state despite a rise in anti-Muslim activity since the events of 9/11 and the ensuing global war on terrorism.[6]

Proponents of a third way in Morocco favour some form of a secular state precisely because it would offer greater freedom to practise religion, especially in cases where someone's faith is at odds with official monarchic discourse on Islam. They see plurality or choice in religious matters as liberating individuals and leading to greater inclusion and public involvement. This, they argue, would allow the country to make fuller use of its human resources. The freedoms that would come with a more secular state certainly would reduce the tension between the monarchy and Islamist movements, because it would take the sting out of the criticism of the king's thus far unassailable religious rulings. Further, such liberalization would force certain Islamists to admit to a political agenda rather than hiding under the mantle of advocating for a purer form of Islam.

The task at hand for each Muslim country is to develop a state and legal system that is at the same time congruent with its own history and with the reality of global interdependence. There is no universal Muslim identity, hence an Indian Muslim may share more in common with an Indian Hindu from the same region on the subcontinent than with a co-religionist in a country on the other side of the world, such as Mali, West Africa. A Moroccan may feel more at home in France than in Somalia, despite the fact that both Morocco and Somalia are predominantly Muslim countries located on the African continent. Muslim culture is indeterminate as a primary marker of identity, not only because of the 'multiplicity of nationalities and ethnicities, but also the varieties of identification of the religion itself, and its adaptations to ideologies, generations and styles of life' as Sami Zubaida rightly observed.[7] In practical matters, religion is a less important factor than economic opportunity. Migration patterns of North Africans show that economic considerations overwhelmingly outweigh religious ones; the largest percentage of Moroccan migrants chooses to move to Western Europe, Canada, or the United States rather than to a fellow Muslim-majority country. While some migration occurs to affluent parts of the Middle East, like Persian Gulf countries, it is not on the scale of the migration to Western Europe or North America. Most telling, virtually no migration takes place from Morocco to other Muslim-majority countries that are less developed. Despite the furore over Islam-phobia and discrimination against Muslims in Western countries, they are still the preferred destination for North African Muslim migrants. Third way proponents take such global realities into consideration in developing a successful domestic discourse. While repeated assertions of a 'Muslim identity' may be a crowd-pleaser, the term connotes a simplistic, reductionist view of what it means to be a Muslim and does not take into account changing notions of identity over time and space. Despite the serious problems European countries encounter with the integration of immigrants into their societies, today significantly more male and female Muslims of immigrant backgrounds hold positions of power in Europe than do non-Muslims in Muslim-majority countries.[8]

Moroccan authorities are keenly aware of the impact of Moroccans living abroad on the communities from which they originated. Given the short geographical distance between Morocco and Europe, and the fact that Morocco is situated on the farthest Western outskirts of the Arab Muslim world, Moroccan authorities are alert to the various influences bearing on domestic discourse. Furthermore, unlike some other Muslim-majority countries, Morocco imposes no limitations on Internet access, though certain sites (mostly Islamist) are difficult to access from within Morocco. With the exception of very remote regions, cybercafés are common all throughout the country. Public Internet access in such cybercafés is cheap and fast and there is no time during the day or night when these locales are not filled with mostly young patrons, chatting or skyping away, playing online games, or checking out various social media sites. Customers even access pornographic sites in these public venues and some cybercafés have partition walls between computers to offer their clients some measure of privacy. On the other end of the spectrum are Muslim religious sites, which are also very popular. Moroccans browse such websites in Arabic, French, and increasingly English. In addition, online forums serve as safe places for romantic exchanges, advice on personal conduct, and queries on religious or philosophical questions that many would not dare to pose openly within their own community. People increasingly turn to sources of information and communication beyond their local borders and network with like-minded people across the world. It is within this globalized context that a third way and a new approach to questions of gender equality in Morocco are being developed.

The above-mentioned legal scholar An-Na'im[9] drew on a variety of sources in proposing a new holistic approach for Muslim-majority countries:

> Part of this inclusive approach is the consideration of concepts and arguments from broader comparative perspectives, including

Western political and legal theories and experiences, all as part of the civic reasoning process ... The point here is not only that including non-Muslims in an Islamic discourse regarding public policy is expedient or tactical, but also that this is the way it has been done throughout Islamic history and should continue to be done in the future. It is neither possible nor desirable, in my view, to identify and deploy purely 'Islamic' arguments, to the exclusion of non-Islamic arguments, as if the two forms of discourse can evolve in isolation or be separated from each other.[10]

Given Morocco's expressed aspiration to forge substantially closer links with its powerful Mediterranean neighbours to the North, insistence on religious identity alone as a basis for domestic discourse is an increasingly untenable stance. The conflict with Europe or the West in general is not based on religious incompatibility between Christianity and Islam but on the historical experiences of conquest and domination. In recent times, this conflict has been intensified by conflicting conceptions of a secular state, as in Western countries, versus a state with an official religion, as in Morocco. Regardless of the nature of the encounters between Europe and Morocco, historic interaction with Europe has left a mark on North African culture. Moroccan sociologist and novelist Abdelkebir Khatibi described this mix of influences, from the early Arab conquest to European colonization, as having created a genuine hybrid Moroccan identity composed of the diverse strands of 'the sacred and the secular, the national and the foreign, the self and the other'.[11] While such hybrid identities emerge in most previously colonized countries, Morocco has continued to maintain active and close relations with its former colonizer, France, and to a lesser extent, Spain. Indeed, the narrowness of the expanse of water that separates Morocco from southern Europe contributes to their shared Mediterranean culture.

Morocco's hybrid identity

A third way for addressing gender equality in Morocco seems a natural outgrowth of Morocco's history and ongoing relationship with Europe.

Yet, such an approach does not enjoy widespread appeal, let alone acceptance, in parts of the Arab-Muslim world. Moroccans are often called 'arabized Berbers' owing to a thousand years of mixing between Arabs and various Berber populations. Hence, Moroccan culture and ways of practising Islam have a distinct North African flavour that differs from the Arab Middle East and is evident in everyday life, as described in previous chapters. When Morocco reformed its Personal Status Code in 2004 much of the official Arab Middle East responded with scepticism or outright criticism. And criticism continues to come from among Islamists or conservative Muslims who fear an interpretation of sacred scriptures that strays too far from literal readings. They worry that if one or two verses are up for interpretation, soon the entire scripture will be newly interpreted; thus, they view re-interpretation as a slippery slope. On the other hand, secular feminists criticize this third way for not condemning polygamy outright, for instance, or for failing to address the issue of violence against women with adequate urgency. They also fear the close link of cultural identity with religion. Because this third way is a work in progress, one cannot expect that it will contain a finely tuned stance on every single issue facing modern Morocco. Because the third way does not represent the development of a new dogma, but rather a pragmatic response to some of the pressing questions of our time, positions necessarily will be refined, altered, and adjusted over time.

In today's Morocco, a sense of urgency about the need to develop a counter-discourse to that which argues either for an Islamist state or a copy of the Western model has arisen in response to events in neighbouring Algeria. Regional factors, in addition to domestic and larger international pressures, have played an important role in exploring a new vision for Morocco – and not only with regard to gender issues. Algeria, situated across Morocco's long eastern border, is a country plagued by a decade of bloody internal strife between rival radical Islamist groupings, the national military, and local militias, resulting in the loss of more than 150,000 lives. Violence against women was an integral part of what is now called 'the black decade' that began in the 1990s. Women were assaulted in public for not wearing the Muslim headscarf and abducted for subsequent use as domestic or sexual slaves for self-proclaimed Islamist warriors. Gang rapes and public aggression, especially against women living alone, occurred frequently. Today, there is virtually no family in Algeria that has not been touched by these years of terror, resulting in a climate of profound distrust and fear.[12] By contrast, since independence from France in 1956, Morocco has enjoyed peace and stability, enforced with an iron grip under Hassan II whose 36 year reign (1961–1999) is today labelled 'the leaden years'. Morocco's natural resources, minerals, and seafood cannot compare with the oil and gas wealth of its neighbour Algeria. Thus, Morocco is pressed to invest and develop its human resources, an objective with direct implications for women's rights.

In Morocco, the sense of urgency for a third way stems in part from the realization that Islamist violence – not only in Algeria but worldwide – has cost the lives of more Muslims than any other population group. Peaceful Muslims are intent on reclaiming their religion from those who have wreaked havoc in the name of Islam. This response, however, should not be viewed simply as a reaction to national or global pressures or exposures. In fact, it is mostly those in religious circles who are thinking about a third way. Secular feminists, due to their generous support from the European Union and the West in general, feel no such need to rethink their positions and consequently remain somewhat out of step with large segments of the population with its decidedly religious inclinations. As previously stated, Moroccan feminists who are firmly entrenched in Western discourse are valued by the West and find much international support. Within Morocco, however, few back positions that do not take cultural specificities into consideration. Certainly class differences also play a major role in secular women's advocacy associations, since these are led and staffed mainly by members of the upper middle class. As Asma Barlas wrote: 'It is safe to say that no meaningful change can occur in these societies that does not derive its legitimacy from the Qur'an's teachings, a lesson secular Muslims everywhere are having to learn at their own detriment.'[13] Today the most vibrant discourse on gender equality in Morocco occurs among Islamic thinkers and organizations rather than between secularists and Islamists who are entrenched in their respective positions.

An important part of the third way is the questioning of foundational Islamic gender myths about male superiority and female inferiority. These beliefs are based on Qur'anic verses that seem to endow men with more rights than women; for example, through polygamy and inheritance conventions. Another central question concerns modernity. Since modernity is most commonly associated with the West, it presents a dilemma for those Muslim women who are seeking to become 'modern' while at the same time retaining their cultural and religious identities. Pertinent to this discussion is the issue of violence against women. In the West violence against women is treated as a social problem and governments have created laws that, at least in principle, allow for protection or legal recourse. By contrast, in North African countries, violence against women, especially domestic violence, is largely considered to be a cultural or religious issue, implying that violence against women is a cultural phenomenon that has roots in the religion of Islam. In the West, few would argue that domestic violence is a natural consequence or outgrowth of the Christian or Jewish religion. Yet the West generally perceives the victim status of women in the Muslim world primarily as a religious and cultural problem and not a social one. According to new Islamic thinkers, women have been sacrificed in the name of the sacred for too long, and now the sacred must be newly interpreted.

Mustapha Safouan is an Egyptian psychoanalyst who has translated the works of Jacques Lacan[14] into Arabic and is a frequent guest speaker in Morocco. Safouan has asserted that theocratic regimes in the Arab world have not been able to respond to modernity in the areas of economy, technology, and culture. Thus, today increasingly louder voices in Morocco and elsewhere are decrying the false idealization of the distant past. That this vigorous debate is currently possible in Morocco can be traced to its history of resistance in more recent times – that is, to repelling the advances of the Ottoman Empire and, later, against the colonial powers of Spain and France. Safouan has insisted that the Qur'an was revealed at a time when women and children largely were considered a necessary nuisance. In the tribal society of Arabia in the seventh century, women represented war booty, personal property of no economic or military value. The majority of the verses in the Qur'an that pertain to women were a response to questions by members of the emerging community of believers in the new faith at a time when converts to the new religion desired a response from God via His messenger. In calling for a re-ordering of society according to newly revealed ideals in which women were granted some status and the right to own property, the Qur'an was at odds with prevailing mores. Thus, Safouan has asserted, rather than justifying the status quo, Muslim thinkers need to recapture the reformist zeal of early Islam. At the same time, Safouan is a proponent of the notion that the Qur'an needs to be treated as a historical document. He argued:

> Arabs at the time did not know anything about snow, so there are no references about winter or cold-climate practices in the Qur'an. We need to distinguish between verses that carry universal meaning and those that address specific issues of the time and place of the Qur'an's revelation.[15]

Safouan also encouraged a re-reading of the text with regard to the role of women in the same manner as fellow Egyptian scholar Oumaima Abu Bakr. According to Abu Bakr, who wrote *Islamic Feminist: What's in a Name?* (2001), contemporary Muslim women scholars are making themselves specialists in order to balance a centuries-long tradition of male interpreters and 'scholars who had nothing to lose by emphasizing discriminating differences and glossing over egalitarian principles, or neglecting to extend these to wives, daughters, sisters, and women colleagues in the work place'. Rather than emphasizing negativism towards the religion or simply using it as a temporary rhetorical position, Muslim feminists approach Islam as an all-encompassing, overarching worldview incorporating divine justice, compassion, egalitarianism, and liberation from slavery or submission to any being other than God. Another important Islamic principle, according to Abu Bakr, is a Muslim woman's right to a direct relationship with God without requiring a human mediator. This, of course, is the prophetic tradition for all believers, but one that has not been applied to men and women equally. Scholars like Abu Bakr propose that a Qur'an-centred discourse needs to involve re-interpretations of relevant verses so as to elicit meanings that support equality and gender justice and run counter to the traditional interpretations that highlight preference and superiority of men over women. Thus she wrote:

> It is a matter of emphasis: Whereas traditional interpretations of gender verses stressed complementarities of different social roles to justify an imbalanced relationship, Muslim feminists insist on reading these verses only in the light of the overarching, more determining verses of egalitarianism and equal public participation of believers, both men and women. Whereas the traditional perspective will never deny Islamic basic and spiritual equality between men and women, the principle will remain isolated in that sphere, never extending to actual practice and application of that egalitarian spirit. Muslim women readers of the Qur'an today are addressing this matter of extending and applying the egalitarian verses to the spheres of family and society.[16]

As previously stated, much of the scholarship on Islamic feminism has thus far come out of Egypt and Iran; Morocco is something of a newcomer on the scene but is now bursting with male and female scholars who aspire to bring together secular and Islamic activists, an approach typical of Morocco's comparative inclusiveness. On a practical level, such collaboration between religious and secular moderates is already in evidence.

Caravans for equality

One organization that is straddling the divide between Islamism and the secular women's rights approach is La Ligue Démocratique pour les Droits de la Femme (LDDF), or the Democratic League for the Rights of Women. Known for its caravans throughout Morocco as well as Spain and France, the LDDF seeks to understand, document, and address in a practical manner specific issues affecting women in Morocco and Marocains Résidant à l'Etranger (MRE), or Moroccans Residing Abroad. It is a human rights organization that operates transnationally in an effort to address specific needs of Moroccans regardless of their country of residence. As previously stated, nearly 10 per cent of the Moroccan population of about 30 million is living beyond the borders of their home country and many maintain close relationships with their country of origin.[17] LDDF activists do not describe themselves as secular or Islamist and are barely familiar with the term 'third way'. But their approach is remarkably inclusive of activists who volunteer out of a sense of religious calling or duty and those who come with a human rights agenda, individuals ranging from highly educated young women to less educated middle-aged women and men. There are few organizations that apply such an intersectional approach, one that seeks to cut across social classes, bridge the rural/urban divide, and bring together Moroccans of many stripes in the cause for gender justice.[18]

One of the aims of LDDF is to collect viable data on the status of Moroccan women inside the Kingdom as well as abroad. Much has been written about the high illiteracy rate of Moroccans, women in particular. After nearly 60 years of independence and repeated instances of government lip service about eradicating illiteracy, the LDDF has found that the number of illiterate women has not significantly decreased in Morocco. While some strides were made at increasing educational levels in the period after independence, illiteracy has remained fairly constant over the past decades. According to the LDDF, 30 per cent of girls around the age of ten are illiterate and about 60 per cent of adult women do not know how to read and write. These estimates do not reflect official government statistics, according to which female illiteracy has significantly decreased. LDDF president Fouzia Assouli asserted that the right to education has not been aggressively pursued by the government: 'To put it simply: If women don't have basic education, the government's agenda of women's rights is not put in place.'[19] She pointed out that though more girls are attending schools, they often do not complete their education, largely due to the economic situation of their families. As Assouli noted, 'the rate at which young girls abandon school is a serious social problem.'

Assouli was also a founding member of the Democratic League for the Rights of Women, which was created in 1993. Prior to assuming leadership of the LDDF, Assouli, a long-time activist, contributed to the Moroccan Association for Human Rights (AMDH), which today is headed by Khadija Ryadi, another outspoken activist. Assouli is part of the generation of Moroccan women who came of age during King Hassan II's period of iron rule in the early 1970s, and became involved in various human and women's rights causes. Over the years, the LDDF has evolved into an organization that accommodates a broader range of viewpoints, including those of moderate, yet overtly religious members. It has also broadened its focus to shed light on the plight of rural women.

Rural in Morocco does not merely mean isolated countryside with a low population density. Visiting rural regions resembles travelling back in time. Life is slow and in some of the large rural areas of Morocco, high in the Atlas mountains and along the Sahara desert, residents are dressed mostly in traditional Moroccan attire. There is an absence of paved roads and running water, electricity is sparse, and subsistence farming remains the main activity. People in these regions use donkeys and mules rather than cars. Women weave carpets and blankets with wool they have spun themselves. Life in such regions feels a world away from the hustle and bustle of the large, modern, urban centres of Morocco, and the two do not often intersect. Such a rural/urban divide is one of the major challenges faced by many global South countries and Morocco is no exception. About 40 per cent of the population resides in the Middle and High Atlas, in the Souss plain, and along the edges of the Sahara. Rural life depends largely on manual labour, supplied to a great extent by a female labour force. Some villages are almost entirely inhabited by women because their men are in the cities looking for work. Even if women migrate to the cities to find work in factories, they earn the equivalent of no more than five dollars per nine-hour workday. Often it is more profitable to work as a domestic where, in 2009, women could be paid as much as $1.20 per hour.

Though it is beyond the scope of any one organization to address the multiple challenges faced by Moroccan women, the LDDF has managed to attract volunteers who reflect the larger landscape of Moroccan women. When I spoke with Halima Benaoui, one of the founding members of LDDF, she told me that, for her, the grassroots component of this organization is especially important. Middle-aged, widowed, and a cancer survivor, Benaoui joined the LDDF because she was looking for a way 'to put my faith into action'. With no more than a basic education, she saw no place for herself in explicitly secular women's organizations that mostly attract highly educated, urban women. As a practical person she also was not interested in joining an Islamist group that places emphasis on studying scriptures and discussing theological issues. Wearing the *hijab* and dressed in a traditional *djellaba*, she explained that she was attracted to LDDF because it is one of the few organizations where veiled and unveiled women work side by side and where her action is valued as an expression of her religious observance.

With 14 branch offices all over Morocco, the LDDF organizes adult literacy classes, manages hotlines for victims of domestic violence, provides legal counsel, and organizes high-school programmes to sensitize the youth to issues of responsible citizenship and women's rights. In the past, the LDDF has used the slogan, 'No to extremism and terrorism, yes to equality and citizenship' for its awareness-raising training in secondary schools and universities. Most of these programmes were held in institutions that are located in Casablanca's working-class districts, which have traditionally been breeding grounds for terrorism. The programmes also include a discussion about *bid'a*, the Arabic term for innovation that in an Islamic context has negative implications. The Prophet is believed to have revealed all there needs to be revealed until the Last Days or the assumed end of the world and, through his life and his immediate successors, established an example of an ideal Muslim community. Therefore, the best way for a believer to improve his or her life is to look back at the precedent set at the time of the Prophet and shortly thereafter rather than coming up with 'innovative' ideas. Benaoui told me that a more forward-looking approach is needed, however, in order to address current problems that are quite different from those in seventh-century Arabia. Unlike those who work with secular women's associations, LDDF activists often wear headscarves, describe themselves as 'observant Muslims', and come from a variety of social and economic backgrounds. Their activism is grounded in an understanding that change needs to be firmly rooted in local culture, which means that volunteers are Moroccan and foreign influence is limited. The League's goal is to offer practical assistance as well as to advocate for women's rights.

Benaoui invited me to accompany her to one of the caravans for which LDDF is best known. These caravans resemble mobile town-hall meetings cum portable medical clinics. There, the otherwise shy and rather mono-syllabic, middle-aged Benaoui suddenly came to life, buzzing from tent to tent, chatting amicably with other volunteers, and making sure that women who entered the tent city received the attention they required. These caravans typically consist of several large tents reminiscent of those used by Amazigh nomads; they are set up in high-school yards, open fields, or town squares. The tents are staffed by volunteers, male and female, young and old, who invite women to fill out a demographic survey and to elaborate on their particular grievances, such as domestic violence, legal disputes as a result of a divorce, sexual violence, and so on. Illiterate women are assisted in filling out these questionnaires. Other tents are set up like discos, broadcasting Arab, Amazigh (Berber), and Western pop music with the intention of attracting younger audiences. Yet another tent offers free medical check-ups. The caravans create somewhat of country-fair type ambiance except for the issues addressed. Speakers elaborate on provisions under the 2004 Personal Status Code reform, on domestic violence, and even on AIDS and sexually transmitted diseases. These caravans usually last two or three days and the diverse group of volunteers who work with them enables these events to have a broad-based appeal. The collected information is processed and made public twice a year.

The most vocal opposition to the caravans comes from law enforcement officers who feel that such large gatherings disturb the public peace; certain Islamists also oppose the caravans because they believe that the LDDF is steering people off the right path. Police officers are concerned that the caravans will incite violence, as their purpose sometimes is not well understood by the population. In the poorer parts of the country where mistrust and dislike for government is high, people often mistake caravans for government functions and organize protests against them. Others think that the caravans are rallies by political parties, which are met with the same suspicion. Conservative Islamists disapprove of the caravans by pointing to the lack of emphasis on religious instruction in LDDF activities.

To reduce opposition rallies and generate public awareness of the purposes of the caravan, volunteers go door to door in the days prior to its arrival to inform people of its goals and let them know about the free medical check-ups that will be available. As access to health care facilities is limited in the socially disadvantaged parts of big cities and rural areas, these medical services are a big draw. The LDDF collaborates with the Organisation Pan-afriquaine contre le SIDA (OPAS), or the Pan-African Organization against AIDS, which sets up a separate tent offering AIDS tests. LDDF activists do not hide the fact that it is mostly because of these free medical facilities that men and women visit the caravans. Opponents charge that using medical services to lure people into the tent city is trickery. Certainly, once inside a caravan, people who are waiting for their turn at a clinic participate in other activities and listen to the talks being delivered.

One of the most surprising problems raised by visitors to the caravans, and one for which organizers were initially not prepared, is incest. Almost at every stop, women and girls confide about some incident of incest in their home. One of the reasons victims feel more at ease talking about such a taboo subject is that many LDDF volunteers resemble people from their own communities and are not perceived as outsiders. Volunteers report that they were initially taken by surprise by such repeated revelations about incest and that it took some time for them to formulate a reasonable response. Mostly, they suggest medical tests and try to help the victim think about ways to get out of the house. In the absence of clear domestic violence laws and frequently corrupt law enforcement, such recourse rarely offers a solution. Volunteers lament that the best service they can offer is to listen with compassion and allow victims to unburden themselves. The fact that people are coming forward with such highly sensitive problems attests to the trust the caravans have earned among the population. Some of the volunteers are so overwhelmed by the stories they hear from caravan visitors that they have to retreat to a small room (which is reserved for such a purpose) and compose themselves. I spent some time at one of these caravans in a room set aside for volunteers, and listened to male and female volunteers exchange information and offer each other tips on how to advise women who confided in them. A pervasive sense of purpose bonds the volunteers, and, as is common throughout Morocco, strong, sweet mint tea is served for them all day long.

The LDDF is an organization with practical goals yet it does not have particular ideological or theological leanings. In its inclusive approach it is emblematic of what is emerging as a third way even though LDDF activities do not use this term. They join others who work on academic or theoretical frameworks in seeking new approaches to gender issues.

A doctor's presciption

In Morocco, one of the early proponents of a third way is Asma Lamrabet, medical doctor and wife of a high-ranking former diplomat. Her husband's Foreign Service career took Lamrabet to various countries in Central and South America where she volunteered her medical expertise to underserved population groups. I met Lamrabet in her luxurious home on the outskirts of Rabat, accompanied her to presentations in front of select audiences of Morocco's high society, and to lectures aimed at students in sparse classrooms at public universities. In all these different settings, Lamrabet was at ease, delivering the same basic message.

The slender, elegant Lamrabet described to me the internal conflict created by her constant moves between her mansion in high-class suburbs and the health centres in which she worked, located in the most impoverished parts of overcrowded shantytowns in Central and South America. Her daily exposure to gross inequalities and misery contrasted sharply with the easy life afforded to her expatriate diplomatic circle. A modern, Western-educated woman with no particular religious inclination, she wanted to find her place in the world. At one point, she recounted, she had something of an epiphany that led her to explore her religious roots. She began researching Islam and in time became a devout believer. Dr. Lamrabet put on the headscarf – highly unusual among the Moroccan elite – and proceeded to write several books and numerous articles on what it means to be a Muslim in today's world. Lamrabet recalled that her concern for marginalized people during her stay in Latin America attracted her to Christian Liberation Theology. Therein she found a religiously motivated path to social work that inspired her own search for a comparable interpretation of Islam. Liberation Theology is a Christian theological movement that started in South America, more precisely with Dom Hélder Câmara and Leonardo Boff of Brazil in the mid 1950s. This approach to Christianity interprets the teachings of the Bible in terms of liberation from unjust economic, political, or social conditions. And just as Liberation Theology went on collision course with the Vatican, Lamrabet's interpretations of the Qur'anic scriptures has set her on a collision course with orthodox readings of Islam. Still, this high-spirited, sophisticated woman said she prefers dialogue to confrontation and does not see herself as a revolutionary or overt rebel.

As Lamrabet studied the history of Islam, the life of the Prophet, and, in particular, that of his wife Aïcha, she began to focus more and more on the role and status of women in Muslim-majority countries. She described herself as an 'independent intellectual', unaffiliated with any institution of higher learning, political party, or religious organization or movement. The absence of any institutional support initially made it difficult for Lamrabet to enter public discourse, after all she represented no one but herself and her religious knowledge was self-taught. After her third book was published, however, scholars began taking note of her writings and she received invitations to speak at domestic and international conferences. In 2010, she accepted a position as the Director of the Centre d'Etudes Féminines en Islam (the Centre for Feminine Studies in Islam) in Rabat. The Centre is connected to the Mohammedian Council of Religious Scholars that was created by the palace. To some, Lamrabet's new role means that she has become part of the Moroccan power structure and has lost her independence. She countered this argument by saying that she does not represent the Council but leads a research centre that deals with religious issues. She readily admitted that she already had spirited arguments with some of the male leadership of the Council so as to ensure her autonomy. She went on to explain to me that one of the advantages of working with the Centre is that it allows her access to resources and people engaged in similar projects that she otherwise would not have had as an unaffiliated researcher. Lamrabet was clear about stating that her task is not the same as that of religious scholars who are charged with matters of interpretation. She told me that she sees her role as posing probing questions that religious scholars should address and critiquing conventional religious discourse on women. Her goal is to steer research into the direction of currently relevant issues pertaining to gender discourse and away from esoteric theological questions that are of little consequence to believers' daily lives. She said she would hold this position as long as she can be effective in spite of inevitable conflicts with male leaders of the affiliated religious council.

In her book, *Le Coran et les femmes* (*The Qur'an and Women*), Lamrabet identified 'two major tragedies' of Muslim history: the status of women and the persistence of slavery.[20] Though several passages of the Qur'an pertain to the liberation of slaves, this practice continued for more than a thousand years in Muslim-majority lands. According to Lamrabet, the disregard for the Qur'an with regard to the freeing of slaves is closely linked to the institutionalization of the oppression of women. She contended that, in Morocco as in other North African countries, an official 'culture of subordination' was passed on from generation to generation until it became synonymous with sanctioned Islamic practice. In its wake, a 'code of fear' evolved that has continued up until the twenty-first century. She debunked the phrases often repeated by sincere Muslims that 'Islam has given all rights to women ... It honours women ... It protects them ...' as rather poor and defensive arguments that fly in the face of reality and create a make-believe world in which women are made to feel that they have all the rights they need.[21] Books with similar ambitions – and almost identical titles to the ones authored by Lamrabet – have been written before, yet it seems that each country needs to produce its own voice and come up with interpretations and conclusions relevant to a specific audience. Morocco's embrace of Lamrabet's work is the reverse of the biblical idea that a prophet has no honour in his country.[22]

Scholars like Amina Wadud of the United States (*Qur'an and Woman: Rereading the Sacred Text from a Woman's Perspective*, 1999), Asma Barlas of Pakistani origin (*'Believing Women' in Islam – Unreading Patriarchal Interpretations of the Qur'an*, 2002) and Nimat Hafez Barazangi of Iran (*Women's Identity and the Qur'an: A New Reading*, 2004) also have written extensively about the gulf between the Qur'anic vision of women and the reality on the ground. This diversity of voices speaks to the fact that, despite its universal message, Islam is not understood and practised in the same way the world over.

Apart from wanting to effect change in her own country, Lamrabet believes in transnational dialogue. With this goal in mind, in 2008 she co-founded an international study group Le Groupe International d'Etude et de Réflexion sur la Femme en Islam (GIERFI), or the International Group for the Study and Reflection on Women in Islam. The group has attracted the attention of government officials, most notably the Rabita Mohammedia des Oulémas du Maroc, or the Mohammedian Council of Religious Scholars, established by the king. I will return to this institution later in this book.

One of the goals of the GIERFI is to explore theological and legal questions pertaining to women. Its statement of purpose reads in part:

It is obvious that predominantly Muslim societies, Muslim communities in the West and Muslims in general face real difficulties and even dread addressing the question of women. This is due to the fact that this issue represents the principal challenge of political modernization in the Islamic space. It remains one of the most sensitive questions and the most difficult one to debate. The question of women presents a multi-dimensional problem, including questions of identity, modernity, tradition and the preservation of an imagined culture. The Muslim world is undergoing a real crisis, the most critical stumbling bloc being the question of women, which is often skirted for reasons of identity, intellectual bias and at times as political strategy, wilfully omitted. The creation of GIERFI is motivated by the urgent need of an alternative discourse, capable of making up for the lack of an official Islamic discourse on women, a discourse that is frequently reductionist, infantilizing and most often lacks substance.[23]

The GIERFI study groups meet on an irregular basis in Morocco, Spain, Belgium, and Canada; the GIERFI maintains a website with links to articles, books, and a forum for exchanging ideas. Because of Lamrabet's ties to diplomatic circles, she can address groups of highly connected women who normally do not spend much time attending lectures with a theological theme. At one such gathering to which I was invited, women dressed in mink coats and Parisian *haute couture* and sat in a large marble sitting room, the scent of luxurious perfumes wafting in the air. They listened attentively to Lamrabet's provocative elaborations on Islam's message of gender equality. The question-and-answer session that followed revealed that these women, privileged by social class rather than gender, had rarely pondered the issues raised by their peer, though most seemed genuinely inspired. After the presentation the participants adjourned to a sumptuous buffet with an exquisite selection of pastries and hors d'oeuvres, where the discussion about religious questions continued. Elegant and highly sophisticated, Lamrabet was keenly aware of the cleavage between the lower class and the upper class, which enjoys rights and privileges denied to the majority of the Moroccan population. As a believer, she finds these class distinctions to be distasteful and unacceptable, especially in a developing country such as hers. She maintained that this reality contradicts Islam's claims of solidarity of the *ummah*, the community of the faithful. She noted that she understands but is saddened by criticism based on her social status, which she encounters when addressing students at public universities. She explained:

In Morocco, people are sceptical when someone like me takes up a religious cause. Especially young people think that upper class women are secular and support women's rights in line with Western goals. In their eyes it is Islamists who stand for the 'common man' and the upholding of our traditions. It is hard for them to believe that someone like me would be on their side.

To avoid obvious signs of the economic disparity between her and her audiences at certain public universities, where most students come from lower-middle-class backgrounds, Lamrabet gets behind the wheel of her own car rather than using her family's chauffeur-driven limousine when driving to these venues and speaking to student audiences. Though Lamrabet's writings are popular among religiously inclined students, they fear that she wants to expand privileges for her own elite peers rather than advocate for the rights of all women. Such suspicion based on class difference is a common phenomenon throughout North Africa, where the opportunity for upward social mobility is not widespread. Furthermore, Lamrabet writes in French, another indication to some that she is more beholding to the West rather than to her Maghrebi roots. This is a somewhat spurious argument against her, however, since Nadia Yassine – whose grassroots and Islamist pedigree is impeccable – wrote her one, and to date only, book in French as well.

Lamrabet's basic position is that Islam was revealed to liberate all human beings, men and women. She insists on a third way that builds bridges between secular Western feminism and Islamists. In an interview, she shared her position with me:

> Women are the last bastions of Islam. I don't see a contradiction between secular laws and Islamic principles. I know this is a difficult position for many Islamists to accept. Legal equality is non-negotiable and it has to be created in a secular sphere. Women's rights have to be achieved on many different levels and in many different spheres. However, when we talk of real equality we are not taking the Western model that makes men the norm and demand that women have the same status as men. We need to rethink this and first make the human being the norm and start from there.

She added vehemently, 'Just because women are perceived to be more emotional than men does not mean they should not have the same legal rights.' She said that Muslims sometimes have an almost irrational fear of the term equality – an issue that needs to be confronted and tackled by intellectuals engaged in this debate.

Lamrabet does not reserve her critical assessments for her co-religionists only; she finds much in the Western approach to women's rights lamentable as well. In this regard, she reiterated what many Moroccan Islamists are saying, namely that women's rights basically means giving women the same rights as men without considering additional sets of rights that are highly pertinent to women, such as paid parental leave and affordable child care. For many Muslim women's rights advocates, an exclusive focus on equal rights with men is a flawed starting point, as in the end women may enjoy legal equality but still have primary responsibility for childcare and household chores while pursuing a professional career. They note that even in more gender-egalitarian societies, raising children is not given the same value as a professional career and is not rewarded financially. In the emancipated West, for example, women's familial obligations are still frequently a hindrance to professional advancement. Such obligations do not only pertain to childcare; it is taken for granted that women more often than men take care of ageing relatives, whether their own or their partner's or husband's. These realities need to be taken into consideration, according to Lamrabet, when developing a gender rights platform. Due to her work with the poor in Latin America, she has developed a deep sense of social responsibility and an admiration for people who turn their religious convictions into social action. Though her social status would allow her a life of leisure common among Moroccan elite women, she has chosen to move beyond the traditional boundaries of a privileged life. In addition to her scholarly pursuits, Lamrabet works in poorly staffed public hospitals in Morocco's capital city. A recurring theme in conversations is Lamrabet's critical stance toward literalist interpretations of Islam. She asserted:

There is an intellectual and emotional block when it comes to discussing the status of women. Reference is made to an idealistic, but what I call fatalistic, past that never existed in this idyllic form nor could we go back in time even if we wanted to.

She also rejects the focus on women's bodies and their appearance — that is, the notion of a biologically determined role and the emphasis on the clothes women should or should not wear and how they should appear in public. Most discussions about Muslim women's rights end up being about the veil, an issue Lamrabet finds particularly tiresome. Veiled herself, she argued that covering the head is the choice and right of an adult woman and should neither be imposed on young girls nor confused with the 'extremist' full-face veil, which impedes women's participation in public life. This centrality of the body, she argued, reduces women to their sexual and maternal roles, ignoring their mental capacity. Similarly, she finds loathsome the preoccupation with the veil in certain Western countries, most notably France. On the other hand, within Muslim religious circles the focus is all too often on women's divinely perceived obligations and not on their rights, according to Lamrabet. On her personal website she characterized her notion of third way activism as follows:

> We are dealing with a timid movement, still somewhat confused, here and there expressing its first stammers on Muslim soil and in the West, trying to emerge as a major force and to make its voice heard. Engaged, believing Muslim women are mobilizing slowly – too slowly even – in order to stop people from making any kind of pronouncements concerning women in the name of religion.[24]

Lamrabet also zeroed in on the issue of fear when discussing women's rights. She acknowledged the widespread alarm that many men would feel if large numbers of women were freed from their traditional domestic roles and from their subservience to them.

The fear of women's rights was openly expressed in my discussions with groups of educated young Moroccans – men especially. They admitted to fearing an unravelling of society if women were free to compete in the open market alongside them. On a personal level, they reported feeling unsure how relationships will work out if women are their equals. They questioned their own male identity in a marriage between equal partners. Young Moroccans will admit without hesitation that they have limited experience with democratic structures as these are not found in their families, at school, at the university, or in society at large. Fear and obedience are instilled early on within the family, where the patriarch expects deference from all members and mothers dominate their children with emotional appeals. The young men I spoke with said openly that they feel at a loss about how to approach gender equality. They have been taught to revere their mothers but admitted that this exaggerated adoration of motherhood does not translate into egalitarian treatment of women.

Particularly for men from lower-middle-class backgrounds who are limited in their own opportunities and choices, a privileged status over women is just about the only power they hold in a highly autocratic and class-stratified society. University students in particular fear attaining a college or graduate degree but then ending up underemployed or unable to obtain a job at all. The prospect of having to compete with equally qualified women for already scarce jobs touches on larger social and economic problems. In these circumstances, gender equality becomes a vital threat to men's livelihoods. Though the official unemployment rate is 9.1 per cent, in reality unemployment is significantly higher, especially among the educated young. Large demonstrations by unemployed university graduates in front of the seat of government in Rabat have become a weekly occurrence. This brings us back to the issue raised at the beginning of this book, namely that the question of women's rights is intersectional, tied in with other pressing social issues like economics, social class, unemployment, and an individual's sense of value.

For Lamrabet, the issue of social class is a crucial one. She is saddened when students at public universities are sceptical of her primarily because of her elite background. She acknowledged, however, that often upper-class women seek to advance their own status rather than demonstrate solidarity with those less fortunate. In Lamrabet's words, 'For most of these students, a religiously inspired activist is someone who comes from the same social background as they do and therefore they find it hard to believe that someone like me could share similar beliefs.' She added:

> Islamists have cornered the market so to speak on social justice issues so I do not fit their image of someone who advocates for

change with their interests in mind. The distrust between people of different social classes is rather deep.

Distrust and fear are two issues that Lamrabet addresses head-on in
her public appearances. She speaks about women's fear of advocating
for emancipation based on religious reasoning. Fear permeates the
lives of women in Morocco who often remain silent in the midst of a
discourse that directly concerns them. Due to the cultural emphasis
on values such as obedience, submission, and patience, women who
are not actively involved in public life (that is, the vast majority of
Moroccan women) remain silent and make the best of their present
situations. Religious concepts such as submission to God are mixed
with concepts of male domination, such that qualities associated
with religious observance are used in the service of male domination. This confluence of meanings creates fear among women that
women's liberation means going against God's will. Such sentiments
are deeply ingrained in the female populace of North African countries, where women have largely internalized their own subservient
status. Third way proponents are trying to disentangle such outmoded links between women's oppression and religious identity by
proposing a new religious identity that is in line with an egalitarian
reading of the scriptures.

The West has largely freed itself from explicitly linking social structures to religious concepts, an important distinction that helped pave
the way for women's rights. Nevertheless, according to Lamrabet, the
Qur'an provides a basis for liberation, not only for women but also for
men, since she views the quest for women's rights as a universal one.
In this sense, there is room for collaboration with the West. Lamrabet
and those who think like her believe that wholesale vilification of the
West is counterproductive.

Though Lamrabet argues from a religious perspective when advocating for human rights and women's rights in particular, she finds
herself at odds with certain Islamists. She considers the Justice and
Charity movement (Al Adl wa Ihsane) to be a sect. In her view, the
cult-like status of its founder and the organization's way of dividing
people into insiders (members) and outsiders (non-members) does not

allow the movement to act as major player in the larger national discussion on women's issues.

What irks Lamrabet the most is an absence of dialogue between different women's groups and genuine debate among Islamic thinkers. She is aware that in the West, feminists or women's rights advocates never did, and to this day do not, agree on every single issue. Furthermore, she recognizes the country-specific differences among Western feminists. Yet she admires the fact that the ongoing debate in the West about how to expand gender equality has occurred without the basic concept ever being drawn into question. In my discussion with Lamrabet, she commented, 'In the absence of developing our own platform, we are bound to either copy from the West or continue to fall prey to the same literalist reading that has dominated religious discourse for too long.' She cited the issue of abortion as an issue of immense importance to feminists in the West but one that has not been fully addressed in Morocco: 'Abortion is forbidden in most Muslim countries but there is no religious justification for this.' She referred to twelfth-century Muslim Sufi scholar Abu Hamed al-Ghazzali, who is quoted as having said that a woman has a right to accept or reject motherhood.

The Mohammedian Council of Religious Scholars

As mentioned above, Lamrabet's work attracted the attention of the Rabita Mohammedia des Oulémas, the Mohammedian Council of Religious Scholars. Though some version of this Council, which functions somewhat like a think tank, has existed since the 1960s, the current King Mohammed VI (after whom the Council is now named) revived it and vested it with new responsibilities. For example, the king has endowed the Council with the sole official authority in the country to issue *fatwas* – that is, pronouncements by religious scholars. Previously, religious scholars in Morocco made such pronouncements on any number of issues, such as condemning video games or declaring popular politician Mehdi Ben Barka (assassinated under still unresolved circumstances in 1965) a martyr. King Mohammed VI brought the Council under his direct control – previously it had been part of the Ministry for Religious Affairs – thus asserting his religious authority. The Council is charged with bringing various factions of Moroccan thinkers to the table with the purpose of developing a vision for the country. As a visible sign of its importance, the recreated Council is located in the centre of the capital city of Rabat, next to the *medina*, the historic and always-bustling part of town, where it is easily accessible.

Ahmed Abbadi, Secretary General of the Mohammedian Council of Religious Scholars, is a charismatic scholar of Islam with a doctorate in Islamic Studies. In Abbadi, the king appointed a Moroccan with an Islamist background who is fluent in English (in addition, of course, to Arabic and French) and conversant with contemporary Western modes of thinking. Previously, Abbadi taught at a university in the United States and was appointed to lead the Council in 2006. The choice of Abbadi is a clear indication that the king understands the rising power of Islamism in his country. Formerly a member of the Islamist Party of Justice and Development (PJD), Abbadi has evolved into a visionary in his own right. His ideas go beyond conservative Islamism and he now advocates a plan for harmony between the different interpretations. This, he explained to me in an interview, is more in keeping with Sufism, the mystical branch of Islam, which has deep roots and is widespread in Morocco.

At the same time, Abbadi stressed that the Qur'an reminds believers that God endowed human beings with reason. Therefore reason needs to be employed when discussing religious tenets. Fond of metaphors, he told me that building a society is like building a house: the architect has the entire plan while different units are charged with individual tasks. He elaborated: 'There may be conflict among electricians and construction workers concerning where to put wires and outlets. In the end, the architect is responsible for the house and that installations are in the right place and work properly.' By the same token, Abbadi believes that religion needs to be understood more broadly as serving the goal of allowing human beings to worship God in their own way while at the same time living in harmony with each other. Forgetting this ultimate purpose of religion gives way to misunderstandings and places emphasis on conflict, not only between religions but within religions as well. To Abbadi, the existence of a variety of discourses is useful and for the purposes of discussion no viewpoint should be excluded. 'We are wasting access to each other's wisdom,' he explained, adding:

> There is danger in an inward-looking West as much as in an inward-looking Muslim world. The wisdom of the world needs to be shared. There is a need for a global, holistic vision that transcends mere tolerance of each other but reaches the level of complete mutual respect.

To this end, Abbadi maintains an open-door policy that tries to exclude no one. The steady comings and goings at the Council attest to his sincerity about this approach. A constant flow of visitors, from American diplomats and scholars to white-robed, bearded Islamists to representatives of the Jewish and Christian communities in Morocco, can be observed at the Council's offices. They all come to discuss their ideas with Abbadi and attend small gatherings or symposia where ideas are exchanged in a climate of respect.

I met Abbadi in his large wood-panelled office, which looks much like a library. Like most Moroccan men who are affiliated either with Islamist organizations or want to show their religious inclination, the Secretary General wore a short cropped, full beard. Even more than the woman who wears a headscarf, the *barbu* (bearded one) identifies a Moroccan often as an Islamist of some sort or another. He enjoyed jumping from topic to topic, making sure the points of interest to him are covered. Abbadi's critique of modernity takes into account the value it places on efficiency, because in dealing with matters of religion or identity he feels patience is more important than aiming at a quick result. From Abbadi's perspective, a careful approach to new Qur'anic interpretations is required in order to bring differing factions on board and ensure a long-term outcome. Abbadi said he is moving towards the goal of gender equality by employing the Islamic interpretive tradition of exploring the 'meaning behind the text', an issue to which we shall turn next.

Intent or purpose

The Islamic tradition of *maqasid* is a method of understanding the ultimate purpose or intention of scriptural verses used as the basis for laws and as such it is different from the study of specific cases or literal readings. Abbadi believes this method is the most appropriate for fulfilling the mission of the Council. In an American context this method is akin to the Supreme Court's task of interpreting the US Constitution. There are those who advocate for a literal reading and those who see it as a living document. Certainly, there is a significant difference in interpreting a man-made Constitution and a divinely revealed text, because when dealing with sacred scriptures one must tackle the challenge of discerning God's immutable design, as it were.

A full discussion of the tradition of *maqasid* exceeds the purpose of this book; suffice it to say that *maqasid* refers to a method of examination of the ultimate objectives of law. The goal or purpose of interpretation and the subsequent pronouncement of laws is intended to ensure the harmonious co-existence of all members of society and to respond to the need for laws to be adjusted to specific societal contexts according to time and place. *Maqasid*, then, forms the basis of the interpretation of religious texts and can in a very simplified way be summed up as pertaining to the preservation of religion, life, lineage, intellect, and property. Abbadi emphasized that *shari'a* (religiously based) laws have always been a contested concept, first because they are understood as God's will, and second because humans can only have a limited understanding of the Almighty and always will have differing interpretations of scripture. A central theme in understanding the intention of a text is that though the Qur'an is the word of God, its teachings are experienced within a specific historical, social, cultural, and geographical context. For many conservative scholars of Islam, however, the word of God is eternal and the revelation would have been no different had it occurred at a different time and in a different place.

An example of how *maqasid* can be applied in a specific context and one that is germane to this book concerns one of most contentious issues in Muslim law, namely the provision in the *shari'a* that deals with inheritance. Inheritance laws touch on all the five areas to be

addressed by *maqasid*. Unlike those who advocate for a literal reading
of the law, Abbadi explained to me that he believes that in today's
society one needs to consider that the interests of society are no longer
best served by adhering to the strict rule that a woman can only inherit
half of what a male member of the family is entitled to. Inheritance
laws are some of the most hotly debated issues in Morocco because the
Qur'an is explicit on this issue and a literalist reading would not allow
for an interpretation that can be viewed as straying from the text. In
order to appreciate the controversy around this particular verse, I will
cite it here in full:

> An-Naissa (the Women)
> As for the children, God decrees
> That the share of the male
> Is equivalent to that of two females.
> If they consist of women only,
> And of them more than two,
> They will get two-thirds of the inheritance;
> But in case there is one, she will inherit one half.
> The parents will each inherit a sixth of the estate
> If it happens the deceased has left a child;
> But if he has left no children,
> And his parents are his heirs,
> Then the mother will inherit one-third;
> But if he has left brothers,
> The mother will inherit one-sixth
> After payment of legacies and debts.
> Of parents and children
> You do not know who are more useful to you.
> These are the decrees of God
> Who knows all and is wise.
>
> (Sura 4:11)

Abbadi argued that the law derived from this passage of the Qur'an,
like other such laws, needs to be evaluated within the historic context
in which it was revealed. The purpose of the law, namely to safeguard

the life of a family in case of death and other unforeseen circumstances, requires a re-reading in light of contemporary reality. Today, men are no longer always the sole breadwinners and often it is daughters, not sons, who assume financial responsibility and take care of their ageing parents. In modern Morocco, literal application of the inheritance law frequently leads to conflict, especially when sons are unemployed, study, or work abroad and it falls onto the daughters to assist their parents, often without any financial support from their male relatives. According to Abbadi, the law is intended for men to use their inheritance in the service of their family, not to personally enrich themselves. Furthermore, at the time such laws were first formulated, women had few, if any, rights, and the mere introduction of inheritance and personal property rights for women was revolutionary. It is this revolutionary early spirit of Islam that people like Abbadi want to recover. Tariq Ramadan called this evolving under-standing of the scriptures a 'divine pedagogy', and characterized it in this way: 'The faithful are thus led to evolve in their understanding of things and critically reconsider some of their cultural or social practices.'[25] In his book *Radical Reform – Islamic Ethics and Liberation*, Ramadan wrote about the era in which the Qur'an was revealed:

> The status of women, who were sometimes killed at birth because of the shame they might bring, was to be reformed in stages, as verses were revealed. It thus appeared more and more clearly that the Qur'an's message and the Prophet's attitude were apt to free women from the cultural shackles of Arab tribes and clans and from the practices of the time.[26]

The same sort of virulent discussion revolves around the issue of polygamy. While some literalist interpretations lead to the conclusion that polygamy is a right, it can also be understood as an obligation in the sense that it obliges men to take care of widows and their children. In the absence of social services and a structure that provides for such individuals, polygamy was a way to ensure the safekeeping of widows and their children. The primary purpose of polygamy, then, was not to provide a legal basis for sexual enjoyment with multiple partners. Looking at the issue of polygamy from the viewpoint of obligation rather than right or privilege not only impacts a re-evaluation of this institution as a safety net but also allows for more dispassionate discourse. While in the West, few circumstances would make polygamy a feasible option, in the global South, where family often provides the only safety net for those without the means to support themselves, there are cases in which polygamy may present a reasonable alternative.

Abbadi's thinking is in line with official government discourse on the question of polygamy. Nouzha Skalli, one of the architects of the Personal Status Code reform and former Ministre du Développement Social, de la Famille et de la Solidarité (Secretary of Social Development, Family, and Solidarity), has repeatedly called for the abolition of polygamy not only in the name of women's equality but also to safeguard the rights of children. Skalli, it should be noted, is one of the founding members of the secular Association Démocratique des Femmes du Maroc (ADFM), or Democratic Association of Moroccan Women, and an outspoken opponent of Islamist positions. The issues surrounding inheritance laws and polygamy illustrate the differences between the Muslim world and the West in relation to the battleground for women's rights. While Skalli invokes universal human rights standards to support her positions, Abbadi prefers to remain within a religious framework and employs the method of *maqasid*, in essence, to achieve the same goals.

In books originally published in French, Tariq Ramadan, philosopher and scholar of Islam and frequent visitor to Morocco, has written extensively about the historical development of *maqasid*. In his *Islam, La réforme radicale: éthique et libération*, which appeared under the above-mentioned English title *Radical Reform – Islamic Ethics and Liberation*, he posed the question:

> ... whether the human social environment has received sufficient attention in the elaboration of Islamic *fiqh*. Indeed, what appears – albeit implicitly, in the works of *maqasid* school scholars is that the social and human environment operates as a potential source of law insofar as the scholar (*al usuli*) must constantly take it into account to understand a ruling, think out its implementation, or state a legal opinion (*fatwa*) when no

text is available. However, stressing awareness of the context is one thing, while it is quite another matter to give its true place and grant the environment the same work of categorization and ranking of priorities.[27]

At times, Ramadan has generated much controversy with statements that made him appear to be a 'fundamentalist', a categorization that led him to be denied entry into the United States in 2004 when he was offered a professorship in Chicago. He accepted a position at Oxford University instead. In 2010, the US Department of State, in a document signed by Secretary of State Hillary Rodham Clinton, lifted the ban on Ramadan's admittance to the United States. A prolific author and perennial presence at international conferences and in various mass media forums, Ramadan straddles the line between maintaining his credibility in devoutly religious circles and acting as a reformer intent on infusing internal discourse with new ideas. His elaboration on *maqasid* goes hand-in-glove with his advocacy for a new understanding of women. In a chapter entitled 'Women: Tradition and Liberation' Ramadan wrote:

> Such studies must be carried out, although two main pitfalls must be avoided. One the one hand, one must of beware of focusing too much on some sensitive issues having to do with text interpretation while neglecting a more comprehensive approach that would link texts, the social environment, and the logics that in this latter case legitimate specific readings and sometimes result in including false religious truisms. On the other hand, one must avoid thinking about this process of critical reconsideration only in terms of the West, no matter whether this latter is praised or rejected.[28]

On the international level, Ramadan is the most vocal proponent of a third way, insisting that, in fact, Islam has become a Western religion and that Muslims in the West subscribe to the values of the countries of which they are citizens. In this sense, reforms in Islam not only affect Muslim-majority countries but Muslims anywhere in the world.

The Mohammedian Council of Religious Scholars uses Ramadan's scholarly work as a basis for their deliberations.

Not quite as well known but equally pertinent is South African scholar Farid Esack, who also is concerned with the meaning or ultimate purpose of Islamic laws. Esack, a South African Muslim theologian, anti-apartheid campaigner, and social activist, rose to prominence when then-President Nelson Mandela appointed him in 1997 as Commissioner for Gender Equality. To put a Muslim man partially in charge of gender equality – in a Christian-majority country no less – was one of Nelson Mandela's trademark appointments and vested Esack with the particular responsibility to come to terms with gender inequalities within his own faith community. Esack describes himself as an 'Islamic liberation theologian' who, unlike Ramadan, does not straddle the Orient/Occident divide but rather the gap between the global South and North. Having a government position gave Esack a political arena rather than confining him to the academic/theological realm, yet led him to arrive at conclusions similar to those of Ramadan. Esack also encourages a historic reading of the Qur'an, which for literalists is a timeless revelation free from historical context. In his book *On Being a Muslim* (2000), Esack tackled Qur'anic verses pertaining to slavery and women, a link made earlier by Mernissi and Lamrabet.

> While exhortations to feed and clothe your slaves and to be gentle with your women were courageous and path-breaking at that time, we cannot get stuck there, because the objectives towards which the Prophet moved are far more important than the premise from which he started. While kindness, gentleness and compassion are always qualities to be welcomed, they can never be substitutes for justice, freedom and equality. Similarly, reforms in women's issues meant that the prophetic intention was the freedom and equality of women.[29]

It is no coincidence that the countries that were among the last to abolish slavery – Sudan, Saudi Arabia, and Mauretania – are also the ones that today have the most restrictive laws pertaining to women. Slavery was reported in Sudan as late as 1995, officially abolished in Saudi Arabia in 1961 and in Mauretania in 1981. Although Islam is clear that all Muslims are to be considered equal without distinctions based on race or gender, slavery has a long tradition in the Muslim/Arab world since tribal economies depended on an unpaid labour force.

Because Muslim law is believed to be divinely inspired, a new interpretation does not only mean a change of law but the possibility of altered religious beliefs as well. Ramadan and Esack are scholars who write for international audiences; their books are translated and distributed throughout the world and frequently read by non-Muslims. On the other side of the Mediterranean are local scholars who write for domestic audiences and address a specific, limited public. This is the case for Moroccan cleric Ahmed Raissouni, one of the founding members and former president of the Mouvement Unité et Réforme (MUR), or Movement of Unity and Reform, the organization that gave birth to the Justice and Development Party (PJD) in 1998. Raissouni primarily addresses himself to Islamist circles within Morocco. Hence, his writing is intended to shed light on issues he considers important in the domestic discourse of his own country:

> The internal battle in the Muslim world is no longer focused –
> and should not focus – on the victory or defeat of modernity over
> tradition, or of tradition over modernity; neither on conservatism
> or renewal over conservatism. It is rather focused on complemen
> tarity and equilibrium ... If preachers and Muslim reformers
> today seek to inspire new religious vigour among Muslims and
> to take them out of what I call religious spontaneity toward a
> conscientious religiosity, the method of *maqasid* is required for
> a deeper understanding, education on mobilization of all toward
> these goals.[30]

Though Raissouni left his leading role in the MUR, he continues to be a formidable presence among Islamic scholars in Morocco. In the past, he has angered the king (much like Sheikh Yassine of the Justice and Charity movement, but not as radically) by advocating for a separation of powers, meaning that the monarch should not also serve as

Commander of the Faithful but leave religious leadership in the hands of Islamic scholars or leaders. While Raissouni and the MUR have reached out to fellow Islamists of the Justice and Charity movement, the political PJD party has not responded and insists on distancing itself from the MUR and other such organizations. Thus, today membership in the MUR is independent of PJD affiliation.

Raissouni's concern has focused mainly on finding new ways of approaching the real or perceived conflict between Islamism and modernity, and he sees a separation of the religious from the political sphere as a step in the direction of allowing religious reforms to occur. Raissouni also has suggested using the method of *maqasid* to reach consensus:

> For reasons pertaining to our time, people more than ever need to think along the lines of *maqasid*. Islam no longer is a unique nor unifying faith. Islam is neither the sole basis of law nor its dominant source. Neither is it the dominant culture. We live in an era of competition where ideas outdo one another – we live in the era of Western globalization.[31]

The method of finding the meaning behind the laws opens new possibilities for 'liberal' interpretations that nevertheless stay true to the essence of Islam. In Morocco, it is a method most commonly employed when grappling with the phenomenon of modernity and in the undeniable influence and presence of the West. The above-cited scholars referred to the method of studying the intended meaning behind the law in order to arrive at an application of law that takes modern reality into consideration while allowing for Muslim law to still remain relevant in this day and age. Raissouni wrote:

> The battle within the Islamic world is not aimed at – or rather should not be aimed at – a victory or defeat of modernity or of the ancient over the new, or conservatism over renewal or renewal over conservatism. The goal of the battle is to find balance and compatibility ... To this end, the methodology of *maqasid* is necessary.[32]

In creating the Council of Oulemas (religious scholars), King Mohammed VI has appropriated Islamic discourse and opened the way for progressive thinkers to shape and influence a vision for the twenty-first century in this North African kingdom. His actions demonstrate recognition of the increasing influence of Islamism in Morocco and the need to develop ideas that are acceptable in an increasingly religious and politically uncertain climate. Having observed the havoc that militant and violent Islamists have wreaked, especially in neighbouring Algeria and other parts of the Muslim world, this is an astute move and sets an interesting precedent. In creating such a body and by investing religious leadership in a council of Islamic scholars, the king is at once deferring to experts while at the same time asserting his role as religious leader, intent on initiating a far-reaching theological reform. It can only be hoped that the Council will in time reach out to all factions of moderate Islamists in Morocco so as to reach a genuine consensus and open the way for a more pluralistic society.

There are other ways in which the king has appropriated the religious debate, such as by appointing female *murchidates* (guides) to roles in mosques. In this way, the monarch has set in motion an important discussion about the role of female religious leaders in Islam.

Female religious leaders

As women gain more overt involvement in discussions about religion and Islam and women's rights, King Mohammed VI once again has proven to be finely attuned to certain current trends. Trying to stay ahead of contemporary tendencies, he has taken the bold and unusual step of appointing women to religious office. Their role – apart from leading Friday prayers in the mosques – fulfils much the same job description as that of *imams*. Two years after the family law reform, the king initiated the *murchidate* programme in 2006 as part of a larger vision of promoting what he calls 'Morocco's moderate Islam'. This vision includes elevating the status of women and advancing gender equality. The pioneer group of *murchidates* brought back a now frequently forgotten or ignored tradition of female religious leaders in this country, namely *muqqamadat* (circle leaders), who were common in Morocco until 1942. Especially within Amazigh (Berber) communities, female religious leaders have a long tradition. Given this context, the monarch's idea is not so much revolutionary but is a revival of a dormant institution. In examining historic Muslim female leadership roles in North Africa, Margaret Rausch observed:

> Throughout Africa, local Muslim scholars, in particular those affiliated with Sufi orders, endeavoured to proliferate Islamic knowledge at the scholarly as well as the popular level. In Morocco, like elsewhere in Africa, women were recognized as indispensable in the transmission of Islamic knowledge to other women.[33]

The appointment of female religious leaders in Moroccan mosques can be seen as symbol of modernity, something new in appearance if not substance. To a large extent, *murchidates* serve the political project of the palace rather than having genuine religious authority. The same, however, can be said about *imams*, who also must follow the directions of the Ministry of Islamic Affairs. Individual *imams* preach or carry out their duties as clergy in accordance with official guidelines. *Imams* in Morocco are civil servants, appointed by the Ministry and in the service of the state. Hence the argument that *murchidates* do not possess genuine religious authority has to be seen in the context of the system of government-appointed clergy in Morocco.

Since the programme's inception, Morocco's Ministry of Islamic Affairs each year selects qualified women from thousands of applicants. The women study for about a year and their courses include such subject areas as religion, communications, history, geography, law, computer science, and psychology. The women also are required to be able to recite large portions of the Qur'an. Upon graduation, the *murchidates*, alongside their male counterpart *imams*, are assigned to serve in one of Morocco's more than 40,000 official mosques. *Murchidates* most commonly are sent to work in the impoverished and marginalized urban areas, townships from where the terrorists involved in the 2003 attacks in Casablanca hailed. Female religious leaders are primarily charged with providing counsel to women on issues such as family planning, domestic abuse, child rearing, and women's legal rights, in addition to tending to their spiritual needs. Assigning female religious leaders to otherwise underserved population groups can be seen as part of a larger plan to stem the tide of radical Islamists who heavily recruit among the poor and unemployed. The rationale is that potential terrorists have mothers, sisters, and wives who can exert influence on their male relatives if they are properly guided. These female guides also compete with moderate Islamists who minister and supply services in socially disadvantaged parts of town.

A recurrent theme of this book has been intersectionality, the notion that women's issues are always tied to other important social issues and need to be examined in a larger socio-economic context. The appointment of *murchidates* is no exception. These women – in their function as civil servants – also serve as the king's eyes and ears in those parts of the country where the *makhzen* has no hold, areas where unemployment, poverty, crime, and lawlessness are rampant and illiteracy is high. In the long run, the assignment of religious leaders will not substitute for the absent health and social services and infrastructure in areas without electricity and water and where dwellings are shacks created from corrugated iron.

The appointment of *murchidates* sent shock waves through much of the Muslim world but was hailed in Europe and the United States as a major step in the right direction. In fact, this transformation goes further than reform efforts within the Roman Catholic Church. The largest Christian denomination worldwide continues to insist that priesthood is the sole prerogative of men. In fact, the Moroccan Minister of Religious Affairs Ahmed Taoufiq has argued that the appointment of female religious leaders is intended to inspire women to get more involved in religious and public matters. His is an official call for moderate Muslim women to become more engaged in religious life beyond their homes rather than leave religious discourse mostly to Islamists.

As stated above, *murchidates*, like *imams*, are civil servants, employed by the State. Thus, they have to follow government-prescribed guidelines. Because national and international interest in this new phenomenon of Muslim female religious leaders has been intense, the government has advised them not to avail themselves for interviews with media and local or international scholars unless previously approved by the Ministry. When the main Islamist daily newspaper in Morocco, *Attajdid*, published a series of approved interviews with *murchidates* and women who are members of their congregations, the paper sold out as soon as it hit the newsstands. Nevertheless, there were no stunning revelations in these interviews; *murchidates* did not divulge any potentially controversial details about their work and avoided theological questions. Likewise, the quoted congregants gave almost formulaic responses, saying they preferred sessions lead by *murchidates* since they addressed issues relating to family relationships, childrearing, and their roles of mother and wife. Some said they learned how to 'pray properly'. Still, the fact that people bought this particular newspaper more than any other edition shows the intense local interest in all things related to the relatively new phenomenon of *murchidates*.

Impetus behind the appointment of *murchidates* also derived from the actions of the above-mentioned American Muslim scholar Amina Wadud. Wadud caused an international controversy in 2005 when she broke with time-honoured tradition and led Friday prayers – attended by men and women – in New York City. She previously had done the same at the invitation of Farid Esack in South Africa. In a Muslim-majority country in the process of modernization, Moroccan thinkers found it irksome that important reforms of Islamic religious practices should originate in the predominantly secular or Christian West, thus leading to a widespread assumption that Islam receives its main momentum for change from Muslims in the West. The same applies to Tariq Ramadan who insists that reform in Islam is spearheaded by Western Muslims, first and foremost of course himself. Nevertheless, in training and subsequently appointing female religious leaders in Morocco, the king enlarged the playing field for women's public engagement and brought the plight of socially and economically disenfranchised population groups into focus.

To refer once more to Amina Wadud whose *Qur'an and Woman* is considered a groundbreaking text, one that is read widely by proponents of a third way. In it, she linked social justice with gender equality:

> With regard to social justice, it becomes necessary to challenge patriarchy – not for matriarchy, but for an efficient co-operative

and egalitarian system, which allows and encourages the maximum participation of each member of society. This system would truly respect gender in its contribution, and all tasks that are contributed. This would allow for the growth and expansion of the individual and consequently society at large.[34]

In sum, the efforts of many in Morocco to create a middle ground between Western secularism and Islamism can be overlooked when more radical voices gain the spotlight and generate media controversy. As a third way develops and gains ground, however, it has the potential to become a genuine agent of change. Given that the developments on the ground in the spring of 2011 have overtaken the careful royal planning in Morocco, it remains to be seen just how the various factions of Moroccan society ultimately will come together to create a more open, democratic, and pluralistic society in which women enjoy equal rights.

CHAPTER 4

THE WAY FORWARD

We live in an age of ongoing pluralization of societies. Governments in Maghreb countries no longer emphasize one identifying indicator of citizenship over all others. In the past, their attempts to instil a sense of Arab identity among their citizens have failed in the face of the prevalence of non-Arabs in their populations; that is, a substantial portion of the population in North Africa is either Amazigh (Berber) or of mixed Arab-Berber origins. Further, many individuals in this region resist being placed in a neat category; increasingly, they insist that their personal set of beliefs and values be accepted. Thus, while a Muslim identity is still very important in the eyes of governments as well as citizens, it is no longer a homogenous marker, as young people in particular are asserting their right to adopt an individualized approach to their faith.

In the same spirit, people throughout North Africa took to the streets in the tumultuous spring of 2011 to demand control over their countries' destinies. Their sustained protests – from Tunisia to Egypt, Yemen, Libya, and Syria – had no overt religious overtones. No one marched to have an Islamist state installed. The demonstrations were remarkable, among other reasons, because they were not driven by any particular ideology. In fact, the initial spark in Tunisia was almost apolitical; the 26-year-old, Mohammed Bouazizi, who set himself ablaze in the small town of Sidi Bouzid in December 2010, did so in desperation after police sought once again to take away his already meagre business, an outdoor vegetable and fruit stall. The demonstrations that ensued throughout North Africa and the Middle East turned into rallying calls for democracy.

An important element of these mass protests was the demand for dignity, reflecting the yearning to shake off excessive domestic or foreign domination and allow individual citizens a larger measure of involvement and choice. The protesters' experience with and acknowledgement of the increasing plurality in their societies was a factor in this demand. Such an emphasis on the individual is an integral aspect of globalization because it leads to identities that are more fluid and no longer limited to one primary marker in the formation of national identity.

Globalization has occurred for good or for ill, and is now a fact of life. Western influences weigh especially heavy in countries of the global South owing to historic connections and subsequent economic reliance. Such global interdependence, coupled with the transnational movements of people and ideas, has led to an invigoration of local discourses and, at the same time, to disorientation. Closer contact between people with differing visions for society carries the potential for conflict as familiar conceptions and worldviews are drawn into question. Social media assume an increasingly important role in facilitating the communication, organization, and dissemination of information across boundaries in a manner that defies government control. In the twenty-first century, tranquil isolation is no longer possible. In such times of uncertainty as these, one can observe a revival of the search for assurances, and even absolutes, within religious experience. Such religious revivals are taking place in many areas of the world today, and Morocco is no exception.

The Tunisian revolution and the Arab Spring

As this book was being put to press, major events had unfolded in North Africa in early 2011, including the overthrow of Presidents Zine El Abidine Ben Ali of Tunisia and Hosni Mubarak of Egypt, the uprising against Colonel Muammar Gaddafi in Libya resulting in his violent death in October 2011, continuing riots in Bahrain, Yemen, and Syria. Interestingly, these mass demonstrations, which spread like wildfire throughout the Arab world, began in the central Maghreb (North African West) and quickly spread to the Mashrek (North African East). Maghreb countries are the ones furthest away from the Arab/Muslim

Middle East and are inhabited by various indigenous Berber populations that historically have straddled different cultures. Though the uprisings did not appear to have a strong ethnic component, they are in keeping with the distinct Maghreb cultural mosaic. Largely peaceful mass demonstrations occurred in Morocco in the wake of the overthrow of Tunisia's long-time ruler Ben Ali. These actions resulted in the king's announcement of constitutional reforms that are intended to vest more power in the prime minister, allow for greater regional independence, and affirm the Amazigh cultures within the Kingdom. Supporters of the demonstrations have thus far decried these reform proposals as cosmetic and demanded more substantial changes, especially limiting executive powers and lifting the 'sacred' status of the monarch.

What is remarkable about the mass movements throughout North Africa is that they reflect alliances between young and old, leftwing politicians and Islamists, secular and religious advocates. In Morocco, the Islamist movement Al Adl wa Ihsane (Justice and Charity) is as prominently represented in these demonstrations as are secular activists, confirming what has been proposed in this book, namely the emergence of a third way; that is, a coming together of various strands of thought, from Islamism to secularism, in an attempt to create a new vision for this North African country. Even experts of the region could not have foreseen what has happened since the beginning of 2011 and the ultimate consequences have yet to unfold. Regardless of the eventual outcome, these uprisings have set in motion events that cannot be undone. The courage of people to make their demands loudly, repeatedly, and consistently heard in countries where public questioning of authority comes at great personal risk is extraordinary.

On the newly established political website lakome.com, Moroccan international relations scholar Nizar Messari published an article entitled 'What do we owe to the youth of February 20?',[1] a reference to the date of the first mass demonstrations in all major cities of Morocco. He observed that the people who took to the streets reinvigorated a seemingly stagnant political process in Morocco:

We owe them a big thank you, finally, because of their great openness of spirit, their tolerance and their inclusive attitude ...

They have brought together people from very different groups, women, Berbers, leftwing democrats, Islamist democrats and Human Rights activists from all sides. They have systematically adopted a non-sectarian attitude and one of inclusion, which is rarely seen in our country and elsewhere.[2]

The 2011 demonstrations and uprisings in North Africa have shattered many Western stereotypes and fears. For one, Arabs and Muslims have shown that they are interested in a free and open society and that they can organize peaceful, sustained demonstrations and collaborate with each other across ideological or religious divides. The thousands of people that marched through the streets of Tunis, Cairo, and Casablanca and camped out in public squares until their demands for greater social justice were met have shown that 'global jihad' – the one linked to criminal extremists like Al Qaeda[3] – is not a viable force in these new social movements and national struggles. Clearly, radical Islamists have not been at the forefront of these popular upheavals since moderate Islamists have joined in popular revolts alongside other groups. Neither have fundamentalists usurped leadership and imposed their will on their fellow citizens. As French scholar Olivier Roy, one of the foremost European experts on the role of Islam in politics, stated:

This is not an Islamist revolution ... Particularly striking is the abandonment of conspiracy theories. The United States and Israel – or France, in the case of Tunisia – are no longer identified as the cause of all the misery in the Arab world.[4]

It still remains to be seen how each of the countries that has undergone such sudden and astounding transformation will develop in the long run. We should remember that more than 20 years after the fall of the Berlin Wall in 1989, East and West Germany still have not achieved complete parity. Though the two parts of the country were separated, after all, for only for 28 years by a highly fortified boundary, the authoritarian system that dominated in communist East Germany and deprived its citizens of free access to information and a democratic process, left its mark on the population. Thus, even in a place where people previously had shared a common history, culture, religion, and language, exposure over only one or two generations to a totalitarian system made it difficult to transition to another system of government, education, economy, and so on. The protests and subsequent transformations sweeping through the Arab world are no less important than those that occurred with the demise of the Soviet Union and the end of communism. Of course, significant differences exist between the two situations in terms of expected outcomes. Post-communist East European countries had the opportunity to join the European Union (EU) and the intergovernmental military alliance, the North Atlantic Treaty Organization (NATO), both of which provided an international incentive and framework for their domestic policies. No comparable transnational structures are available to newly emerging Arab governments.

Regardless of what the 2011 uprisings in North Africa and the Middle East are called – the Arab Spring or the Arab revolution – they mark the end of the post-colonial era in that region. In each of the countries concerned, the call and subsequent action for change emanated from local populations who organized themselves without direct input from outside the country. Western Europe, the United States, and the dictators of these countries themselves were caught by surprise. In the case of the Soviet Union, the fall of the Berlin Wall in 1989 and its subsequent demise can, at least in part, be attributed to President Ronald Reagan's policies towards the communist world, best summarized in his powerful appeal at the Brandenburg Gate in 1987: 'Mr. Gorbachev, tear down this Wall!'[5] No Western leader can claim to have issued a similar call to any of the rulers in North Africa or the Middle East. To the contrary, the West overtly and tacitly had propped up most of the regimes in North Africa and the Arab world for several decades. Thus, on many levels, the events in the spring of 2011 demand a re-evaluation of prevailing conceptions of post-colonialism, the nature of Arab societies, and the role of the religion of Islam. Ordinary people in North African and Middle Eastern Muslim-majority countries have proven, then, that they can join together to assert their collective will without the support of a superpower. In the case of North Africa, for example, former colonial master France stood embarrassingly at the sidelines – particularly in the case of Tunisia, where it backed strongman Ben Ali until the last moments before his hasty departure. Further, Islamist organizations joined the movements but were not the prime instigators. Of particular interest in the context of this book is the fact that women participated and contributed alongside men in these protests. In fact, some women were instrumental in organizing demonstrations, mobilizing like-minded individuals and disseminating updates via social media. Whether young or middle-aged, women were front and centre of the popular revolt. Veiled women were anything but submissive, marching in the front rows of protesters in Casablanca, Rabat, and other cities throughout North Africa, except for Libya.[6]

How women will be represented in the new governments that evolve remains to be seen, however. Certainly, the new governments have serious pressing issues to tackle – eradicating unemployment and poverty, limiting corruption, and creating mechanisms for a democratic process – and it is likely that the issue of women's rights will not be at the top of their agendas. Starting a revolution is different from setting up a government, designing a constitution, and putting in place new gender norms. Until all of these tasks are accomplished, past and present models still hold sway. In fact, we cannot really speak of a revolution, as representatives of the people who overthrew governments in Tunisia and Egypt are not the ones who have assumed positions of power there. Yet there can be no doubt that women will demand their rights. This new wave of unrest is unlike the battles for independence fought against colonial powers, in which the achievement of liberation from occupation left women assigned to their pre-colonial, subservient roles in the name of asserting an Islamic identity. In Algeria, the collective memory of women fighting on the forefront of the Algerian war for independence from 1954 to 1962, only to be relegated to the margins of politics afterwards, remains a stark reminder that there are no guarantees for women who actively involve themselves in movements for change. This time, however, it is likely that the majority of educated, professional women throughout North Africa, some of whom have reclaimed their identity as Muslims, will refuse to be relegated to a second-class status.

Of the women I interviewed for this book, the most active in the demonstrations calling for democratic change was Merieme Yefout of the Al Adl wa Ihsane (Justice and Charity) movement. She is an example of a woman who expertly used social networking to garner support for the demonstrations in Morocco, even putting videos on her Facebook page that showed police brutality against protestors. In an interview, she told me about her involvement with the movement for democratic change in Morocco:

> Of course, we support the February 20 movement. The objectives of this movement represent part of what we have called for all along. We have always decried despotism, injustice, and corruption. With all that is happening in the Arab world, it is now or never to support these demands. As for women, we are very much present in the demonstrations and in coordinating events.

Nadia Yassine, for her part, also lent her support to the demonstrators, particularly those of the younger generation. In talking with her, I learned that she believes the call of the Justice and Charity movement to limit the powers of the king finally resonated with the larger population, which no longer is afraid to march in the streets to make such demands known.[7] But she warned that what she calls 'cosmetic changes to the constitution' proposed by the king would not solve Morocco's problems. As she has for years, she insisted on 'genuine public discourse' with the goal of eliminating the entitlement mentality of a small group of elite Moroccans. As expected, members of the political, economic, and military elite, Les Forces Armées Royales (FAR), or Royal Moroccan Armed Forces, as well as the circle of the *makhzen* (the powerful circle of people associated with monarch) have stayed away from the demonstrations and refrained from supporting calls for democracy. Naturally, it is the national elite connected to the palace that stands to lose the most if the current system were to change in favour of one that allows for greater transparency, less corruption, and genuine democracy.

Yet, even among the elite, there are those who support the movement for change. Chief among them is Asma Lamrabet, who shared her position with me:

> The changes we are experiencing now can only be positive even if it is difficult to adequately evaluate the perspectives. A page of history is about to be turned and authoritarian regimes can no longer endure. This is the first time since independence that the people have rebelled, especially the youth, who are demanding change in the name of dignity, freedom and universal values. There is a real awakening of consciousness and this is extraordinary! I am very optimistic for our future generations.

What distinguishes the uprising in Morocco from those in other North African and Middle Eastern countries is the absence of a demand for the king – the supreme leader – to step down. Rather, up to now the call for reform is focused on changes to the existing system. This focus has enabled the monarch to respond to the demonstrators with a more measured tone. Further, because many of the protestors are unemployed and routinely demonstrate in front of the parliament building in Rabat, the palace was able to deflect the political dimension of the recurring demonstrations by framing the protests as an expression of social and economic problems rather than discontent with the king in particular. Indeed, some of the most vocal demonstrators in Morocco have been plagued by longstanding under- or unemployment, exacerbated by the widespread lack of economic and professional opportunities. In addition, the mass demonstrations in Morocco revealed a crack in the palace's efforts to take the lead in religious reforms. While the palace created various organizations like the Mohammedian Council of Religious Scholars to spearhead the modernization agenda of Morocco's official moderate Islam, the continued persecution, incarceration, or at the very least vilification of non-violent Islamists like Adlists, demonstrate that religious freedom – a key component of any democratic society – is still a far cry from reality.

Regardless of the exact outcomes of the current struggles, outcomes that cannot be determined at the time of this writing, it is likely that the epochal changes underway in North Africa and the Arab world eventually will put to rest real or perceived dichotomies between the Muslim and the Western world. Just as discourse in the West concerning 'Muslim women' is typically reductionist and often influenced by stereotypes, discourse about the West in parts of the Muslim world is equally simplistic. Mervat Hatem referred to this phenomenon as 'Occidentalism',[8] which can be thought of as a counterpart to Orientalism. Actually, however, part of the reason for the contentious relationship between the West and the Muslim world may be due to their similarities rather than their differences. With regard to the status of women, some of the practices that continue in the Muslim world were, until recently, the norm in some of the Western world, southern Europe – the Mediterranean region – especially. Wearing a headscarf was required for entrance to a church, for example, and widows in Europe routinely covered their heads in public. Exaggerated notions of family honour vested in female family members were as common in Sicily as they are in today's North Africa. Many of the significant economic and cultural differences that have evolved between the countries of the Mediterranean region have occurred only within the past century.

Understanding a culture on its own terms is always difficult, as our own reference points and perspectives are shaped by our particular cultural experiences. Many in the West share the perception that Islam is a hindrance to women's rights. Conversely, many in Morocco fear that feminism is an imperialistic, Western, anti-religious project. Yet, it is neither Islam, nor religion in general, that is the main stumbling block to women's emancipation in North Africa and elsewhere; rather, it is the existence of entrenched patriarchal structures, extending from within the family through the educational system and the government. Women are a focal point in the dismantling of such structures. Gender provides a prism through which modernity can be imagined, yet everyone looking through that prism sees something different. Gender issues are at the core of society and, as most people interviewed for this book have made clear, working for increased rights for women is best seen not as a battle between men and women but as an endeavour that aims to benefit all members of a society. Of course, because women are not a homogeneous group their goals and aspirations differ. Moroccan women's rights activists across the spectrum have emphasized women's role as mothers and urged that laws be enacted to accommodate special needs relating to parenthood. Additionally, because the mother is considered the bearer and first transmitter of culture, most people have strong opinions, and thus a vested interest, in what she is supposed to project and pass on to the next generation. As Newcomb wrote: 'Women serve as signifiers of religion, of modernity, national identity or religiosity, not as actual beings with agency but as representations of competing ideologies.'[9]

Religion and culture are linked to some extent in every country. In the West, separation of church and state legally limits the influence of the state over religious matters and guarantees freedom of religion. In most of the Middle East and North Africa, there is no such separation. Countries in North Africa generally have a Ministry of Religious Affairs because Islam is the official religion of the state and religious leaders like *imams* are civil servants, beholden to government authorities. Morocco is something of a special case because of the status of the monarch, who is believed to be a descendant of the Prophet, and whose position is considered 'sacred'. Furthermore, for most Moroccans, the monarchy is a source of pride and a unifying factor. Still, as the 2011 uprisings made clear, the sacred nature of the monarchy has come increasingly under popular scrutiny. In the past, only the Justice and Charity movement openly criticized the constitutionally protected status of the king and his role as supreme religious leader. That thousands of people took to the streets of major Moroccan cities in 2011 to demand that the powers of the king be limited was an entirely new phenomenon, even if the people did not call for the monarch's resignation. Perhaps one reason for this is that monarchs are expected to live in splendour – unlike dictators who are reviled and overthrown because they live lavish lifestyles out of step with their impoverished populations. Moroccans compare their king to royalty in Britain, Belgium, the Netherlands, Sweden, and other monarchs in the Arab world, but not with the presidents of republics. What is more, kings and queens do not serve at the will of the people; thus, they never sit on the throne as a result of fraudulent elections.

Gender and religion

The three religions of the book – as the religions of Judaism, Christianity, and Islam are referred to – are all based on divine revelations that include a creation story in which God made living beings, male and female, and assigned different roles to each. For believers, such expressions of divine design can be the basis of the social order. Thus, debates about gender issues that take place in Morocco must be understood beyond their political or social contexts and include a significant religious dimension as well. The understanding of what constitutes a marriage, for instance, is derived from religious dogma; in the West it is traditionally the union between one man and one woman, in the Muslim world between one man and up to four wives. Thus, if laws concerning marriage, divorce, and inheritance are to be changed in North Africa, it is necessary for feminists and women's rights activists to communicate a revised explanation of how the world should be ordered in modern times. In the West, one sees conflict with such decidedly religious undertones in controversies surrounding gay marriage or abortion; in Morocco, conflict occurs in relation to issues like polygamy and inheritance laws. In all these conflicts pertaining to marriage and the family, the laws governing them are essential in shaping the gender norms of a culture.

Among Western feminists, the quest for women's rights was grounded not in religious beliefs but in the notion of a social contract. In contrast, Morocco's King Mohammed VI proclaimed that the 2004 Personal Status Code reform was achieved *because of* and not *in spite of* religion. In Morocco, religious and social reforms must go hand in hand. Thus, the Personal Status Code reform actually paved the way for the appointment of female religious leaders in Morocco. This relationship is unlike that in the West, where the separation of church and state allows religious entities largely to abide by their own rules. Religious institutions in the West are at liberty to remain out of step with modern notions of gender equality and anti-discrimination requirements because laws applied in the public sphere have no bearing on internal rules of a religious denomination. The Personal Status Code reform in Morocco has been one important step in achieving gender equality and is directly linked to the institutionalizing of female religious leaders, the *murchidates*. Still, achieving gender equality remains a long and often arduous process, as cultural and religious norms passed from one generation to the next offer stability, continuity, and a sense of identity.

Gender and democracy

Under former President George W. Bush, the US government in 2002 embarked on a campaign to promote women's rights in the Arab world, most notably through the Middle East Partnership Initiative (MEPI). The campaign was based on the faulty perception that Muslim women need the help of the West on their way to emancipation, a point that has been refuted in this book. Even more misinformed was the fundamental idea behind the initiative – that democracy is integral to women's rights. This was a flawed assumption, since non-democratic states in former socialist and communist countries achieved women's rights without democratic governments. The notion of an inextricable link between democracy and equal rights for women is also weakened by historical evidence, since Western countries were democratic long before they endorsed gender equality. In fact, the United States developed democratic institutions more than a hundred years before women – and men of colour, for that matter – had the right to vote. Another example of the uncertain relationship between democracy and women's rights can be found in democratic India, where the practice of 'gendercide' – that is, abortion in cases where the foetus is female – is even more common today than in the past owing to the widespread use of ultrasound.

Democracy, then, is not necessarily the prime engine of change with regard to women's rights. Had the Personal Status Code reform been decided by plebiscite in Morocco, it most likely would not have passed, as evidenced by the demonstrations against the reform by thousands of people in the streets of Casablanca in 2000 and the results of a 2009 survey that concluded that the majority of Moroccans think that the king has gone too far in advancing women's rights. By the same token, had civil rights legislation been up for a popular vote in the United

States, it may not have been enacted in 1964. Thus, enlightened leaders can be as important in advancing large-scale social transformation
as the expressed 'will of the people'. Nevertheless, it is important to
cultivate the acceptance of new legislation by citizens if it is indeed
to propel society forward. For this to happen, public discourse is
necessary.

Public discourses do help shape individual opinions, but because
academics as well as the mass media often emphasize the differences
between viewpoints, it is easy to overlook points of convergence.
Despite the title of this book, three distinctly separate discourses on
women's issues do not exist in Morocco. The boundaries between the
various positions are fluid and often overlap, despite vehement claims
to the contrary by proponents of certain positions. This ambiguity
of stance is especially the case for those women's rights activists who
base their positions on religious texts. Because of the absence of a central authority figure for all Muslims, much like in Judaism, divergent
interpretations of Islam can and have co-existed throughout the centuries. Thus, consistent with historical precedents, one can find a range of
positions among those who call themselves Islamists, both within and
between Muslim-majority countries. As shown in previous chapters,
within Morocco there are even mutually exclusive strands of Islamism.
Some groups uphold the legality of polygamy and unequal inheritance laws as non-negotiable tenets of Muslim life, while others wish to
abolish it in the name of Islam. That said, supporters of polygamy and
traditional inheritance laws, such as members of the PJD, MUR, and
ORCF, have more extensive rationales for their position. They argue
that polygamy is not widely practised in Morocco, and that the majority of Moroccans are relatively poor, with little or nothing to inherit in
the first place, so changing laws on these two issues would affect only
a very small portion of the population. Islamists of various persuasions emphasize religion as their most important point of reference,
and share a focus on women's rights issues and a critique of the West,
however. Western consumer society, unbridled individualism, and a
concept of gender equality that aims to neutralize differences between
men and women are rejected as aberrations of modern civilization. On
these points, Moroccans of many different stripes agree.

Though I have spoken of a third way in this book as a new phenomenon, it is in some ways a return to ideas proposed by Moroccan thinkers around the time of the country's independence from France. They called for a reinterpretation of sacred scriptures that would acknowledge modernity as well as preserve their cultural and religious identity. During the early part of the twentieth century, Moroccan leaders had no sense of what we now think of as Muslim particularism – that is, the notion of Islam as being unique as a religious as well as state project. According to this concept, Islam is unlike Christianity, the predominant religion of countries that are today modern and secular states. In fact, Moroccan thinkers in the early part of the twentieth century believed that modernity could very well take root in their Muslim society and supported development in this direction. Thus, third way discourse nowadays actually picks up where early modernists left off, and after years of acrimonious division between secularists and certain elements of Islamism, they have begun to demonstrate a nascent inclination to find common ground. This convergence was most evident in early 2011, in the countrywide demonstrations calling for more democracy and accountability in Morocco. As in other North African countries with extraordinary upheavals, like Tunisia, Libya, and Egypt, in Morocco a wide range of the population – young and old, Islamists and secularists – demonstrated together to demand political reforms. Importantly, though members of Islamist organizations participated widely, there was a conspicuous absence of banners calling for an Islamist state.

Gender and Islamists

Interesting developments are occurring within various Islamist movements in Morocco. The leading female members are shifting their positions on gender and are now, on some issues, closer to the ideas of secularists than of traditional, conservative Islamists. They embrace equal rights for women and even advocate for men to become more involved in household chores and childrearing. Some Islamists have joined the democracy movements sweeping throughout North Africa and the Middle East. These loose coalitions are mostly composed of idealistic people who believe above all in the collaboration of like-minded individuals. They are people who want their governments to become more democratic, less corrupt, and more aggressive about producing economic opportunities for their citizens. They may differ in their religious or political beliefs but are driven by the quest for more egalitarian and participatory societies and a rebuilding of their nations. It remains to be seen if proponents of gender complementarity (a concept described in previous chapters) will in time replace this notion with the concept of equality or if they will continue to insist that women's role in society should be defined primarily by their function as wives and mothers.

However, proponents of a third way and some conservative Islamists in Morocco part ways around the concepts of gender complementarity and gender equality. A belief in gender complementarity justifies inequality because it emphasizes the inherent differences between men and women. Viewing men and women as intrinsically different cannot result in laws that render them legal equals. The idea behind complementarity is analogous to the thinking behind the 'separate but equal' doctrine in the United States in the pre-civil rights era. This disingenuous approach to equal rights meant that facilities, public services, and educational institutions could remain racially segregated as long as they were 'equal' for African Americans. The principle ultimately failed and was abolished because, in reality, separate never meant equal. Particularly in regard to education, schools for African Americans remained inferior to those for white students. Similarly, in Morocco, the idea of complementarity can be used to justify not sending girls to school or restricting women's access to professional careers. Undoubtedly, the quest for gender complementarity will not result in women's emancipation.

While ideas about women's rights in Morocco are many, concrete proposals are few. At this point in time, Islamists and third way proponents are concerned mainly with changing mentalities and attitudes. Altering people's understandings about women's rights, while important, is a long-term task, however, and there are few measurable outcomes of this process. What is needed immediately in Morocco is a new reality on the ground, above all educational and professional opportunities. Women's empowerment has to include sustained government efforts to bring women from the economic margins into the mainstream. Secular women's associations have been successful in the past because they have advocated for specific, tangible goals, such as the Personal Status Code reform and the signing of the Convention on the Elimination of all Forms of Discrimination against Women (CEDAW). Because their demands were specific, the palace felt compelled to respond. However, since the passing of the Personal Status Code reform several years ago, secular women's rights organizations have not evolved to keep pace with societal trends, particularly the increasing emergence of religious performance in public spaces. Whether wearing the veil is an act of piety or a fashion statement is ultimately irrelevant; the fact that increasing numbers of young women now put on the *hijab* in Morocco is a sign that religion is asserting itself in the public sphere and is a major element of the public discourse on gender.

On Internet sites and through hundreds of Arab satellite TV channels, religion is a recurring theme, and a variety of viewpoints are advocated and discussed with vehemence. In this regard, Islam is likely the most dynamic religion in the world at present. In addition to conversions to Islam among people of other faiths or no faith, internal conversion – that is, turning to a more stringent form of Islam by a Muslim – occurs with greater frequency.

Who is a proper Muslim?

In Morocco, Islamists proselytize among their fellow religionists in the cities as well as in rural areas, where approximately 44 per cent of the population resides. Actually, before the Arab Spring eclipsed all other events in North Africa, there was a great deal of competition for the souls of rural Moroccans. In the predominantly Berber regions, Islamists solicited stricter adherence to Islam by offering financial incentives to heads of households in return for the veiling of their wives and daughters. Anecdotal accounts from rural areas reveal that government-appointed *imams* have haggled with representatives of various Islamist factions – to the bewilderment of a local population that is more preoccupied with its subsistence than with theological minutiae.

Islamists in rural areas also offer grassroots services, such as literacy classes and, through charitable outlets, occasionally food and clothing distribution.[10] In slums surrounding big cities (in Morocco the French term *bidonville* is routinely used for such areas) this type of proselytizing has been taking place for some time. The government is actively trying to counter these efforts by sending officially appointed religious leaders out into the rural areas and *bidonvilles* near Casablanca and Rabat, attempting to implant its own version of moderate Islam in disenfranchised population groups. Something of a competition exists between state-sponsored Islam and Islamist organizations, a competition that intensified in the spring of 2010, when the Moroccan government expelled a number of expatriates suspected of proselytizing in the name of Christianity.[11] Also affected by these drastic measures were orphanages run by Christians, which were nearly closed after their expatriate staff members were given an ultimatum to leave the country. Small associations assisting refugees from sub-Saharan countries came under scrutiny as well, the irony being that the majority of refugees were Christian and not in danger of rejecting Islam. Most Western media reported on these expulsions as a sign of growing religious intolerance towards non-Muslims in Morocco, when in fact they reflected domestic wrangling over who best defends and represents Islam, the government or the Islamist organizations. The widely publicized show of force that occurred actually represented an attempt by the palace to demonstrate to the local population that it was the prime institution upholding Islam, and that the interventions of the Islamists were not needed to protect the country's Muslim heritage. The implied message was that while all Islamists are Muslims, Muslims need not be Islamists. This internal strife foreshadowed the rebellions that took place in early 2011. The demonstrations revealed that regardless of how modern and religiously and culturally authentic the palace and the government presented themselves, masses of people wanted more say in how their country is run, and were capable of incorporating people with differing religious beliefs to mobilize in support of that goal.

Gay rights

Gay rights are excluded from Moroccan discussions about gender equality, though gender discourse is deeply connected to issues of identity and boundaries. Androgyny, transsexuality, and homosexuality all question widely held certainties about gender, body, spacial, or proxemic norms, and boundaries. In her seminal book *Gender Trouble* (1999), Judith Butler argued – as other feminist scholars before her – that because gender norms are constructed and performed they are not pre-determined. Further, since clear categories for appropriate behaviour provide meaning and are reinforced over generations, in time they confirm a belief that they reflect the natural order of things. Most Moroccans agree that homosexuality should remain illegal in their country despite timid efforts by some human rights and gay rights advocates to establish gay rights organizations. Though the monthly gay publication *Mithly* was denied a circulation licence in 2010, it exists underground and online and is the first Arab-language gay publication in Morocco.

Novelist Abdellah Taïa caused a stir as the first Moroccan writer to open up about his homosexuality. In his 2008 semi-autobiographical novel *Une mélancholie arabe* (*An Arab Melancholy*) the young novelist chronicled the coming of age of a gay Moroccan boy in a religiously conservative urban environment. Taïa now lives in France and has said that his literary success offers him protection when he returns to his home country to speak about gay and minority rights. Not surprisingly, Taïa became one of the first outspoken supporters of calls for a more open, democratic, and transparent society, as expressed in the spring 2011 mass demonstrations, even though gay rights were not part of the protestors' agenda at all. Certainly, there is no intrinsic link between gay rights and women's rights in Morocco, which is a long way from granting sexual minorities protection under the law. Still, the fear among Islamists that gender equality will ultimately lead to a broader rethinking of gender norms is not unfounded. Thus, the alliance of a diverse cross-section of Moroccan citizens with seemingly irreconcilable positions on gender diversity in the 2011 spring uprisings is rather tenuous. Nevertheless, though some activists remain apprehensive about rethinking gender norms and boundaries, many are now questioning other inequalities, such as those created by social class. This line of thinking is consistent with the focus of the protesters on inequities other than women's rights and gender diversity.

New activists, new demands

The emergence of the women's rights movement in Morocco followed the success of the nationalist movement for independence from France. Just as the nationalist drive in mid-twentieth-century Morocco was spearheaded by urban, educated men of the elite, the women's rights movement in Morocco today is spurred by secular women's rights associations led by members of the bourgeoisie who stand to gain the most from its successes. This situation leaves educated women from modest backgrounds dissatisfied, since despite their university education they find themselves excluded from opportunities to rise to decision-making roles in these established secular women's rights associations. Though they lack social connections, they still wish to play a part in the shaping of their country, are frustrated with the status quo, and often feel alienated from such secular associations. In addition, they tend to be attracted to religiously inspired action, are critical of the authoritarian state and patriarchal structures, and seek meaningful engagement in social change. These women do not support a totalitarian Islam; to the contrary, they insist on liberal access to their religion and the right to individualize their beliefs. A third way has the potential to tap into these unrealized human resources and seize on their social, political, intellectual, and economic disappointment by offering avenues of involvement on various levels.

Women who turn to religiously inspired feminism point out that Islam envisions a social project; it offers a blueprint for a particular social order. Obviously there is a difference between Islamic norms and reality. No matter how eternal the revelation on which Islam was founded, the *fiqh* (jurisprudence) that developed based on the Islamic scriptures changed over time and responded to the challenges of specific eras. Such shifts demonstrate how laws can evolve and change without disrespecting the sacred revelation. New discourses have emerged throughout Islamic history, and clearly current trends are in keeping with historical precedents. Iranian anthropologist Ziba Mir-Hosseini, who lives in the United Kingdom, has conducted extensive research in Morocco. She is a founding member of *Musawah* ('equality' in Arabic), a global movement that advocates for equality and justice in the Muslim family. She argued:

> One of the paradoxical consequences of the late twentieth century rise of political Islam is that it helped create space in which Muslim women could reconcile their faith and identity with the struggle for gender equality. This is not because Islamicists[12] offered an egalitarian vision of gender relations, but because their return to *shari'a* and attempt to translate the patriarchal notions inherent in traditional interpretations of Islamic law into state laws and policies provoked many women to increasing criticism of these notions and spurred them to greater activism.[13]

Activism of all sorts is evident all over Morocco. From social media activists who rally around calls for democracy and social justice, to informal partnerships of activists from a variety of backgrounds, to female members of the Islamist Justice and Charity movement, many Moroccans feel energized by the relatively peaceful uprisings in the fellow Maghreb country of Tunisia, though they reject the violence that has engulfed Libya. Those with strong religious leanings are applying a central concept of Islamic scripture and philosophy – justice – to modern norms of equality, individual agency, and calls for democracy. Yet, however universal the idea of justice appears in theory, conflict occasionally erupts between those who seek to apply it differently, or in different contexts. At the transnational level, for example, collaboration between Muslim women's advocacy groups is not always smooth. A case in point is the French NGO Ni putes, ni soumises (NPNS), or Neither Whores nor Submissive, founded in France in 2003 by French women of North African origin with the goal of combating intra-communal violence against women. Founded primarily by Muslim women, NPNS members have taken up the cause of Muslim women who are seen by traditionalists as

not conforming to 'proper Muslim standards'. The event that initiated the formation of NPNS occurred in a *banlieue* (socially disadvantaged neighbourhoods on the outskirts of Paris and other large
cities in France) where several young women who did not put on the
Muslim headscarf were gang raped and beaten by young men of their
communities who sought to punish them for their immodest attire
or behaviour. When French NPNS activists attempted in 2009 to
establish a branch of the organization in Morocco, however, they were
met with widespread criticism. Although some of the NPNS activists
were of Moroccan origin, Islamists joined ranks with the government
in rejecting their presence on the south side of the Mediterranean.
They considered not only the name of the organization offensive but
also its overly frank public discussion of delicate matters like sexual
morals and male-on-female violence.

Members of NPNS say they deliberately chose their provocative
name because, in their experience, Muslim women of North African
origin are often portrayed as being either overly permissive with
loose morals or subservient and oppressed. The decision to call their
association 'Neither Whores nor Submissive', expressed their aim to
affirm a Muslim identity that provocatively refutes such stereotypes.
NPNS has worked mostly in the socially disadvantaged immigrant
neighbourhoods in France and addressed a variety of problems in
these communities. Theirs is a new type of feminist Muslim wom-
en's organization, and its contributions were eventually recognized
by the French government. In 2007, founding member Fadela Amara
was even appointed Secretary of State for Urban Policies in France.
Yet, on the other side of the Mediterranean, no such recognition
was forthcoming. To the contrary, only the Moroccan organization
Solidarité Féminine,[14] or Feminine Solidarity, openly welcomed
NPNS members in Casablanca. Though it originated in Morocco,
Solidarité Féminine is also controversial there because it addresses
the needs of unwed mothers and victims of domestic abuse. The
case of NPNS is but one example of how complicated transnational
cooperation can be – even when the organization in question is predominantly Muslim and its leading members share a similar or even
identical cultural heritage.

Intra-communal and domestic violence are, of course, not unique to any particular population group. In fact, some Islamists frequently assert that Western feminists have not been able to eradicate the problem of domestic violence within their own borders and therefore cannot serve as an example for women's rights in Morocco. They find unconvincing the argument that legal equality does not correlate with violence against women. In all, Muslim women's rights activism in Morocco and elsewhere extends over a large spectrum, with differing individuals and groups focusing on different issues based on their importance to them. While such differences should be expected, the point bears repeating because it illustrates the heterogeneity of Muslim women, who are often viewed by non-Muslims as a homogeneous group.

International conventions

Transnational cooperation between women's advocacy groups, whether on a relatively small bilateral NGO level (such as the failed effort to establish a branch of the French NPNS in Morocco) or on a grand international scale, is almost always fraught with complications. A case in point is the United Nations Convention on the Elimination of all Forms of Discrimination against Women (CEDAW), to which I have referred in previous chapters. Secular women's rights associations in Morocco have successfully pushed the Moroccan government to sign on to this convention, providing another example of the responsiveness of the palace when confronted with specific demands, in this case backed by the United Nations, an international body of which it is a member. The following section contains a closer look at the issues surrounding the implementation of this international agreement, since it sheds light on the complexity of gender issues beyond narrowly defined domestic women's rights demands.

In 1979, the General Assembly of the United Nations adopted the CEDAW, which defines discrimination against women as 'any distinction, exclusion or restriction made on the basis of sex which has the effect or purpose of impairing or nullifying the recognition, enjoyment or exercise by women of human rights and fundamental freedoms'. The CEDAW can be likened to an international bill of rights for women;

it consists of 30 articles defining discrimination and also offers strategies to help minimize or eliminate discrimination against women.[15]
Countries that have ratified the CEDAW are required to submit
reports to the United Nations every four years to describe their current status of implementation and offer a gap analysis; that is, explain-
ing the steps to be taken for full implementation. Morocco expressed
specific reservations about the convention and for decades refused to
sign it. After years of deliberation, the Moroccan government finally
acceded in 1993 but with such numerous and detailed reservations
that it rendered the signing almost invalid. In marking the 60th anniversary of the Universal Declaration of Human Rights in 2008, the
king announced the lifting of Morocco's reservations to CEDAW but
full implementation has yet to be achieved.

To most Western readers, the CEDAW appears reasonable and not
particularly controversial. Yet governments of most MENA countries
have voiced reservations about articles they deem to be in contrast
with their national constitutions or in conflict with Islamic law. It
should be noted here that Muslim-majority countries are not the only
ones expressing such reservations. The Israeli government also considers certain articles of the CEDAW as contradicting its particular version of religiously based Judaic family law.

In international practice, reservations are used to reconcile two
opposing interests. In the case of the CEDAW, the interests are individual states on one side and the international community, as represented by the United Nations, on the other. When there is an inherent
conflict between the provisions of the State's constitution and the
Convention, states can register a reservation, meaning in principle they
agree to the Convention and ratify it while at the same time making
clear that certain provisions cannot be implemented in their respective countries. In this day and age of global interdependence, most
governments cannot outright ignore or reject a convention such as the
CEDAW. Recognizing that interests may differ, the UN has demonstrated substantial flexibility in the handling of conventions as the
case of Morocco demonstrates. However, the United Nations does not
possess the power to prosecute states for not upholding a convention
that it has signed.

When Morocco first considered agreeing to the CEDAW in 1993 it did so with major reservations. At the time, it was attempting to strike a balance between internationally accepted norms while at the same time retaining its national autonomy. However, by all accounts the reservations of the Moroccan government were so numerous that its accession to the CEDAW was, in effect, meaningless.[16] One of the points of concern for the palace was Article 2 of the CEDAW, which concerned the issue of succession to the throne. According to the Moroccan constitution only a male heir can become monarch. Though the CEDAW's Article 2 may seem general, the Moroccan government clearly understood that ratification would mean the possibility of changing the face of the monarchy. Article 2 of the CEDAW reads:

> States Parties condemn discrimination against women in all its forms, agree to pursue by all appropriate means and without delay a policy of eliminating discrimination against women and, to this end, undertake:
>
> (a) To embody the principle of the equality of men and women in their national constitutions or other appropriate legislation if not yet incorporated therein and to ensure, through law and other appropriate means, the practical realization of this principle;
>
> (b) To adopt appropriate legislative and other measures, including sanctions where appropriate, prohibiting all discrimination against women;
>
> (c) To establish legal protection of the rights of women on an equal basis with men and to ensure through competent national tribunals and other public institutions the effective protection of women against any act of discrimination;
>
> (d) To refrain from engaging in any act or practice of discrimination against women and to ensure that public authorities and institutions shall act in conformity with this obligation;
>
> (e) To take all appropriate measures to eliminate discrimination against women by any person, organization or enterprise;

(f) To take all appropriate measures, including legislation, to modify or abolish existing laws, regulations, customs and practices which constitute discrimination against women;

(g) To repeal all national penal provisions which constitute discrimination against women.

Thus, in that the guidelines of the CEDAW conflict with a specific Moroccan constitutional provision concerning the gender of the monarch, its acceptance would require a fundamental rethinking of the monarchy. Further, Morocco is a hereditary monarchy, so according to the CEDAW a daughter should be able to ascend to the throne. Allowing for a queen would be akin to imagining a female pope of the Roman Catholic Church. Though one of the demands of the Moroccan demonstrators in the spring of 2011 was the revocation of Articles 19 and 23[17] of the Moroccan Constitution, which enshrine the king's role as *Amir al-Muminin*, or Commander of the Faithful, and uphold the sacredness of the person of the king, the protestors were not concerned with the possibility of a female monarch.

Another contentious issue related to the CEDAW concerned nationality. Article 9 of the CEDAW pertains to a woman's right to pass her nationality on to her children. In the past, children of Moroccan fathers had a right to Moroccan citizenship, but not those of a Moroccan mother and a foreign father. In part due to the CEDAW, this provision was changed, and women now can pass their nationality to their children regardless of the father's nationality. The law now states that a child born in Morocco to a Moroccan mother and a foreign father is entitled to the mother's nationality on the condition that the child declares a desire to acquire Moroccan nationality two years before reaching the legal age of majority. In addition, at the time of this declaration the child must be a full-time resident of Morocco. By contrast, in the United States current law states that anyone born on United States soil is an American citizen; place of birth, *jus solis*, is the prime determining factor for citizenship. This system is different from that in most countries in the world, where *jus sanguinis* (the law of blood) co-determines the right of citizenship according to ancestry.

The CEDAW's Article 16[18] presents the biggest stumbling block for countries that have a religious set of laws pertaining to personal status. This is the case in all countries that have a Personal Status Code rooted in religious laws, which includes most Muslim-majority countries as well as Israel. As discussed in previous chapters, with the 2004 Personal Status Code reform, Morocco has established a family law that largely conforms to the CEDAW stipulations. Twenty years after the original CEDAW document was drawn up (though not ratified by many countries worldwide), the United Nations developed an Optional Protocol (OP), a separate treaty that, while not creating a new set of rights, provided procedures by which women can claim certain rights contained in the convention.

In 2006, the previously mentioned Association Démocratique des Femmes du Maroc (ADFM), or Democratic Association of Moroccan Women, organized a regional conference entitled 'Equality without Reservation' in order to assess Morocco's progress in abiding by the CEDAW and exert domestic and international pressure on Morocco to do so more fully. That same year, on the occasion of International Women's Day, the Moroccan Ministry of Justice issued a statement announcing the withdrawal of Morocco's reservations to Articles 2, 9, 15, and 16 of the CEDAW, which had been approved conditionally, meaning that certain passages were substituted with alternative phrasing. Two years later, on the 60th anniversary of the Universal Declaration of Human Rights, King Mohammed VI declared: 'Given the advanced legislation adopted by our country, the said reservations are now obsolete.'[19] However, since removing its reservations to the CEDAW, the Moroccan government still has not clearly defined how it plans to implement all the stipulations contained in the convention. Nevertheless, in acceding to the convention without reservations, the Moroccan government has expressed its intention to move forward and anchor itself firmly within the international community.

From a Western perspective, it is easy to underestimate the importance of such international conventions, as they do not occupy a prominent place in public discourse. It should be noted, however, that to date the United States has not ratified the CEDAW. Conventions do reflect the will of international bodies like the United Nations to enact certain universal norms and legal codes, and are a vital aspect of creating an 'international community'. The role of the United Nations in putting together the building blocks for women's rights in a globally interconnected world frequently is not fully appreciated in the West. Certainly, it is correct to argue that international conventions commonly reflect Eurocentric norms and typically are not as applicable in countries with different sets of values, norms, and laws.

Just as in other countries that experienced sustained foreign domination, Morocco insists on its right to self-determination. Thus, Morocco experiences a dilemma: it would like to be a member in good standing of the international community, the organizations of the United Nations included, and at the same time it wants to retain a sense of ownership of the domestic process of change that their participation in the international community requires. International pressures bear most heavily on nations whose social or business activities are in the process of growth and industrialization, referred to as emerging markets. These countries have the most to gain – or lose – by being considered accepted global team-players; this puts countries such as Morocco, which is an emerging market, in an awkward situation.

International relations scholars have coined the term 'norm cascading' to describe a process in which norms like human rights or women's rights emerge in a set of places, gain transnational legitimacy, and eventually, upon reaching a tipping point, cascade and are adopted throughout the international system.[20] This process erodes national sovereignty to a certain extent, because non-state actors such as the United Nations or NGOs undermine state sovereignty by proposing or operating under certain norms that are not fully accepted by individual countries. The women's rights discourse in Morocco has to be understood in the larger context of international systems. The insistence of the Moroccan government as well as certain women's rights activists on developing a culturally authentic approach to women's rights is necessary for the Kingdom to maintain its internal legitimacy. Consequently, sometimes concessions to international conventions are tactical rather than substantive and the CEDAW is a good example of this.

In addition to the CEDAW, there are several other international agreements that have an effect on women. First and foremost among these are trade accords, because many of the jobs created as a result of the accords will be held by them. One example is the Euro-Mediterranean Association Agreement (EMAA), also referred to as the Barcelona process, which Morocco signed with the European Union in 1996. The European Union is the Kingdom's most important trading partner, and the agreement is scheduled to lead to the successive establishment of a free trade area beginning in 2010. The EU signed similar agreements with the southern Mediterranean countries of Lebanon, Egypt, Israel, and, in North Africa, Algeria and Tunisia. In addition to liberalizing trade, the goal of such accords is also political, social, and cultural cooperation. From a European standpoint, these accords are also intended to stem the tide of tens of thousands of migrants who use Morocco as a transit migration country. Most of these migrants are from countries south of the Sahara, and they cross Morocco on their way across the Strait of Gibraltar to southern Spain.

While in the past, the majority of refugees and migrants fled from war and political crisis in their homelands, today a substantial number leave for economic reasons. With stricter European border controls, many now remain in Morocco or are immediately returned to North Africa before they even land on the shores of southern Europe. These migrants add to the already substantial number of unemployed in Morocco and are resented by many Moroccans in part because they make more difficult the efforts of Moroccans who themselves are trying to make the narrow sea passage in hopes of finding better economic opportunities in Europe. Because the most important reason for transnational migration is lack of employment prospects, the EMAA is supposed to lead to large-scale, income-generating projects in Morocco, especially in the northern region around the port city of Tangier. Such increased employment opportunities will benefit women, even though many of the jobs initially may be in lower-level manufacturing or service industries. The efforts of the EMAA also stand to accelerate the urbanization process in Morocco, as much of the labour force comes from the Moroccan hinterland, especially the rural areas of the Rif Mountains that lie beyond Tangier.

Conclusions

In spite of the uncertainties that come with the rapid landslide of change sweeping through North Africa and the Middle East, this is indeed a time of hope. The disenfranchised masses of the population, educated but unemployed or underemployed young people, women, moderate Islamists, disillusioned former political activists, all came together to show their clout in the spring of 2011. Armed with nothing but laptops and cell phones, courageous youth left fear behind and overthrew rulers that had been in office all their lives, like the ageing dictators Hosni Mubarak of Egypt and Ben Ali of Tunisia, who had long lived in their presidential bubbles, out of touch with their fellow countrymen. The dictators' systems of control of information and mass media failed in the age of satellite television and social media. Though major upheavals erupted over a five-month period in six countries – Tunisia, Egypt, Yemen, Bahrain, Libya, and Syria – in none of the countries where regimes were overthrown have the leaders of the revolution taken power. This is largely because these uprisings were not guided by proponents of a single ideology, but by people with different religious and political dispositions who came together to call for dignity and self-determination for all citizens. The lack of a coherent organization by protestors made impossible a rapid transition to a new form of government.

Morocco has enjoyed peace and relative stability since its independence from France in 1956, but as a large portion of the population has remained rural and illiterate, the expectations of the people for democratic change have been limited. What people felt they could envision for their country changed in the spring of 2011. Change can be slow in the making, but suddenly can be propelled forward by an unexpected turn of events. In the small Tunisian town of Sidi Bouzid, the self-immolation of Mohammed Bouazizi, which led to his death on 4 January 2011, was the spark that set off a wave of unrest from Tunisia to the rest of North Africa and parts of the Middle East. Tunisian dictator Zine El Abidine Ben Ali fled his country a mere ten days after the unrest started, followed by Egypt's Hosni Mubarak, who was ousted only 18 days after demonstrations began in Cairo and Alexandria in February of that same year. Within days, ordinary people had collapsed half a century of autocratic rule in these two countries. Other leaders in Libya, Yemen, Bahrain, and Syria held out longer, ordering their armies, police, and secret service forces to fire on and kill their own people. It seems evident that the avalanche set in motion by the desperate act of a single individual can no longer be stopped, though it is too early to assess the full impact of the changes in North Africa.

In the transition period – the time between the overthrow of the old governments in Tunisia and Egypt and elections, constitutional reform, and the setting up of a new government – wealth creation either stopped or was hindered significantly. Countries like Tunisia and Egypt depend heavily on tourism, which came to a halt in the wake of the unrest. Morocco had to deal with the devastating consequences to its own tourism industry as well, not as a result of the mass demonstrations but due to the 28 April 2011 terrorist attack in the well-known Café Argana restaurant in Marrakesh, in which at least 17 people were killed. Since the attack, some have speculated that terrorists linked to Al Qaeda wanted to strike at the heart of Morocco's economy by bombing a place that was particularly popular with international tourists.

The use of fear as an integral part of patriarchal authoritarian societies has been addressed variously in this book. The uprisings during the Arab Spring were remarkable for many reasons, not least of all because they amply demonstrated that people in the Arab-Muslim world – men and women alike – are capable of overcoming their often-justified fear once a tipping point has been reached. In Morocco – as in other MENA countries – this point was reached for some with publication of documents from Wikileaks that exposed even further the extent of corruption and what some have called cleptocracy of the ruling elite there. No doubt, these revelations poured fuel on the fire of existing social discontent.

The women's rights discourses that have been described in this book bode well for a future gender egalitarian society in Morocco. As evidenced by talk of a third way, there is clearly a concerted effort in Morocco to bring together various strands of society and to develop a vision for the country in which men and women jointly contribute. The challenges for women lie not only in overcoming patriarchal structures but also in opening educational and professional opportunities to women, since lack of social mobility entrenches social class divisions. The masses of individuals mobilized during the Arab Spring did not demand gender equality, but implicit in their calls for dignity, democracy, and the right to self-determination was the notion of inclusiveness for all members of society.

Inasmuch as the final decade of the twentieth century was marked by the end of communism, the beginning of the twenty-first century will be remembered by the changes occurring in North Africa and the larger Arab world. Of course, the divisions between men and women and secular and religiously motivated activists will not disappear once the revolutionary fervour has ebbed, and the task of building a new society must be tackled. There are reasons for cautious hope that the unforeseen mass movements of 2011 will eventually lead to a more gender-egalitarian society. Yet as the fall of communism and the subsequent changes in the former Soviet bloc have shown, it will likely take a generation to eradicate entrenched authoritarian systems.

The transitional period following mass uprisings inevitably brings instability. Developments described in this book with regard to women's rights show that uncertainty is part of Morocco's path. This North African country seems neither headed towards a theocracy nor a continuation of its entrenched authoritarian system. Rather, Morocco is in the midst of exciting changes that in time will lead to a more gender-egalitarian society.

GLOSSARY OF ARABIC TERMS

Allahu akbar   God is great

Al Qur'an   literally 'the recitation'; also spelled Quran, Koran, central religious text of Islam. Muslims believe the Qur'an to be the literal word of God as revealed to Mohammed, over a period of 23 years by the angel Gabriel. It is understood as God's final revelation to mankind

Aid   festival, holy day

Aid al-Fitr   the day of celebration that marks the end of Ramadan. Children receive gifts or money from their relatives

Aid al-Adha   the Feast of Sacrifice, takes place during the traditional time of pilgrimage to Mecca. It is celebrated by pilgrims in Mecca and by those who remain at home. It commemorates Abraham's obedience to God by being willing to sacrifice his son. Each family is supposed to kill a sheep and prepares a feast using the meat

Al Adl wa Ihsane   Justice and Charity, name of the largest Islamist movement in Morocco

Amazigh   Amazigh people, Berber people, pl. *Imazighen*

Amir al Mouminin	Commander of the Faithful, one of the dual titles held by the king of Morocco which makes him the highest religious authority in the country
Ayat	verses in a *sura* (chapter) of the Qur'an
Baraka	holiness, special blessing, good fortune
Bled Bilad (or bled) -al siba,	lit. place (city) of youth, meaning 'Lands of Dissidence' (until 1930s, Berber-dominated Rif, Atlas and Sahara) today often used by French to refer to countryside or Morocco
Bismi'll-ahi	opening phrase of all Qur'anic *suras* except one
Chorfa	elevated place in the mosque for the *imam*
Dereja	dialectical Arabic spoken in Morocco, containing Berber and French words and expressions
Dhikr	remember, collect. Spiritual exercise designed to render God's presence throughout one's being
Djellaba	floor-length, loose-fitting hooded garment, worn by men and women in Morocco
Fatwa	legal opinion rendered by an Islamic scholar
Fiqh	religious law
Ftour (or *iftar*)	the festive meal after sunset that breaks the daily fast
Habous	religious foundation; in Morocco there is a Minister for Islamic Affairs and *Habou*s
Hadith	collection of customs, sayings of the Prophet
Hajj	ritual pilgrimage to Mecca; *hajja*, honorific title of a woman who has performed the pilgrimage
Halal	permissible. In French and English this terms refers mostly to food. In Arabic it refers to all that is permissible under Islam
Haram	forbidden

Hijab	Muslim headscarf
Hshuma	forbidden, shameful; common expression in Morocco
Ijtihad	rightful interpretation of sacred texts
Imam	leader in public worship
Imazighen	pl., the free people, original name for Berbers, original inhabitants of North Africa, sing. *Amazigh*
Jihad	striving along the mysterious path, also used in the sense of holy warfare
Jinn	category of spirits, common belief in Morocco
Kabyle	ethnic (Berber) group in Algeria; the *Kabyle* language
Lalla	respectful way to address a woman in Morocco
Madhab	Sunni juridical school
Maghreb	the West, Al Maghrib also meaning Morocco
Marabout	French version of *Murabit*, in North Africa a general term for any kind of professional religious man
Mashriq	the East, region of Arabic-speaking countries in the Eastern hemisphere
Mirhab	a niche in the wall of a mosque indicating the direction of prayer
Muqqadam	sectional leader in a Sufi order
Murshid	Sufi guide
Murchidate	guide, leader, new title given to female religious leaders in Morocco
Nafs	soul, in Islam used to describe the lower self
Ribat	strong point, frontier post, also walled-in city, origin of Rabat, the capital city of Morocco
Shahada	testimony, the profession of faith
Sheikh	master, head

Shari'a	the path to be followed, Islamic jurisprudence
Sharif	one who claims to be a descendant of the Prophet
Sidi	Mister; in Morocco respectful way to address a man
Suf	wool
Sufi	a Muslim mystic
Sunna	custom, tradition of a custom of the Prophet
Sura	chapter of the Qur'an
Talib	(law) student, candidate
Ta'lim	teaching, instruction
Tafasir	exegetical works
Talaq	the right of a man to single-handedly repudiate (divorce) his wife
Tamazight	Berber language(s)
Tachelhit	Berber language spoken in Morocco
Tarifit	Berber language spoken in Morocco
Ulema	sing. *alim*, those who are trained in the religious sciences
Umma	community or nation (often spelled *ummah*), is used to mean the community of the believers (*ummat al-mu'minin*)
Wali	guardian
Waqf	religious foundation, in Morocco called *Habous*
Zawija	in Morocco from French: *zaouia*, small mosque, saint's tomb

The five pillars of Islam: 1. *Shahada*: profession of faith (There is no God but God and Mohammed is His prophet) 2. *Salat*: daily prayers 3. *Zakat*: giving of alms or charity. 4. *Swam*: fast during the month of *Ramadan* in commemoration of the revelation of the Qur'an completed with the feast of *Id-al-Fitr* 5. *Hajj*: pilgrimage of every physically and economically able Muslim to Mecca.

NOTES

Introduction

1. All quotations in this book are from *Al-Qur'an. A Contemporary Translation* by Ahmed Ali. Princeton University Press, revised version 1988.
2. Ndeti, Kivuto and Gray, Kenneth. *The Second Scramble for Africa*. Nairobi: PWPA, 1992.
3. According to Human Rights Watch, the Group against Racism and for Assisting and Defending Foreigners and Migrants (*Groupe Anti-raciste d'Accompagnement et de Défense d'Etrangers et Migrants*, GADEM) monitors the treatment by Moroccan authorities of migrants, in particular sub-Saharans living in Morocco or crossing Moroccan territory in the hope of reaching Europe.
4. Non-membership in the African Union is largely due to the fact that the AU supports independence of the Western Sahara, a territory that Morocco claims as its own.
5. For a brief introduction on Berbers see: 'The Berber Awakening – Amazightié is rapidly climbing down from the Atlas mountains', *The American Interest*, vol. VI, no. 5 (May/June 2011), pp. 29–35.
6. Gross, Rita. *Feminism and Religion*. Boston: Beacon Press, 1996, p. 5.
7. Simone de Beauvoir (1908–1986) is credited with having postulated in the 1950s: 'One is not born a woman, one becomes one.' This statement became one of the cornerstones for feminist theory.

Chapter 1   And God Created Eve ...

1. *The Economist* January 2–8, 2010, p. 7 'We did it.'
2. Gender equality, equality between men and women, entails the concept that all human beings, both men and women, are free to develop their personal

abilities and make choices without the limitations set by stereotypes, rigid gender roles, and prejudices. Gender equality means that the different behaviour, aspirations, and needs of women and men are considered, valued, and favoured equally. It does not mean that women and men have to become the same, but that their rights, responsibilities, and opportunities will not depend on whether they are born male or female. *ABC of Women Workers' Rights and Gender Equality*, Geneva: ILO, 2000, p. 48.

3. 'Bob Jones University drops interracial dating ban.' *Christianity Today*, March 2000, vol. 44.

4. Article 6 of the Moroccan Constitution reads: Islam shall be the state religion. The state shall guarantee freedom of worship for all. Article 19 reads: The King, Amir Al-Muminin (Commander of the Faithful), shall be the Supreme Representative of the Nation and the Symbol of the unity thereof. He shall be the guarantor of the perpetuation and the continuity of the State. As Defender of the Faith, He shall ensure the respect for the Constitution. He shall be the Protector of the rights and liberties of the citizens, social groups and organizations. The King shall be the guarantor of the independence of the Nation and the territorial integrity of the Kingdom within all its rightful boundaries.

5. Johnson, Allan G. *The Gender Knot: Unraveling Our Patriarchal Legacy*. Philadelphia: Temple University Press, 1997, p. 255.

6. Plantade, Nedjma. *La guerre des femmes*. Paris: La Boite à Documents, 1988, p. 137.

7. ibid, p. 165.

8. See Larbi Messari's definition thereof in *Journal Islam Today*, Nr. 20-1424H, 2003, p. 1.

9. In France, Italy, and the Netherlands, the Muslim population hails mostly from North Africa and to a smaller degree West Africa; in Germany the largest number of Muslims comes from Turkey; whereas in the United Kingdom, Muslims most often come from Asia, most notably Pakistan, Bangladesh, and India.

10. Ramadan, Tariq. *Radical Reform – Islamic Ethics and Liberation*. Oxford, New York: Oxford University Press, 2009, p. 207.

11. French saying: The more things change, the more they stay the same.

12. Essafi, Tahar. *La Maroccaine: Moeurs – Condition Sociale – Evolution*. Marrakesh: Imp. du Sud, 1935, p. 2.

13. Pèsle, Octave. *La femme musulmane dans le droit, la religion, et les moeurs*. Rabat: Ed. De la Porte, 1946, p. 91.

14. Mernissi, Fatima. *Rêves de Femmes*. Casablanca: Le Fennec, 1997, p. 314.

15. ibid, footnotes to Chapter 17. These footnotes do not appear in the original English language edition *Dreams of Trespass – Tales of a Harem Girlhood*. New York: Basic Books, 1994.

16. ibid, p. 315.

17. Dialmy, Abdessamad. *Féminisme, islamisme et soufisme.* Paris: Publisud, 1997, p. 52.

18. ibid.

19. Alal al Fassi was one of the founders and leaders of the political party Istiqlal. Among other things he promoted a 'greater Morocco' meaning the post-colonial borders of the Kingdom should extend from Senegal into parts of Algeria. He also opposed the Berber *dahir* of 1930, a decree that separated the Moroccan population into two distinct ethnic groups, Berbers (Imazighen) and Arabs. The decree stipulated that Islamic law did not apply to Berbers instead they were to apply traditional tribal laws. This was an explicit divide and rule policy by the French who felt that Berbers were not as deeply committed to Islam as the Arab populations. The French also discouraged use of the Arabic language by Berbers and created schools for Berbers that only taught French, most notably in the Berber College of Azrou in the Middle Atlas mountains. Al Fassi by contrast promoted a greater Arab identity. He was imprisoned and exiled several times under the French rule.

20. Sadiqi, Fatima and Ennaji Moha. 'The feminization of public space: Women's activism, the family law, and social change in Morocco', *Journal of Middle East Women's Studies*, vol. 2, no. 2 (Spring 2006), pp. 86–114.

21. Gaudio, Attilio. *Allal El Fassi ou l'histoire de l'Istiqlal.* Paris: Alain Moreau, 1972, p. 120.

22. Dialmy, *Féminisme, islamisme et soufisme*, p. 58.

23. There are four main legal schools of Islamic jurisprudence: Hanafi, Maliki, Shafi'i, and Hanbali. Morocco's laws are based on the Malekite School.

24. Quoted in Dialmy, *Féminisme, islamisme et soufisme*, p. 361.

25. Fernea, Elizabeth. 'Introduction'. In Abouzeid, Leila. *The Year of the Elephant.* Austin: Center for Middle Eastern Studies, 1989, p. 11.

26. The Maghreb (also spelled Maghrib), literally the West in Arabic, also meaning the place where the sun sets, is separated from the rest of the African continent by the Atlas mountains and the Sahara. It refers to the most arabized of African countries and includes Libya: Tunisia, Algeria, and Mauretania. When the French speak of the Maghreb they generally only mean their former colonial possessions: Tunisia, Algeria, and Morocco.

27. 'Berber' is considered a derogatory term and has been replaced by Amazigh (person), Imazighen (plural) and Tamazight (language). Though there are numerous linguistic variations, Tamazight has been accepted as the umbrella term for all Amazigh languages. In Morocco, Tarifit and Tachelhit are also spoken.

28. Psychoanalysis, counselling and psychological services are not common in Morocco.

29. The verses in the *Qur'an* (53: 19–23) refer to Lāt, al-'Uzzā and Manāt, three pagan goddesses worshipped by residents of Mecca during the Prophet's lifetime.

30. Rhouni, Raja. *Secular and Islamic feminism the work of Fatima Mernissi*. Leiden, Boston: Brill, 2010, p. 227.

31. Majid, Anouar. *A Call for Heresy: Why Dissent is Vital to Islam and America*. Minneapolis: University of Minnesota Press, 2007.

32. Mernissi, Fatima. *Islam and Democracy: Fear of the Modern World*. New York: Perseus Books, 1992, p. 160.

33. Roy, Olivier. *Secularism Confronts Islam*. New York: Columbia University Press, 2007, p. 40.

34. Benradi, Malika. *Le Code de La Famille – Perceptions et pratique judiciaire*. Rabat: Friedrich Ebert Stiftung, 2007, p. 13.

35. United Nations Development Programme Human Development Report, 2004, p. 58.

36. Moghadam, Valentine. 'State, Gender, and Intersectionality', *International Journal of Middle East Studies*, vol. 40, no. 1 (2008), pp. 16–19.

37. Esposito, John L. and Delong-Bas, Natana J. (2002). *Women in Muslim Family Law – Contemporary Issues in the Middle East*. Syracuse University Group, p. xi.

38. Rosen, Lawrence. *The Anthropology of Justice: Law as Culture in Islamic Society*. Cambridge University Press, 1989, p. 17.

39. *Discours du trône*, 30 July 2005, reported in *Matin du Sahara*, 31 July 2005.

40. Eddouada, Souad. *Women, Gender and the State in Morocco: Contradictions, Constraints and Progress*, Ph.D. dissertation Université Mohammed V, Rabat, 2003.

41. Huntington, Samuel P. 'The Clash of Civilizations', *Foreign Affairs*, vol. 72, no. 3 (Summer 1993), pp. 22–49. Huntington, Samuel P. (1996). *The Clash of Civilizations and the Remaking of World Order*. New York: Simon & Schuster.

42. Khatibi, Abdelkebir. *L'Alternance et les parties politiques*. Casablanca: Eddif, 1998, p. 32.

43. An unofficial English translation is available at www.hrea.org/moudawana.html.

44. This statement applies to Algeria but not Morocco or Tunisia, which do not possess such natural resources as oil and gas.

45. www.transparencyinternational.com.

46. Article 23 of the Moroccan Constitution reads: 'The person of the King shall be sacred and inviolable.' Hence criticism of the king is not permitted.

47. *Le Monde*, 3 August 2009.

48. Quoted in the Abu Dawoud collection of *hadith*, which are sayings and traditions attributed to the Prophet.

49. Unemployment in Morocco affects mostly young people; according to Human Rights Watch, nearly 24 per cent of university graduates are unemployed.

50. The Moroccan weekly journal *Tel Quel* introduced the larger Moroccan audience to female rappers with its article 'Rap au féminine'. No. 450, 4–10 December 2010, p. 48.

Chapter 2   Feminism and Its Discontents

1. Ahmed, Leila. *Women and Gender in Islam*. New Haven: Yale University Press, 1992, p. 149.

2. ibid, p. 151.

3. *Feminist Review*, vol. 97, no. 1, March 2011.

4. ibid, p. 1.

5. ibid.

6. ibid, p. 32.

7. *Femmes du Maroc*, no. 159, March 2009, p. 60.

8. Badinter, Elisabeth. *Dead End Feminism*. Polity, 2006. *XY: On Masculine Identity*. Columbia University Press, 1997.

9. Moi, Toril. 'I am not a feminist but . . . How feminism became the F-word', *Publications of the Modern Language Association (PMLA)*, October 2006, p. 1735.

10. hooks, bell. *Feminism is for Everybody*. Cambridge: South End Press, 2000, p. 1.

11. Olivier, Roy. *Secularism Confronts Islam*. New York: Columbia University Press, 2007, p. xii.

12. As French census data does not include ethnicity or religion, the number of Muslims in France can only be estimated.

13. Websites: EEWC – Christian Feminism Today. Christians for Biblical Equality. Faith and Gender: A Necessary Conversation. Book: Hunt, Mary E. and Neu, Diann (eds) *New Feminist Christianity: Many Voices, Many Views*. Skylight Paths, 2010.

14. Abu-Lughod, Leila. 'Dialects of Women's Empowerment: The International Circuitry of the Arab Human Development Report 2005.' *International Journal of Middle East Studies*, vol. 41, no. 1 (February 2009), pp. 93–103.

15. ibid.

16. Geertz, Hildred. 'The Meaning of Family Ties', *Meaning and Order in Moroccan Society: Three Essays in Cultural Analysis*. Cambridge: Cambridge University Press, 1979.

17. Kapchan, Deborah. *Gender on the Market – Moroccan Women and the Revoicing of Tradition.* Philadelphia: University of Pennsylvania Press, 1996, p. 29.

18. ibid, p. 277.

19. Ottaway, Marina and Abtellatif, Omayma. 'Women in Islamist Movements: Toward an Islamist model of Women's Activism', *Carnegie Papers*, no. 2 (2007).

20. ibid, p. 1.

21. Badran, Margot. *Feminism beyond East and West: New Gender Talk and Practice in Global Islam.* New Delhi: Global Media Publishers, 2007.

22. Muñoz, Gema Martín. 'Islamistes et pourtant modernes', *Confluences Méditerranée*, no. 59 (Fall 2006), pp. 97–108.

23. Gray, Doris H. *Muslim Women on the Move: Moroccan Women and French Women of Moroccan Origin Speak Out.* Lanham: Lexington Books, 2008.

24. From www.musafira.de/islamwissenschaft/interview-with-omaima-abou-bakr-on-science-islamic-feminism-and-history, 2008.

25. Ramadan's work is referred to in Chapter 3.

26. Göle, Nilüfer (ed.) *New Public Faces of Islam.* Istanbul: Metis Publishing, 2000.

27. Tozy, Mohammed. *Monarchie et Islam politique au Maroc.* Paris: Presses de Sciences Politiques, 1999.

28. Abderrahmane Yousoufi was prime minister from 1998 until 2002.

29. Maddy-Weitzman, Bruce. 'Islamism Moroccan style: The ideas of sheikh Yassine', *Middle East Quarterly*, Winter 2003, pp. 43–51.

30. Yassine, Abdessalam. *Islamiser la modernité.* Rabat: al ofok impressions, 1998, p. 191.

31. Tozy, *Monarchie et Islam politique au Maroc.* See above.

32. Club Méditerranée, commonly referred to as Club Med, is a French corporation of international vacation resorts.

33. *Psalms* 84:6

34. Rieder, Johnathan. *The Word of the Lord is Upon Me: The Righteous Performance of Martin Luther King, Jr.* Cambridge: Harvard University Press, 2008.

35. *Le Monde*, 24 June 2009, p. 3.

36. United Nations Millennium Campaign (2008). 'Goal #3 Gender Equity'.

37. For definitions of equality and equity see: www.unfpa.org/gender.

38. Moi, Toril. 'Feminist Theory after Theory', Payne, Michael and Schad, John (eds). *Life After Theory.* London: Continuum, 2003.

39. ORCF is sometimes referred to by its English acronym, ORWA, though the French acronym is more commonly used.

40. *Moroccan Women: Reform Must Stem from the Needs and Expectations of Society.* Interview with Bassima Hakkaoui. www.arab-reform.net/spip.php?article4002. 25 January 2011.

Chapter 3   A Third Way

1. Schimmel, Annemarie. *My Soul is a Woman: The Feminine in Islam.* New York: Continuum, 2003.

2. For example, Dr. Fred Dallmayr proposed 'Islam and Democracy: A Third Way' in a presentation in Rabat in 2007. A selection of his books is listed in the bibliography.

3. Boroujerdi, Mehrzad. *Iranian Intellectuals and the West: The Tormented Triumph of Nativism.* Syracuse: Syracuse University Press, 1998, p. 12.

4. Roy, Olivier. *Secularism Confronts Islam.* New York: Columbia University Press, 2007, p. 40.

5. *Tel Quel,* issue of 31 July 2010, no. 343.

6. Similar studies have been conducted in France which found that young Muslims of immigrant backgrounds consider themselves French and Muslim at the same time without finding a contradiction between the two. For further reading see Cesari, Jocelyne (2006). *When Islam and Democracy Meet: Muslims in Europe and the United States.* Basingstoke: Palgrave Macmillan; and Tribalat, Michèle (1996). *De l'immigration à l'assimilation. Enquête sur les populations étrangères en France.* Paris: Editions La Découverte.

7. Zubaida, Sami. *Beyond Islam: A New Understanding of the Middle East.* London, New York: I.B.Tauris, 2011, p. 9.

8. Ahmed Aboutaleb, a practicing Muslim of Moroccan origin, is mayor of Rotterdam, the second largest city in the Netherlands. Cem Özdemir, of Turkish descent, is co-leader of the German political party The Greens. In France Azouz Begag, Rachida Dati, and Fadela Amara have been or still are high-ranking government officials of North African immigrant background.

9. Dr. Abdullahi Ahmed An-Na'im is professor of law at Emory University School of Law, Atlanta. His specialties include human rights in Islam and cross-cultural issues in human rights. Originally from the Sudan, he is the author of *Islam and the Secular State: Negotiating the Future of Shari'a.* Cambridge, MA and London: Harvard University Press (2008) and *An Islamic Reformation: Civil Liberties, Human Rights and International Law.* Syracuse, NY: Syracuse University Press, 1990, among other titles.

10. An-Na'im, Abdullahi Ahmed. *Islam and the Secular State: Negotiating the Future of Shari'a.* Cambridge: Harvard University Press, 2008, p. 270.

11. Khatibi, Abdelkebir. *Penser le Maghreb.* Rabat: SMER, 1993.

12. Gray, Doris H. 'Women in Algeria Today and the Debate over Family Law', *The Middle East Review of International Affairs,* vol. 13, no.1 (March 2009).

13. Barlas, Asma. 'The antimonies of "Feminism" and "Islam": The limits of a Marxist analysis', *Middle Eastern Women's Study Review*, vol. 18, no. 1–2 (March 2003), p. 3.

14. Jacques Lacan (1901–1981) was a French psychoanalyst and psychiatrist who contributed significantly to psychoanalysis and philosophy. His theories impacted on fields such as critical theory, literary theory, French philosophy, sociology, and feminist theory.

15. Public lecture and discussion at the French Institute in Rabat, March 2009.

16. Abu Bakr, Oumaima. 'Islamic feminism: What's in a name?' *Middle East Women's Studies Review*, vol. xv, no. 4 (Winter-Spring 2001).

17. In order to maintain close links with its overseas residents, the government has established the Council for the Moroccan Community Abroad (CCME) and the Ministry in Charge of the Moroccan Community Living Abroad (MCMRE).

18. The term 'intersectionality' is part of contemporary feminist theory and refers to the intersection of gender with race, social class, ethnicity, religion, etc. With regards to women's rights, intersectionality means that gender alone is most often not the reason for oppression or discrimination, but it is gender plus certain other criteria.

19. Speech delivered at roundtable, 20 March 2009, Casablanca.

20. Lamrabet, Asma. *Le Coran et les femmes: une lecture de libération.* Lyons, Paris: Tawhid, 2007, p. 214.

21. ibid, p. 16.

22. See: Matthew 13:57, Mark 6:4, Luke 4:24, John 4:44.

23. From www.gierfi.org, 2008.

24. From www.asma-lamrabet.com.

25. Ramadan, Tariq. *Radical Reform – Islamic Ethics and Liberation.* Oxford, New York: Oxford University Press, 2009, p. 210.

26. ibid.

27. ibid, p. 76.

28. ibid, p. 208.

29. Esack, Farid. *On Being a Muslim: Finding a Religious Path in the World Today.* Oxford: Oneworld Publications, 1999, p. 117.

30. Raissouni, Ahmed. *Al fikr al-maqasid – La pensée théologique.* Casablanca, 1999, p. 269.

31. ibid, p. 270.

32. ibid, p. 125.

33. Rausch, Margaret. 'Ishelhin women transmitters of Islamic knowledge and culture in southwestern Morocco', *The Journal of North African Studies*, vol. 11. no. 2 (June 2006), p. 173.

34. Wadud, Amina. *Qur'an and Woman: Rereading the Sacred Text from a Woman's Perspective.* New York: Oxford University Press, 1999, p. 103.

Chapter 4   The Way Forward

1. Messari, Nizar. 'Que devons-nous aux jeunes du 20 février?' 14 March 2011. www.lakome.com.

2. ibid.

3. The death of Osama bin Laden on 1 May 2011 was not nearly as big a news story in North Africa as it was in the United States, though Morocco, Algeria, and Tunisia have all been victims of attacks by terrorists linked to Al Qaeda. The most recent one in Morocco occurred in Marrakesh on 28 April 2011, killing 17 people. At the time when bin Laden was killed, people in the Maghreb were preoccupied with the largely peaceful revolutions and uprisings occurring in their region, in which the terrorist organization played no role.

4. *New Statesman*, 15 February 2011.

5. At that time, Mikhail Gorbachev was General Secretary of the Communist Party of the Soviet Union and the call for bringing down the Berlin Wall stood for increasing freedom in the Eastern Bloc.

6. Libyan society is marked by an absence of civil society and allegiances are primarily based on ethnicity or tribe.

7. The king's cousin, Hicham Ben Abdallah El Alaoui, respectfully referred to as Moulay Hicham, who lives in the United States, has also stated that the sacredness of the king is incompatible with democracy. See the French journal *L'Express*, 15 May 2011, where he reiterated this position in an article entitled 'La solution au Maroc: une monarchie réformée' ('The solution for Morocco: a reformed monarchy').

8. Hatem, Mervat F. 'In the Eye of the Storm: Islamic Societies and Muslim Women in Globalized Discourses', *Comparative Studies of South Asia, Africa and the Middle East*, vol. 26, no. 1 (2006), pp. 22–35.

9. Newcomb, Rachel. *Women of Fes – Ambiguities of Urban Life in Morocco.* Philadelphia: University of Pennsylvania Press, 2009, p. 45.

10. For a more detailed description about grassroots-level mobilization by Islamist groups, see an article by Stephanie Willman Bordat, Susan Schaefer Davis, and Saida Kouzzi, 'Women as Agents of Grassroots Change: Illustrating Micro-Empowerment in Morocco', *Journal for Middle East Women's Studies*, vol. 7, no. 1 (Winter 2011), p. 98.

11. See *USA Today*, 29 March 2010 and BBC World News, 12 March 2010. More detailed reporting can be viewed in French media such as *Le Monde*, 6, 8, 10 April 2010.

12. Mir-Hosseini prefers the term 'Islamicist' to 'Islamist' as there are so many misunderstandings about Islamism.

13. Mir-Hosseini, Ziba. 'New Feminist Voices in Islam', *Baraza*. Selangor, Malaysia, no. 4 (2010), p. 3.

14. Aïcha Ech-Channa founded the association Solidarité Féminine in 1985 with the goal of providing unwed mothers, who are highly stigmatized in Morocco, with education, income generating activities, and childcare.

15. The full text can be accessed at www.un.org/womenwatch/daw/cedaw/cedaw. htm.

16. Morocco's reservations:

Declarations:

1. *With regard to article 2:*

The Government of the Kingdom of Morocco express its readiness to apply the provisions of this article provided that:

– They are without prejudice to the constitutional requirement that regulate the rules of succession to the throne of the Kingdom of Morocco;
– They do not conflict with the provisions of the Islamic Shariah. It should be noted that certain of the provisions contained in the Moroccan Code of Personal Status according women rights that differ from the rights conferred on men may not be infringed upon or abrogated because they derive primarily from the Islamic Shariah, which strives, among its other objectives, to strike a balance between the spouses in order to preserve the coherence of family life.

2. *With regard to article 15, paragraph 4:*

The Government of the Kingdom of Morocco declares that it can only be bound by the provisions of this paragraph, in particular those relating to the right of women to choose their residence and domicile, to the extent that they are not incompatible with articles 34 and 36 of the Moroccan Code of Personal Status.

Reservations:

1. *With regard to article 9, paragraph 2:*

The Government of the Kingdom of Morocco makes a reservation with regard to this article in view of the fact that the Law of Moroccan Nationality permits a child to bear the nationality of its mother only in the cases where it is born to an unknown father, regardless of place of birth, or to a stateless father, when born in Morocco, and it does so in order to guarantee to each child its right to a nationality. Further, a child born in Morocco of a Moroccan mother and a foreign father may acquire the nationality of its mother by declaring, within two years of reaching the age of majority, its desire to acquire that nationality, provided that, on making such declaration, its customary and regular residence is in Morocco.

2. *With regard to article 16:*

The Government of the Kingdom of Morocco makes a reservation with regard to the provisions of this article, particularly those relating to the equality of men and women, in respect of rights and responsibilities on entry into and at dissolution of marriage. Equality of this kind is considered incompatible with the Islamic Shariah, which guarantees to each of the spouses rights and responsibilities within a framework of equilibrium and complementary in order to preserve the sacred bond of matrimony. The provisions of the Islamic Shariah oblige the husband to provide a nuptial gift upon marriage and to support his family, while the wife is not required by law to support the family.

Further, at dissolution of marriage, the husband is obliged to pay maintenance. In contrast, the wife enjoys complete freedom of disposition of her property during the marriage and upon its dissolution without supervision by the husband, the husband having no jurisdiction over his wife's property.

For these reasons, the Islamic Shariah confers the right of divorce on a woman only by decision of a Shariah judge.

3. *With regard to article 29:*

The Government of the Kingdom of Morocco does not consider itself bound by the first paragraph of this article, which provides that any dispute between two or more States Parties concerning the interpretation or application of the present Convention which is not settled by negotiation shall, at the request of one of them, be submitted to arbitration.

The Government of the Kingdom of Morocco is of the view that any dispute of this kind can only be referred to arbitration by agreement of all the parties to the dispute.

17. The Moroccan Constitution. Article 19: The King, *Amir Al-Muminin* (Commander of the Faithful), shall be the Supreme Representative of the Nation and the Symbol of the unity thereof. He shall be the guarantor of the perpetuation and the continuity of the State. As Defender of the Faith, He shall ensure the respect for the Constitution. He shall be the Protector of the rights and liberties of the citizens, social groups and organizations. The King shall be the guarantor of the independence of the Nation and the territorial integrity of the Kingdom within all its rightful boundaries. Article 23: The person of the King shall be sacred and inviolable.

18. CEDAW article 161 states: Parties shall take all appropriate measures to eliminate discrimination against women in all matters relating to marriage and family relations and in particular shall ensure, on a basis of equality of men and women: a. the same right to enter into marriage; b. the same right freely to choose a spouse and to enter into marriage only with their free and full consent; c. the same rights and responsibilities during marriage and at its dissolution; d. the same rights and responsibilities as parents, irrespective of their marital status, in matters relating to their children; in all cases the interests of the children shall be paramount; i. the same rights to decide freely and responsibly on the number and spacing of their children and to have access to the information, education and means to enable them to exercise these rights; f. the same rights and responsibilities with regard to guardianship, wardship, trusteeship and adoption of children, or similar institutions where these concepts exist in national legislation; in all cases the interests of the children shall be paramount; g. the same personal rights as husband and wife, including the right to choose a family name, a profession and an occupation; h. the same rights for both spouses in respect of the ownership, acquisition, management, administration, enjoyment and disposition of property, whether free of charge or for a valuable consideration.

19. From maghrebia.net, 12 December 2008, last accessed 23 April 2009.

20. For a detailed analysis of the norm cascading process see: Finnemore, Martha and Sikkink, Kathryn. 'International Norm Dynamics and Political Change', *International Organizations*, vol. 52 (October 1998). Cambridge University Press.

BIBLIOGRAPHY

Abed Al-Jabri, Mohammed (1994). *Introduction: la critique de la raison Arabe*. Paris: La Découverte.
—— (1999). *Arab-Islamic Philosophy*. Austin: University of Texas Press.
Ablal, Ayad (2009). *L'émigration clandestine*. Casablanca: Imp. Info-Print.
Abou El-Fadl, K. (2001). *Rebellion and Violence in Islamic Law*. Cambridge: Cambridge University Press.
—— (2001). *Speaking in God's Name: Islamic Law, Authority and Women*. Oxford: Oneworld Publications.
Abouzeid, Leila (1993). *Return to Childhood*. Austin: Center for Middle Eastern Studies.
—— (1989). *The Year of the Elephant*. Austin: Center for Middle Eastern Studies.
Abu Bakr, Oumaima. 'Islamic feminism: What's in a name?' *Middle East Women's Studies Review*, vol. xv, no. 4 (Winter-Spring 2001).
Abu Khalil, As'ad. 'Toward the Study of Women and Politics in the Arab World: The Debate and the Reality', *Feminist Issues*, vol. 13, no. 1 (Spring 1993), pp. 3–22.
Abu-Lughod, Leila. 'Dialects of Women's Empowerment: The International Circuitry of the Arab Human Development Report 2005', *International Journal of Middle East Studies*, vol. 41, no. 1 (February 2009), pp. 93–103.
—— (ed.) (1998). *Remaking Women – Feminism and Modernity in the Middle East*. Princeton: Princeton University Press.
Afsaruddin, Asma (1999). *Hermeneutics and Honor: Negotiating Female 'Public' Space in Islamic Societies*. Cambridge: Harvard Center for Middle Eastern Studies.
Ahmed, Leila (1992). *Women and Gender in Islam*. New Haven: Yale University Press.

Al Gharbi, Ikbal. 'Les Femmes dans les Mouvements Islamists: Aliénation ou tentative de liberation?' *Journal d'étude des relations internationales au Moyen-Orient*, vol. 1, no.1, article 5 (July 2006).

Ali, Kecia (2006). *Sexual Ethics and Islam: Feminist Reflections on Qur'an, Hadith and Jursiprudence.* London: Oneworld Publicatons.

Alili, Rochdy (2000). *Qu-est-ce que l'Islam?* Paris: La Découverte.

Al-Marouri, Abderazzak. 'Regards sur la question de la femme: sur le concept de la relation.' *Risalat al-Ousra*, no. 1 (1989).

Altavista Maroc (2003). Moroccan web portal. 'Plan d'intégration de la femme au development.' www.ilo.org/maroc.

Amir-Ebrahimi, Masserat. 'Transgression in Narration: The Lives of Iranian Women in Cyberspace', *Journal of Middle East Women's Studies*, vol. 4, no. 3 (2008), pp. 89–118.

Anderson, Benedict (1991). *Imagined Communities: Reflections on the Origin and Spread of Nationalism.* London: Verso.

An-Na'im, Abdullahi Ahmed (2008). *Islam and the Secular State: Negotiating the Future of Shari'a.* Cambridge: Harvard University Press.

Arkoun, Mohammed (2005). *Humanisme et Islam: Combats et propositions.* Paris: Librairie Philosophique Vrin.

—— (2002). *The Unthought in Contemporary Islamic Thought.* London: Saqui Books.

Asad, Talal (1993). *Genealogies of Religion. Discipline and Reasons of Power in Christianity and Islam.* Baltimore: Johns Hopkins University.

Babès, Leïla (2003). *Islam en France: Foi ou Identité.* Paris: Albouraq.

—— (1997). *L'Islam Positif – La religion des jeunes musulmans de France.* Paris: Les Editions de l'Atelier.

—— (ed.) (1996). *Les Nouvelles Manières de Croire. Judaïsme, christianisme, Islam, Jamal nouvelles religiosités.* Paris: Les Editions de l'Atelier.

Badawi, Jamal (1995). *Gender Equality in Islam: Basic Principles.* Plainfield: American Trust Publications.

Badinter, Elisabeth (2006). *Dead End Feminism.* Boston: Polity.

—— (2003). *Fausse route: Réflexions sur 30 années de féminisme.* Paris: Odile Jacob.

—— (1997). *XY: On Masculine Identity.* New York: Columbia University Press.

Badran, Margot (2007). *Feminism beyond East and West: New Gender Talk and Practice in Global Islam.* New Delhi: Global Media Publishers.

—— (2006). *Islamic Feminism Revisited.* www.countercourrants.org.

—— 'Understanding Islam, Islamism and Islamic Feminism', *Journal of Women's History*, vol. 13, no. 1 (Spring 2001), pp. 47–52.

Baker, Alison (1998). *Voices of Resistance: Oral Histories of Moroccan Women.* Albany: SUNY Press.

Bargach, Jamila (2002). *Orphans of Islam: Family, Abandonment and Secret Adoption in Morocco.* Lanham: Rowman and Littlefield.

Barlas, Asma. 'The antimonies of "Feminism" and "Islam": The limits of a Marxist analysis', *Middle Eastern Women's Study Review*, vol. 18, no. 1–2 (March 2003).

—— (2002). *'Believing Women' in Islam: Unreading Patriarchal Interpretations of Islam*. Austin: University of Texas Press.

—— 'Sex, Texts and States: A Critique of North African Discourses on Islam', *The Arab-African and Islamic Worlds: Interdisciplinary Studies*. R. Kevon Lacey and Ralph Coury (eds). New York: Peter Lang, 2000, pp. 97–116.

Barot, Rohit (ed.) (1999). *Ethnicity, Gender and Social Change*. Hampshire, UK: Palgrave Macmillan.

Barreau, Jean-Claude (2005). *Tous les dieux ne sont pas égaux*. Paris: Lattès.

Bassis, Sophie (2007). *Les Arabes, les Femmes, la Liberté*. Paris: Albin Mchel.

Bayes, Jane and Tohidi, Nayereh (2001). *Globalization, Gender, and Religion: The Politics of Women's Rights in Catholic and Muslim Contexts*. New York: Palgrave Macmillan.

Belghazi, Taieb and Madani, Mohammed (2001). *L'action collective au Maroc: De la moblisation à la prise de parole*. Rabat: Publications de la Faculté des Lettres et des Sciences Humaines.

Belyazid, Samia. 'La femme marocaine entre tradition et modernité: le prix d'une Indépendence', *Actes du colloque international*. Rabat, 2004, pp. 21–24.

Benhaddou, Ali (2009). *Les élites du royaume. Enquête sur l'organisation du pouvoir au Maroc*. Paris: Riveneuve.

Benradi, Malika (2007). *Le Code de La Famille – Perceptions et pratique judiciaire*. Rabat: Friedrich Ebert Stiftung.

Benzine, Rachid (2004). *Les Nouveaux Penseurs de l'Islam*. Paris: Albin Michel.

Bertelsmann Transformation Index (2007). Bertelsmann Stiftung, *BTI 2008 – Morocco Country Report*. Gütersloh: Bertelsmann Stiftung.

Bidar, Abdelnour (2008). *L'Islam sans soumission*. Paris: Albin Michel.

Bordat, Stephanie Willman, Schaefer Davis, Susan, Kouzzi, Saida. 'Women as Agents of Grassroots Change: Illustrating Micro-Empowerment in Morocco', *Journal of Middle Eastern Women's Studies (JMEWS)*, vol. 7, no. 1 (Winter 2011), pp. 90–119.

Boroujerdi, Mehrzad (1998). *Iranian Intellectuals and the West: The Tormented Triumph of Nativism*. Syracuse: Syracuse University Press.

Boudhiba, Abdelwahab and Kegan, Paul (1985). *Sexuality in Islam*. London, New York: Routledge.

Butler, Judith (1999). *Gender Trouble: Feminism and the Subversion of Identity*. London, New York: Routledge.

—— 'Performative Acts and Gender Constitutions: An Essay in Phenomenology and Feminist Theory', *Feminist Theory Reader: Local and Global Perspectives*, McCann, Carole R. and Kim Seung-Kyung (eds). New York, London: Routledge, pp. 415–427.

Brand, Laurie (1998). *Women, the State, and Political Liberalization: Middle Eastern and North African Experiences*. New York: Columbia University Press.

Brett, Michael and Fentress, Elizabeth (1997). *The Berbers: The Peoples of Africa*. Hoboken, New Jersey: Wiley Blackwell.

Calvert, John (2008). *Islamism: A Documentary and Reference Guide*. Westport, CT: Greenwood Press.

Cesari, Joycelyne (2003). *L'islam a l'épreuve de l'Occident*. Paris: La Découverte.

Charrad, Mounira (2001). *States and Women's Rights: The Making of Postcolonial Tunisia, Algeria and Morocco*. Berkeley: University of California Press.

Chebel, Malek (2004). *Manifeste pour un Islam des lumières – 27 propositions pour réformer l'Islam*. Paris: Editions Hachette.

Clark, Janine A. and Young, Amy E. 'Islamism and family law reform in Morocco and Jordan', *Mediterranean Politics*, vol. 13, no. 3 (November 2008), pp. 333–352.

Combe, Julie (2001). *La condition de la femme marocaine*. Paris: L'Harmattan.

Cooke, Miriam (2001). *Women Claim Islam*. New York, London: Routledge.

—— 'Multiple Critique: Islamist feminist rhetorical stratégies', *Nepantala*, vol. 1, no. 1 (2001), pp. 91–110. Reprint in L. Donaldson and K. Pui-Lan (eds). *Postcolonialism, Feminism and Religious Discourse*. London: Routledge.

Cross, Rita (1996). *Feminism and Religion*. New York: Routledge.

Dakhila, Jocelyne (2005). *Islamicités*. Paris: PUF.

Dallmayr, Fred (2010). *Integral Pluralism: Beyond Culture Wars*. University Press of Kentucky.

—— (2001). *Achieving our World: Toward a Global and Plural Democracy*. New York: Rowman and Littlefield.

—— (1996). *Beyond Orientalism: Essays on Cross-Cultural Encounters*. Albany, NY: SUNY Press.

Daoud, Zakia (1993). *Féminisme et politique au Maghreb: Soixante ans de Lutte*, Casablanca: Eddif.

Darif, Mohammed (2010). *Monarchie marocaine et acteurs religieux*. Casablanca : Afrique Orient.

De Haas, Hein. 'Morocco: From emigration country to Africa's migration passage to Europe', *Migration Information Source*. www.migrationinformation.org/feature/display.cfm?ID=339 (October 2005).

Deutscher, Irwin (2002). *Accommodating Diversity – National Policies that Prevent Ethnic Conflict*. Lanham: Lexington.

Diaconoff, Suellen (2009). *The Myth of the Silent Woman : Moroccan Women Writers*. Toronto: University of Toronto Press.

Dialmy, Abdessamad (2008). *Le féminisme au Maroc*. Casablanca: Editions Toubkal.

—— (1997). *Féminisme, islamisme et soufisme*. Paris: Publisud.

Discours Royal sur Le Code de la Famille (2005). www.mincom.gov.ma/french/generalites/codefamille/discours.html.

Dore-Audibert, Andreé and Khodja, Souad (1998). *Etre femme au Maghreb et en Mediterranée – du mythe à la réalité*. Paris: Karthala.

Doumato, Eleanor (2003). *Women and Globalization in the Arab Middle East: Gender, Economy, and Society*. Boulder: Lynne Rienner.

Ech-Channa, Aïcha (2004). *Miseria-Témoignages*. Casablanca: Eddif.

Eddouada, Souad (2003). *Women, Gender and the State in Morocco: Contradictions, Constraints and Progress*, Ph.D. dissertation Université Mohammed V, Rabat.

Eickelman, Dale. 'Islam and Ethical Pluralism', Hashimi, Sohail H. (ed.) *Islamic Political Ethics: Civil Society, Pluralism, and Conflict.* Princeton: Princeton University Press, 2002, pp. 115–134.

El Aoufi, Noureddine (ed.) (1992). La *Société Civile au Maroc.* Rabat: Imprimerie El Maarif.

El-Sohl, C Fawzi and Marbro, Judy (eds) (1994). *Muslim Women's Choices: Religious Belief and Social Reality.* Oxford: Berg.

Enloe, Cynthia (1989). *Bananas, Beaches, and Bases: Making Feminist Sense of International Politics.* Berkeley: University of California Press.

Entelis, John P. (1996). *Culture and Counterculture in Moroccan Politics.* Lanham, Maryland: University Press of America.

Esack, Farid (1999). *On Being a Muslim: Finding a Religious Path in the World Today.* Oxford: Oneworld Publications.

—— (1997). *Qur'an, Liberation and Pluralism.* Oxford: Oneworld Publications.

Essafi, Tahar (1935). *La Maroccaine: Mœurs – Condition Sociale – Evolution*, Marrakesh: Imp. du Sud (available at Archives d'Outre Mer, Aix-en-Provence).

Esposito, John L. and Haddad, Yvonne Yazbeck (1997). *Islam, Gender and Social Change.* Oxford: Oxford University Press.

Esposito, John L. and Delong-Bas, Natana J. (2002). *Women in Muslim Family Law: Contemporary Issues in the Middle East.* Syracuse University Group.

Etienne, Bruno (2003). *Islam, les questions qui fâchent.* Paris: Bayard.

Ferguson, James (2006). *Global Shadows: Africa in the Neoliberal World Order.* Durham: Duke University Press.

Fernea, Elizabeth (1998). *In Search of Islamic Feminism.* New York: Doubleday.

Fernea, Elizabeth and Berzigan, Basima (1977). *Middle Eastern Women Speak.* Austin: University of Texas Press.

Filali-Ansary, Abdou (1997). *L'Islam est-il hostile à la laïcité?* Casablanca: Le Fennec.

Gaudio, Attilio (1972). *Allal El Fassi ou l'histoire de l'Istiqlal.* Paris: Alain Moreau.

Geertz, Hildred (1979). 'The Meaning of Family Ties', *Meaning and Order in Moroccan Society: Three Essays in Cultural Analysis.* Cambridge: Cambridge University Press.

Geoffeoy, Eric (2009). *L'Islam sera spirituel ou ne sera plus.* Paris: Seuil.

Gerholm, Tomas and Lithman, Y.G. (eds) (1988). *The New Islamic Presence in Western Europe.* Thousand Oaks, CA: Sage Publications.

Ghazi, Walid-Fala and Nagel, Caroline (2005). *Geographies of Muslim Women: Gender, Religion and Space.* New York: Guildford Publications.

Göle, Nilüfer (ed.) (2000). *New Public Faces of Islam.* Istanbul: Metis Publishing.

Gottreich, Emily (2007). *The Mellah of Marrakesh: Jewish and Muslim Space in Morocco's Red City.* Bloomington: Indiana University Press.

Gray, Doris H. (2008). *Muslim Women on the Move: Moroccan Women and French Women of Moroccan Origin Speak Out.* Lanham: Lexington Books.

Gray, Doris H. 'Women in Algeria today and the debate over family law', *The Middle East Review of International Affairs,* vol. 13, no.1 (March 2009).

Gross, Rita (1996). *Feminism and Religion.* Boston: Beacon Press.

Hafez Barazangi, Nimat (2004). *Women's Identity and the Qur'an: A New Reading.* Gainesville: University Press of Florida.

Hammoudi, Abdellah (1997). *Master and Disciple. The Cultural Foundations of Moroccan Authoritarianism.* Chicago: University of Chicago Press.

Hatem, Mervat F. 'In the eye of the storm: Islamic societies and Muslim women in globalized discourses', *Comparative Studies of South Asia, Africa and the Middle East,* vol. 26, no. 1 (2006), pp. 22–35.

—— 'Gender and Islamism in the Nineties', *Middle East Report,* vol. 222 (Spring 2002), pp. 44–47.

Heck, Paul (2009). *Common Ground: Islam Christianity, and Religious Pluralism,* Washington: Georgetown University Press.

Hegasy, Sonya (1997). 'Staat, Öffentlichkeit und Zivilgesellschaft in Marokko. Die Potentiale der sozio-kulturellen Opposition', *Politik, Wirtschaft und Gesellschaft des Vorderen Orientes.* Hamburg: Deutsches Orient Institut.

Hessini, Leila (1994). 'Wearing the *hijab* in contemporary Morocco', *Reconstructing Gender in the Middle East Tradtion, Idenity, Power.* Gösek, Fatma Müge, and Shiva Balaghi (eds). New York: Columbia University Press, pp. 40–56.

Hobswam, Eric and Ranger, Terence (eds) (1992). *The Invention of Tradition.* Cambridge: Cambridge University Press.

Hoffman, Katherine E. and Gilson Miller, Susan (2010). *Berbers and Others: Beyond Tribe and Nation in the Maghrib.* Indiana University Press.

hooks, bell (2000). *Feminism is for Everybody.* Cambridge: South End Press.

Hunke, Sigrid (1960). *Allah's Sonne über dem Abendland – Unser Arabisches Erbe.* Stuttgart: Deutsche Verlagsanstalt.

Huntington, Samuel (1996). *The Clash of Civilizations and the Remaking of World Order.* New York: Simon and Schuster.

Joffe, George (1997). 'Maghrebi Islam and Islam in the Maghreb', *African Islam and Islam in Africa: Encounters Between Sufis and Islamists.* Rosander, Eva Evans and Westerlund, David (eds). Athens: Ohio University Press.

—— (ed.) (1993). *North Africa: Nation, State, and Region.* London: Routledge.

Johnson, Allan G. (1997). *The Gender Knot: Unraveling Our Patriarchal Legacy.* Philadelphia: Temple University Press.

Jørgensen, Julie Pruzan. 'New female voices within the Islamist movement in Morocco', *Portuguese Institute of International Relations and Security,* Lisbon, Portugal. October/November 2010, no. 6, pp. 15–18.

Joseph, Suad (ed.) (2000). *Gender and Citizenship in the Middle East*. Syracuse: Syracuse University Press.

Kapchan, Deborah (1996). *Gender on the Market – Moroccan Women and the Revoicing of Tradition*. Philadelphia: University of Pennsylvania Press.

Karam, Azza M. (1998). *Women, Islamism, and the State – Contemporary Feminisms in Egypt*. New York: Palgrave Mcmillan.

Kepel, Gilles (1984). *Les banlieues de l'Islam. Naissance d'une religion en France*. Paris: Editions du Seuil.

—— (2003). *La revanche de Dieu: Chrétiens, juifs et musulmans à la reconquête du monde*. Paris: Seuil.

—— (2004). *The War for Muslim Mind – Islam and the West*. Cambridge: Harvard University Press.

Khatibi, Abdelkebir (1998). *L'Alternance et les parties politiques*. Casablanca: Eddif.

—— (1993). *Penser le Maghreb*. Rabat: SMER.

Kilito, Abdelfettah (1995). *La querelle des images*. Casblanca: Eddif.

Knauss, Peter (1987). *The Persistence of Patriarchy – Class, Gender, and Ideology in Twentieth Century Algeria*. New York: Praeger.

Kozma, Liaf. 'Moroccan women's narratives of liberation: A passive revolution?', *Journal of North African Studies*, vol. 8, no. 1 (2003).

Laala Hafdane, Hakima (2003). *Les femmes marocaines – une société en mouvement*. Paris: L'Harmattan.

Lamrabet, Asma (2007). *Le Coran et les femmes: une lecture de libération*. Lyons, Paris: Tawhid.

—— (2003). *Aïcha, epouse du prophète où l'Islam au féminine*. Lyons, Paris: Tawhid.

—— (2002). *Musulmane tout simplement*. Lyons, Paris: Tawhid.

Lapid, Yousouf (ed.) (1996). *The Return of Culture and Identity*. Boulder: Lynne Rienner.

Laroussi, M. Ben Ali. 'Les jeunes marocaines entre frustration et résignation', *Psychologie de l'éducation*, no. 4 (2003), pp. 75–106.

Layachi, Azzedine (1998). *State, Society and Democracy in Morocco: The Limits of Associative Life*. Washington: Center for Contemporary Arab Studies. Georgetown University Press.

Maddy-Weitzman, Bruce. 'Islamism Moroccan style: The ideas of sheikh Yassine', *Middle East Quarterly* (Winter 2003), pp. 43–51.

Maddy-Weitzman, Bruce and Zisenwine, Daniel (eds) (2007). *The Maghreb in the New Century – Identity, Religion, and Politics*. Gainesville: University Press of Florida.

Maher, Vanessa (1978). 'Women and social change in Morocco', *Women in the Muslim World*, Beck, Lois and Keddie, Nikkie (eds), Cambridge: Harvard University Press.

Mahmood, Saba (2004). *The Politics of Piety: The Islamist Revival and the Feminist Subject*. Princeton University Press.

Mahmoud, Hussein (2009). *Penser le Coran*. Paris: Grasset.

Majid Anouar. 'The politics of feminism in Islam.' *Signs: Journal of Women in Culture and Society*, vol. 23, no. 2 (1998), pp. 321–361.

—— (2004). *Freedom and Orthodoxy*. Stanford University Press.

Manji, Irshad (2005). *The Trouble with Islam Today*. St. Martin's Griffin.

Mernissi, Fatima (1987). *Beyond the Veil: Male-Female Dynamics in Modern Muslim Society*. Bloomington: Indiana University Press.

—— (1991). *Women and Islam: A Historical and Theological Inquiry*. Oxford: Blackwell Publishers.

—— (1992). *Islam and Democracy: Fear of the Modern World*. New York: Perseus Books.

—— (1996). *Women's Rebellion and Islamic Memory*. London: Zed Books.

—— (1997). *Rêves de Femmes*. Casablanca: Le Fennec.

—— (ed.) (1991). *La femme et la loi au Maroc*. Alger: Ed. Bouchene.

Mernissi, Fatima, Lakeland, Mary Jo (1992). *The Veil and the Male Elite: A Feminist Interpretation of Women's Rights in Islam*. Cambridge: Perseus Publishing.

Messaoudi, Khalida (1998). *Unbowed – An Algerian Woman Confronts Islamic Fundamentalism*. Philadelphia: University of Pennsylvania Press.

Miller, Susan Gibson and Rahma, Bourquia (eds) (1999). 'Introduction', *In the Shadow of the Sultan: Culture, Power, and Politics in Morocco*. Cambridge: Harvard University, pp. 1–16.

Minces, Juliette (1996). *Le Coran et les Femmes*. Paris: Hachette.

Mir-Hosseini, Ziba (2010). 'New Feminist Voices in Islam', *Baraza*. Selangor, Malaysia, no. 4, p. 3.

—— (2000). *Marriage on Trial: Islamic Family Law in Iran and Morocco*. London: I.B.Tauris.

Moghadam, Valentine. 'State, Gender, and Intersectionality', *International Journal of Middle East Studies*, vol. 40, no. 1 (2008), pp. 16–19.

Moghissi, Haideh (1999). *Feminism and Islamic Fundamentalism: The Limits of Postmodern Analysis*. London: Zed Books.

Mohsen-Finan, Khadija (2008). *L'image de la femme au Maghreb*. Paris: Actes Sud.

Moi, Toril. 'I am not a feminist but .... How feminism became the F-word', *Publications of the Modern Language Association* (PMLA) (October 2006), pp. 1735–41.

Mojab, Sharzad. 'Theorizing the politics of Islamic feminism', *Feminist Review*, vol. 69, no. 1 (November 2001), pp. 124–146.

Monshipouri, Mahmood (1998). *Islamism, Secularism, and Human Rights in the Middle East*. Boulder: L. Rienner.

Mouhtadi, Najib (2008). *Pouvoir et communication au Maroc*. Paris: L'Harmattan.

Muñoz, Gema Martín. 'Islamistes et pourtant modernes', *Confluences Méditerranée*, no. 59 (Fall 2006), pp. 97–108.

Munson, Henry (1993). *Religion and Power in Morocco*. New Haven: Yale University Press.

Nashat, Guity and Tucker, Judith (1999). *Women in the Middle East and North Africa: Restoring Women to History*. Bloomington: Indiana University Press.

Nasr, Seyyed Hossein (2000). *Ideals and Realities of Islam*. Chicago: ABC International Group.

Ndeti, Kivuto and Gray, Kenneth (1992). *The Second Scramble for Africa*. Nairobi, Kenya: PWPA.

Newcomb, Rachel (2009). *Women of Fes – Ambiguities of Urban Life in Morocco*. Philadelphia: University of Pennsylvania Press.

New Lawyers Committee for Human Rights (1999). *Islam and Equality*.

Nökel, Siegrid (ed.) (2001). *Der neue Islam der Frauen*. Bielefeld: transcript Verlag.

Nouama-Guessous, Soumaya (2007). *Au-delà de toute pudeur*. Casablanca: Eddif.

Ottaway, Marina and Abtellatif, Omayma. 'Women in Islamist Movements: Toward an Islamist Model of Women's Activism', *Carnegie Papers*, no. 2 (2007).

Pèsle, Octave (1946). *La femme musulmane dans le droit, la religion, et les moeurs*. Rabat: Ed. De la Porte (available at Archives nationales d'outre-mer, Aix en Provence, France).

Plantade, Nedjma (1988). *La guerre des femmes*. Paris: La Boite à Documents.

Raissouni, Ahmed (1999). *Al fikr al-maqasid – La pensée théologique*. Casablanca.

Ramadan, Tariq (2010). *What I Believe*. Oxford University Press: 2010.

—— (2009). *Radical Reform – Islamic Ethics and Liberation*. Oxford, New York: Oxford University Press.

—— (2003). *Arabes et musulmans face à la mondialisation: le défi du pluralisme*. Lyon: Tawhid.

Rassan, Amal. 'Women and domestic power in Morocco', *International Journal of Middle Eastern Studies* (September 1980), pp. 171–179.

Rausch, Margaret. 'Ishelhin women transmitters of Islamic knowledge and culture in southwestern Morocco', *The Journal of North African Studies*, vol. 11. no. 2 (June 2006), p. 173.

Rchid, Abderrazak Moulay. 'La Mudawana en question', *Femmes, culture et société au Maghreb*, vol. 2. Bourqia, Rahma, Charrad, Mounira and Gallagher, Nancy (eds) (1996). Casablanca: Afrique Orient.

Rhouni, Raja (2010). *Secular and Islamic Feminism the Work of Fatima Mernissi*. Leiden, Boston: Brill.

Rieder, Johnathan (2008). *The Word of the Lord is Upon Me: The Righteous Performance of Martin Luther King, Jr.* Cambridge: Harvard University Press.

Roded, Ruth (2008). *Women in Islam and the Middle East: A Reader*. London: I.B. Tauris.

Rosello, Mireille (2005). *France and the Maghreb – performative encounters*. Gainesville: University Press of Florida, 2005.

Rosen, Lawrence (1984). *Bargaining for Reality: The Construction of Social Relations in a Muslim Community*. Chicago: University of Chicago Press.

—— (1989). *The Anthropology of Justice: Law as Culture in Islamic Society*. Cambridge University Press.

—— (2002). *The Culture of Islam: Changing Aspects of Contemporary Islam*. Chicago: University of Chicago Press.

Roy, Olivier (2004). *Globalized Islam*. New York: Columbia University Press.

—— (2007). *Secularism Confronts Islam*. New York: Columbia University Press.

—— (2008). *La Sainte Ignorance – Le temps de la religion sans culture*. Paris: Seuil.

Ruedy, John (ed.) (1994). *Islamism and Secularism in North Africa*. New York: St. Martin's Press.

Saaf, Abdellah. (1999) *Maroc: L'Esperance d'état moderne*. Beirut: Afrique Orient.

Sadiqi, Fatima. 'The central role of the family law in the Moroccan feminist movement', *British Journal of Middle Eastern Studies*, vol. 35, no. 3 (December 2008), pp. 325–337.

Sadiqi, Fatima and Ennaji Moha. 'The feminization of public space: Women's activism, the family law, and social change in Morocco', *Journal of Middle East Women's Studies*, vol. 2, no. 2 (Spring 2006), pp. 86–114.

Safi, Omid (2003). *Progressive Muslims: On justice, gender, and pluralism*. Oxford: Oneworld Publications.

Safouan, Moustapha (2008). *Pourquoi le monde arabe n'est-il pas libre*. Paris: Denoël.

Said, Edward (1979). *Orientalism*. New York: Vintage Press.

Salim, Zakia. 'The war on terrorism: Appropriation and subversion by Moroccan Women', *Signs: Journal of Women in Culture and Society*, vol. 33, no.1 (2007).

Salwa, Ismail (2003). *Rethinking Islamist Politics: Culture, the State and Islamism*. London: I.B.Tauris.

Schimmel, Annemarie (2003). *My Soul is a Woman: The Feminine in Islam*. New York: Continuum.

—— (1992). *Meine Seele ist eine Frau*. Müchen: Kösel Verlag.

Sebti, Fadéla (1989). *Vivre musulmane au Maroc: Guide des droits et obligation de la femme marocaine*. Casablanca: Le Fennec.

Seddik, Youssef (2004). *Nous n'avons jamais lu le Coran*. Paris: Editions de L'Aube.

Sen, Amartya (1999). *Development as Freedom*. New York: Oxford University Press.

Sharabi, Hicham (1988). *Neopatriarchy: A Theory of Distorted Change in Arab Society*. Oxford: Oxford University Press.

Sikkink, Kathryn and Finnemore, Matha. 'International norm dynamics and political change', *International Organization*, Autumn 1998, pp. 887–917.

Sölle, Dorothee (2001). *The Silent Cry: Mysticism and Resistance*. Minneapolis: Fortress.

Souaiaia, Ahmed E. (2008). *Contesting Justice: Women, Islam, Law, and Society*. State University of New York Press.

Stowasser, Barbara Freyer (1996). *Women in the Qur'an: Traditions and Interpretations.* Oxford, Oh: Oxford Press.

Strauss, Anselm and Corbin, Juliet (1998). *Basics of Qualitative Research. Techniques and Procedures for Developing Grounded Theory.* Thousand Oaks: Sage Publications.

Syed, Mohammed Ali (2004). *The Position of Women in Islam.* Albany: State University of New York Press.

Taïa, Abdellah (2008). *Une mélancholie arabe.* Paris: Seuil.

Tamam, Hussam. 'Separating Islam from political Islam: The case of Morocco', *Arab Insight*, vol. 1, no. 1 (Spring 2007), p. 7.

Tozy, Mohammed (1999). *Monarchie et Islam politique au Maroc.* Paris: Presses de Sciences Politiques.

—— (2007). *Islam au quotidian.* Casablanca: Marsam.

Transparency International. www.transparency.org/content/download/53842/859258/ MoroccanExecutiveSummary_web+(ENGLISH).pdf.

Tucker, Judith E. (2008). *Women, Family, and Gender in Islamic Law.* New York: Cambridge University Press.

Umar Naseef, Fatima (1999). *Women in Islam – A Discourse in Rights and Obligations.* Cairo: International Committee for Women and Children.

Wadud, Amina (1999). *Qur'an and Woman. Rereading the Sacred Text from a Woman's Perspective.* New York: Oxford University Press.

—— (2006). *Inside the Gender Jihad – Women's Reform in Islam.* Oxford: Oneworld Publications.

Webb, Giesela (ed.) (2000). *Windows of Faith: Muslim Women Scholar-activists in North America.* New York: Syracuse University Press.

Wood, Julia T. (2010). *Communication Mosaic.* Wadsworth Publishing.

Yamani, Mai (ed.) (1996). *Feminism and Islam: Legal and Literary Perspectives.* London: Ithaca Press.

—— (1996). *De l'immigration à l'assimilation. Enquête sur les populations d'origine étrangère en France.* Paris: Éditions La Découverte.

Yassine, Abdessalam (1998). *Islamiser la modernité.* Rabat: al ofok impressions.

Yassine, Nadia. *Le féminisme islamique: combats et résistances.* www.oumma.com. December 2008.

Zakaya, Daoud (1993). *Féminisme et politique au Maghreb.* Casablanca: Eddif.

Zayzafoon, Lamia Ben Youssef (2005). *The Production of the Muslim Woman,* Lanham: Lexington Books.

Zeghal, Malika (2008). *Islamism in Morocco: Religion, Authoritarianism, and Electoral Politics.* Markus Wiener Publishers.

Ziai, Fati. 'Personal Status Codes and women's rights in the Maghreb', *Muslim Women and the Politics of Participation: Implementing the Bejing Platform.* Afkhami, Mahnaz and Fried, Erika (eds) (1997). Syracuse University Press.

Zoubir, Yahia (2008). *North Africa: Politics, Religion and the Limits of Transformation.* New York: Routledge.

Zubaida, Sami (2011). *Beyond Islam: A New Understanding of the Middle East.* London, New York: I.B.Tauris.

INDEX